ABORIGINE

ABORIGINALS OF THE NORTH MUSGRAVE RANGES

Photo Taylor's Collotype Series

ABORIGINE
MYTHS AND LEGENDS

WILLIAM RAMSAY SMITH

SENATE

Aborigine Myths & Legends

First published in 1930 as *Myths & Legends of the Australian Aboriginals* by George G. Harrap, London

This edition first published in 1996 by Senate, an imprint of Random House UK Ltd, Random House, 20 Vauxhall Bridge Road, London SW1V 2SA

ISBN 0 09 185039 8

Printed and bound in Guernsey by The Guernsey Press Co. Ltd

TO THE MEMORY OF
GREATLY VALUED AND REVERED FRIENDS
PRINCIPAL SIR WILLIAM TURNER
AND
PROFESSOR D. J. CUNNINGHAM
WITH WHOM I WAS PRIVILEGED TO BE A FELLOW-WORKER
IN AUSTRALIAN ANTHROPOLOGICAL RESEARCH
THIS REGARDFUL OFFERING IS DEDICATED

PREFACE

THE mythology of any and of every people has become a subject of profound and meaningful interest to anthropologists. The Australian race is recognized as one of the oldest and most compact now existing. Its mythology, however, has been a matter of only slight general interest and fragmentary record, and apparently little attempt has been made to set it forth in such a form as would demand or entitle it to serious scientific study.

A few years ago I wrote, regarding the Australian aboriginal: " The more we know of the blackfellow, the more we are convinced that there are whole subterranean rivers of anthropology unmapped and untapped." I also said : " The aboriginal, like every other citizen of the world, has his stock of fables, for the benefit of the youth principally—stories obviously intentionally invented for the purpose of pointing a moral or enforcing some useful truth or precept. He also has his parables of the same nature and for the like purpose. His legends, using the term in a somewhat loose sense, are fairly numerous. It is when we come to mythology, however, that real interest is aroused and practical difficulty arises in connexion with the aboriginal's beliefs. If we accept a myth as ' a tale handed down from primitive times, and in form historical, but in reality involving elements of early religious views, as respecting the origin of things, the powers of nature and their workings, the rise of institutions, the history of races and communities and the like,' then we find that in dealing with the aboriginal we are studying ' folklore in the making.' This is where the interest lies."

This volume is not intended to give any scientific exposition, general description, abstract, or epitome of Australian aboriginal mythology. It is a collection of narratives as told by pure-blooded aboriginals of various tribes who have been conversant with the subject from childhood. If some of the stories may seem to touch the verge of tediousness, they resemble in this respect the legends of other races, Eastern and Western, civilized and uncivilized alike. Such changes as have been made in the narratives are few and slight, and do not go beyond what were considered to be necessary in order to make clear the meaning, or to give some degree of grammatical correctness to the text without changing the 'aroma' of the story when using equivalent English terms or phrases.

The myths as they were told are allowed to speak for themselves. There has been no searching for evidence either to support or to disprove any anthropological or other theories. On the other hand, no pains have been spared in the endeavour to find out accurately what was in the minds of the narrators. A sympathetic study of the psychology of the aboriginal, extending over a period of thirty years, has proved useful when checking, comparing, and verifying the facts with which the narratives deal in order to arrive at a correct understanding of what the language was meant to convey.

The myths here narrated refer to only a few localities in Australia, and to certain tribes in these. Some of the customs, beliefs, and traditions recorded may be found to exist elsewhere, either in varied forms or in apparently similar forms; and one may be tempted to draw inferences from such occurrences or resemblances. In this connexion it must be remembered that in logic generally there is always a risk of fallacy in arguing from the particular to the universal or the general. In subjects like the present such a method of inference is fatal to scientific research.

A good deal of what is set forth relates more or less intimately to the physical conditions of the country and to the habits, religion, customs, observances, relationships, occupations, and recreations that go to make up the life of the aboriginal. A certain amount of information on these subjects is required for an intelligent understanding of the mythology and a proper appreciation of its meaning and its moral value. This desideratum is supplied partly in the narratives and partly in the notes. Although these in some instances may not give the actual words of the 'actors' in the incidents or of their conversations, they sound natural, as if they were the language of the reciter of the story. They help to give a physical setting and a local colour, and to provide a human atmosphere.

The subject of nomenclature has been found to be beset with difficulties. Despite the care that has been expended in endeavouring to secure uniformity in usage, the result leaves a great deal to be desired. It comes far short of the accuracy that was aimed at and hoped for. In the matter of the names of animals and vegetables it would appear absurd, and in many instances meaningless, to use the nomenclature employed in scientific classification. Similarly, aboriginal names would in most instances give rise to difficulties as many and as great. In the case of words that have become generally adopted in English books and usage the *Century Dictionary* has been taken as a general guide. In dealing with terms that have not become quite acclimatized in scientific and general literature account has been taken of native Australian origin, common Australian modern usage, and Morris's *Austral English Dictionary*. For example, in the case of *Phascolarctus cinereus*, the native Australian name koala, also written coala, has been adopted, since the term ' bear ' would be misleading as regards both the structure and the habits of this little animal, which differs so much from the whole zoological class of Ursidæ. The name 'Teddy-bear,' which was used by a narrator, would perhaps be aptly applicable descriptively, but its modernity might appear objectionable.

W. R. S.

CONTENTS

CHAPTER   PAGE

  I. ORIGINS   17

 II. ANIMAL MYTHS   94

III. RELIGION   173

IV. SOCIAL   209

 V. PERSONAL MYTHS   242

    INDEX   351

CHAPTER I : ORIGINS

The Customs and Traditions of Aboriginals

THE aboriginals of Australia have a vast number of legends, myths, and folklore stories. They take great delight in telling stories to the younger members of the tribe. These stories and traditions have been handed down orally for thousands of years. In fact, a knowledge of the tribal laws and customs is first of all made known to the children of the tribe through the medium of stories. The mothers or the elders of the tribe tell the stories with a great deal of gesture.

The aboriginals have always known the four points of the compass and the four winds of heaven—the north, the south, the west, and the east. Traditions say that the aboriginals came to Australia from another land in the north-west. One of these tells that they were forced to Australia by fierce ants. This may mean that they were pursued by a plague of huge, deadly ants, or by a prehistoric race as fierce and as numerous as ants.

Since coming to Australia, thousands of years ago, the people have probably made little or no change in their habits and customs. They kept the balance of nature even, and for centuries they neither advanced nor retrograded. Their tribal laws and customs were fixed and unchangeable. Generation after generation has come and gone, and all have passed through the same unchanging, rigid tribal training.

Every race has had a great traditional leader and law-giver who gave it its first moral training, as well as its social and tribal customs. Nurunderi [1] was the great leader of the aboriginals, and his laws are taught to the children in their infancy. He distributed the hunting-grounds among the various tribes and families, and the boundaries of these tribal hunting-grounds have remained unaltered from the remotest times.

[1] A great chief or god of the Narrinyeri, who came down the Darling to the Lower Murray. He was the creator of the Narrinyeri country, its flora, its fauna, and its people. He was the teacher of the people and their legislator. He made his ascent to heaven from Lake Victoria.

The boys have to pass through the ceremonial rites of initiation, and they bravely and patiently undergo the grievous tests to which they are subjected by the tribal elders. These rites are accompanied by much solemnity, and cause great excitement among the tribes. When they have been concluded there is an end to the anxiety of the mothers, fathers, sisters, brothers, and relatives, and especially of the young girls who will one day become the wives of the boys. In the minds of the children there is aroused a curiosity

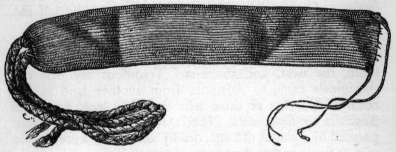

BROW-BAND FROM CENTRAL QUEENSLAND
From *Among Cannibals*, by Carl Lumholtz (Murray).

regarding a mysterious something which they were strictly forbidden to witness or to inquire into.

The chanting of a song, accompanied by the regular beating of a yam-stick upon the ground, produces the effect of the 'tramp, tramp' of a great marching army. At sunset there is an interval, during which all the tribes partake of food and discuss matters of importance. This may occupy two hours. Then the ceremony begins.

Suddenly from a distance of two or three miles there floats upon the still air the soft, vibrating hum of a dozen or more bull-roarers.[1] Some of these are large—about eighteen inches long, four inches wide at the middle, and tapering toward both ends like a cigar. Some, on the other

---

[1] The Australian pattern of this instrument is similar to that found in various countries throughout the world. In parts of Scotland it is used in children's play, and is known by the name of 'thunner-spale.' It plays a great and important part in many ceremonies.

hand, measure only six inches in length. The volume of sound varies. Sometimes it will increase like the noise of a mighty wind, and then gradually diminish into a moan like the voice of departed spirits in distress. This performance lasts until sunrise on the following morning. Then there follows another interval of two hours, during which the tribes break their fast. These celebrations continue for six weeks or more at a time; and the full curriculum of initiation and ceremonial rites extends over several years.

The elders are conscious that the mind in childhood is

BULL-ROARERS
British Museum

more ready to accept and conform to their teaching than when it is more mature. So at eventide an elder will sit by the fireside, chanting a song and inviting the children to come and listen while a story is being told. The children cluster round him, eager to hear some tale that may relieve them from the strain of the mystery of the past weeks. Whatever the stories may relate to—animals,[1] birds, reptiles, fish, insects, land, sea, lakes, rivers, trees, shrubs, plants, or human giants—all symbolize something either good or evil in mankind.

While the children of the tribes are learning from the elders all the traditions and legends of the race, they are at the same time gaining the knowledge of bush-craft and acquiring the skill that is necessary in hunting. They also undergo the three great tests or initiations into manhood

[1] 'Animals' is used throughout the myths to designate animals of the class Mammalia, and no others.

and womanhood. These tests are generally commenced at puberty, and extend over a period of several years.

The first of the tests is the overcoming of appetite. This involves their doing a two days' walk or hunt without food, and then being brought suddenly before a fire on which

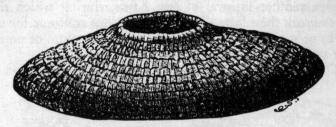

POUCH FOR CARRYING PITURI

Pituri is a native name for a shrub of the genus *Duboisia* of which the leaves contain a stimulant. They are chewed by the aboriginals.

From *Among Cannibals*, by Carl Lumholtz (Murray).

some choice kangaroo steak or other native delicacy is being cooked. They are required to take only a small portion of this.

The next is the test of pain. The young boys and girls submit to having their noses pierced, their bodies marked, and to being laid down upon hot embers thinly covered with boughs.

FOOD BOWL FROM CENTRAL AUSTRALIA

British Museum

The third is the test of fear. The young people are told awesome and hair-raising stories about ghosts and the *muldarpe*, the Evil Spirit or the Devil-devil. After all these tests they are put to sleep in a lonely place, or near the burial-place of the tribe. During the night the elders, who are made hideous with white clay and bark headdresses, appear, making weird noises. Those of the candidates who show no signs of having had a disturbed night are then admitted as fully initiated members of the tribe.[1]

No youth or maiden is allowed to marry without having passed these tests. A proposed marriage is talked over first by all the old members of the tribe. The uncle on the

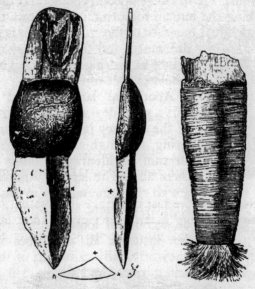

A FLINT KNIFE AND ITS SHEATH
From *Among Cannibals*, by Carl Lumholtz (Murray).

mother's side is the most important relative, and it is he who finally selects the wife. The actual marriage ceremony takes place during the time of festivals. The husband does not look at or speak to his mother-in-law, although he is husband in name to all his sisters-in-law. Under native conditions of living the sex laws are very strict.

A fully developed aboriginal has, in his own way, a vast amount of knowledge. Although it may not be strictly what is called scientific, still, it is very exact knowledge; and his

---

[1] See pages 173-174.

powers of physical observation are developed to the utmost. For instance, an aboriginal living under primitive conditions knows the anatomy and the haunts and the habits of every animal in the bush. He knows all the birds, their habits, and even their love-language—their mating notes. He knows from various signs the approach of the different seasons of the year, as well as from the positions of the stars in the heavens. He has developed in the highest degree the art of tracking the human footprint. He knows the track of every individual member of the tribe. There is as much difference and individuality in footprints as in fingerprints. There is a whole science of footprints.

SMALL BASKET FOR CARRYING ABOUT THE NECK

From *Among Cannibals*, by Carl Lumholtz (Murray).

Aboriginal language and customs vary a great deal according to the nature of the country in which the tribes are living, although there is a great substratum of identity running through them all. The legends and traditions are all the same tales or myths, told in slightly different language or manner on account of local or other colouring. For instance, all the tribes in South Australia agree that they originally came out of the northwest, struck the Darling river, and followed it down to Lake Alexandrina. They did not all come at once, but came in successive waves, and they have preserved the names of the tribes and the order in which they arrived. There is not the slightest hint in any of the traditions that there were any previous inhabitants in Australia.

The greatest time of the year for the aboriginals is the spring-time. It is then that all the great corrobberies take place. At these the sacred traditions are chanted or told.

All the stars and constellations in the heavens, such as the Milky Way, the Southern Cross, Orion's Belt, the Magellan Cloud, have a meaning. There are legends connected with all of them. The heavens are called Waiirri, and the ruler of the heavens is Nepelle.

22

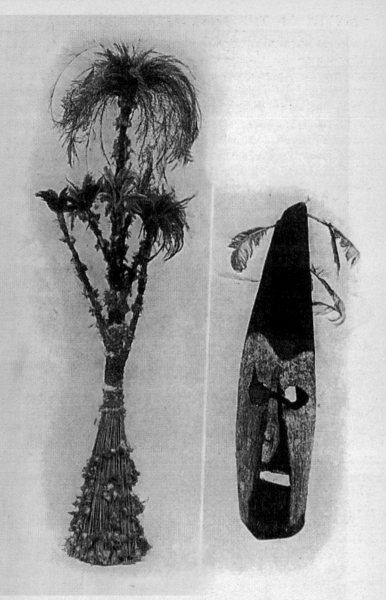

(1) HEAD ORNAMENT WORN AT INITIATION CEREMONIES IN
CENTRAL AUSTRALIA

(2) MASK OF BARK, WITH NOSE ORNAMENT, FROM NORTHERN
QUEENSLAND

British Museum   22

THE STREAM FAILS TO REACH THE SUN

THE STORY OF THE CREATION

From time immemorial the aboriginals have known and practised the art of mental suggestion. Their medicine-men have used charms and other similar means to drive out pain.

The aboriginals, when living under native and tribal conditions, have a very strict and effective code of laws by which the race is kept pure. It is only when they come in contact with white civilization that they disregard their tribal laws and customs. They have nothing to take the place of those old laws and well-established customs. The result is that civilization tends to cause disease and deterioration among them.

The Story of the Creation [1]

The voice of the Great Spirit spake unto Bajjara and Arna in a dream, and said, " Go forth and tell this story, for I have chosen you as my messengers." This is the story :

There was a great darkness which covered all space. This darkness was silent and still, and in it the earth dwelt cold and lifeless. Upon the surface of the earth were mountains with lofty peaks. There were also hills and valleys and plains, and deep caves and caverns. In these caves there were forms of life, but they were unconscious of their surroundings. There was no wind, not even a gentle breeze.

For a long, long time an awful, deathlike stillness pervaded everything. Within the darkness and stillness of the earth there slept a beautiful young goddess.[2] One day the

[1] This story of the Creation was told by a Karraru woman of the west coast of South Australia. She is sixty-five years old, and speaks her language fluently. Her name has a pleasing sound : Kardin-nilla. It means a laughing stream rushing and leaping onward, eager to reach the great and mighty ocean and to be lost in it.

[2] According to this story, the sun, who is female, is called by the names ' Sun Goddess,' ' the Young Goddess,' ' the Mother,' ' the Mother Goddess,' ' the Sun Mother,' ' the Mother Sun Goddess,' and ' the Goddess of Light and Life.' The moon, here also female, is ' the Lady of the Night.' The moon and the morning star, who is male, gave origin to the human race. When human beings die they become stars in the sky.

Great Father Spirit whispered gently to her, " You have slept and fulfilled my will. Now awake and go forth and give life to the universe and to everything therein. Do all as I command you. First awaken the grass, then the plants, and then the trees. After you have covered the face of the earth with grass, plants, and trees you will bring forth insects and fish, reptiles and lizards, snakes, birds, and animals. Then rest until all things that you have created shall have developed so as to fulfil the purpose for which they have come on the earth. Nothing shall come forth that is not for the benefit of other parts of the creation."

The Young Goddess took a great breath that caused the still atmosphere to vibrate, and she said to the Great Father Spirit that she was ready to do his bidding. She opened her eyes, and her whole being appeared to be flooded with light. Darkness disappeared before her. She looked abroad on the earth, and saw how empty it was. She looked beneath the earth, and she saw a tiny speck. Then from out of the distance she came toward the earth, swifter than a meteor. She alighted very gently, as if she feared to disturb the many living things that were upon it and beneath it. She made her home on the Nullarbor Plain,[1] and soon her influence began to be felt upon the cold life of earth.

From her home on the plain she set out on a journey, and continued on a western course until she came back to her starting-point in the east. As she walked the grass, the shrubs, and the trees sprang up in her footprints. Then she turned north, and walked straight on in that direction until she passed to the south and came back to her starting-point. She repeated these journeys round the earth until it was completely covered with vegetation. Then she rested from her labours, and made for herself a home on the Nullarbor Plain, and thus the Sun Goddess, the Mother, and the giant trees and vegetation all lived together in peace.

All at once the Sun Goddess heard a voice commanding

[1] This looks, and sounds, like an aboriginal name, but it is probably a Latin derivative descriptive of the country and meaning ' No Trees.'

her to go forth into the caverns of the earth and to bring forth life. She set out, taking warmth and brightness with her, into the dark, cold regions of the world. The spirits from beneath the earth cried out, " O Mother, why have you disturbed us? We have ruled over this part of the earth for millions of years." The Mother Sun Goddess stayed beneath the earth for one whole day, exploring all parts, and shedding her brightness on everything. Then there came forth from the earth swarms of beautiful insects. They were of all colours, sizes, and shapes ; and they began flitting from bush to bush and blending their colours with everything, and making the earth still more beautiful. Then the Mother Sun rested.

She continued resting in order that the insects might adapt themselves to their new condition of living. Then she rode in her chariot of light, and visited the mountain-tops to behold the glory that covered the face of the earth. After this she rose upon a mighty wind that carried her to every part of the earth in an instant of time. Upon this same wind she returned to her home on the Plain of Null-arbor. She rested for a time that would be equal to two sunrises. But at this stage of creation there was no setting of the sun. She shone continually during an eternal day, and there was no darkness except within the bowels of the earth. After resting, the Sun Goddess visited another cave or abyss. She looked down into its depth, and her radiant face shone with love, and drove the darkness away before her presence. She stepped down to the dark, cold, lifeless bottom. The solid ice there melted before her presence. Then she came forth, and went back to her home on the Nullarbor Plain. From out of this abyss there came forth snakes and lizard forms without legs, which crept upon their bellies upon the surface of the earth. A river also came forth from out of the cavern, and wended its way through a valley, and in the water of this river there were fish of all kinds, great and small.

Then the Sun Mother came and beheld her work, and saw that it was good. She commanded that the new life that she had created should be everywhere harmonious. The Sun Goddess again visited the mountain-top, and saw the trees, shrubs, grass, butterflies, beetles, snakes, and lizards, and the dry land and the water, and she was satisfied with her work. Again the wind came and bore her round on a visit to all corners of the earth, and brought her back to her home on the Plain of Nullarbor. There she rested for some time before resuming her work of creating.

When the Mother Goddess next went forth she was accompanied by insects, snakes, and lizards, who venerated her, and wished to see her create life from the next cavern. Once again the darkness of the cavern was driven out by her brightness as she descended to the bottom. All along the ledges and the bottom were the spirit forms of birds and animals. The Mother Goddess came out of the abyss, and the mighty wind again acted as her chariot, and took her back to her home on the Plain of Nullarbor. Some days after her visit to the cavern there came out of it birds in great numbers and colours. Then there came out animals of all shapes, sizes, and colours. These came straight to the Mother Goddess and looked upon her glory. They went away contented, and glad to be alive. The Sun Goddess rested a while. She saw that the Father of All Spirits was satisfied with all that she had created.

Then the Sun Mother commanded that the earth should be subject to short periods of seasonal changes. She ordained that first, for a certain length of time, there should be a hot period, and then that there should be a cold period ; but that there should not be any such extremes of heat and cold as would harm any of the creatures or the vegetation upon the earth. The Sun Mother said that this heat and cold should be felt throughout the various parts of the earth. From the very hottest parts the heat should gradually grow less and less until they became quite cold. Light and darkness were also to visit the earth, and were to succeed each other.

At the beginning of spring the Sun Mother called the insects, the reptiles, the birds, and the animals together, and a great multitude came from the north, the birthplace and the home of the north wind. Other great multitudes came from the south, the abode of the south wind; and from the west, the birthplace of the west wind. The greatest numbers came from the east, the royal palace, the cradle of the sunshine and sunbeams. When they all had assembled the Sun Mother spoke in a soft and gentle voice to the animals, the birds, the reptiles, and the insects. She said, " Listen, O children; I am your foster-mother. The Great Father Spirit has given me power to take you from the earth. My work on earth is completed, and now I go to a higher sphere, where I shall be your light and life. When I go I shall give you another being who shall govern you. You shall be his servants, and he shall be your lord and ruler. You all in part shall be changed. Your bodies shall go back into the earth, and that life that I called forth and that the Great Father Spirit gave you shall no longer dwell in form on the earth. It shall be transferred into those regions near my abode, and shall shine and be a guide to those who come after you. Your abode will be in the Spirit Land. But this shall not be until you have lived and followed the desires of your own hearts, and have reached a condition in which you are prepared to meet this change. And now I leave you."

Suddenly the Sun Mother rose from the earth, and soared up and up into the great heights. All the animals, the birds, the reptiles, and the lizards watched with fearful eyes the departure of the Goddess of Light and Life. As they stood gazing the face of the earth became dark, and they were all sore afraid of this strange happening. It filled them with fear and sadness, and when the darkness became greater they ceased their crying, thinking that the Mother Sun had forsaken them, and thus they remained until they saw the dawn in the east. Then they watched and were puzzled to see the gradual appearance of light behind them. They spoke among themselves, and said, " Did we not see the Mother Sun go to the west, and what is this that we see coming from the east?" They all stood facing the Sun Mother as she rose smiling upon them out of the eastern sky. They stood, rooted to the ground, watching the behaviour of their beloved Sun Goddess.

She did not remain still, but seemed to be continually moving on her journey toward the west. Suddenly it dawned upon them that this meant that the radiant smile of the Mother Sun Goddess would always be followed by a period of darkness, and that it was intended that the period of darkness should be a time of rest. So they all ran hither and thither, seeking shelter in the dense forests by burrowing in the ground or resting on the boughs of trees. The flowers that had opened to the bright sun closed up and went to sleep. The wattle-blossoms still kept awake all through the silent night. They wished to preserve their form and colour in darkness as in daylight. The water-spirit of the little streamlet loved the brightness of the sunshine so much that it rose and rose far beyond mortal vision. It wept and wept so bitterly in its efforts to reach the brightness that it became exhausted with grief, and it came back to earth and rested upon the trees, the bushes, and the grass in beautiful, sparkling dewdrops.

When dawn appeared in the eastern sky the birds were the first to behold the herald of the coming of the Mother Sun. They became so excited that some began to twitter and chirp, while others were so filled with joy that they laughed and laughed, and others sang a joyful song of praise. When the Mother Sun peeped up in the eastern sky the dewdrops rose up skyward, anxious to meet and accompany the Sun Mother. And this became the beginning of morning and night. All things living understood the plans of the Great Sun Mother.

After a great many years had gone by the animals and the birds began to weary. They were dissatisfied with their state of being. Some of the animals began to weep because they could not fly like the birds. The fishes became dissatisfied because they lived too much in the water. They felt that they would like to have a share in the beautiful sunshine, so they wept and wept, and pined away because they could not be animals, birds, or reptiles. The insects shared in the discontent, and some of them too began to pine away, while others slept and slept, and refused to eat or to enjoy life.

Then the Sun Mother came back to the earth, and gathered the people together, and said, " O children of the earth, have I not brought you forth from the womb of the earth? Have I not shone upon your shapeless forms and breathed life into them? O dissatisfied beings, I have given you life and the right to choose for yourselves. Do as you think best, but you shall all repent of the choice you make."

All the animals, the birds, the reptiles, the insects, and the fishes chose as they severally desired. Oh, what funny creatures some of them were—the kangaroo, the frilled lizards, the bats of all types, the pelican with its big bill, the platypus, the flying-fox, the stupid-looking old wombat, and the frog that grew to maturity in such a strange fashion ! First of all it came forth from the spawn, all belly and tail, then gradually it developed legs peeping out from where the body and the tail joined ; after a while the tail shrank and the body became well developed, four legs appeared, and then the frog was complete.

The mouse family of the bats wished to be birds ; so now the bat is able to fly, although it cannot grow feathers. The seal, not satisfied with being able to roam round the forests and hills, wished to live as it does to-day. The owl wept most bitterly for large and bright eyes, capable of seeing in the dark ; it was given its wish, but it is unable to see in the daylight ; so, during the day, it hides in a cave or in a hollow tree, because it cannot bear the glare and brightness. The owl is not able to look into the face of the Sun Mother. The koala [1] thought it a shame to be in possession of a brush or tail, and he wished to be rid of the beautiful tail that was the envy and admiration of all the animals, so the tail died off, and now the poor koala looks shy when in the company

---

[1] The aboriginal name for the *Phascolarctus cinereus*, known as the native sloth, native bear, tree-bear, and kangaroo-bear, a small, tree-climbing, heavy-looking marsupial that lives on the tender leaves of the eucalyptus.

of the dingo, who prides himself on his beautiful tail, and wags it proudly when he meets dogs or other animals. See, also, how some of the insect tribe have had their desires fulfilled. Some resemble bits of bark of trees, or twigs, or dried sticks.

This heterogeneous creation shows what can be brought about by discontent and foolish desire. When the Sun Mother saw that such strange beings would cause a difference between her and the children of the earth she said, " I will send unto you a part of myself, O children of the earth. My heart's desire shall come to you before I visit you to-morrow." So next morning, when the animals, the birds, the reptiles, and the insects arose, they saw the bright morning star rising out of the eastern sky and settling on the Nullarbor Plain. There the animals, the birds, and the reptiles congregated about him, but he did not speak to them. He sat with his eyes fixed on the east. When the Mother Sun rose she said, " I have given to you a son of the Spirit World, but he shall be one of you." Then she said to the bright morning star, " O my son, rule thou here, and I shall send you a friend. Watch, and when I dip beyond the western sky and darkness covers all the earth you will see a bright form coming out of the western sky. This is the Lady of the Night, who will help you to shine, and will share with you the joys of light."

And so it came to pass that when the Goddess of Light, the Sun Mother, rode on her chariot of light across the sky, and passed over to the west, and darkness drew her veil across the sky, the promised visitor came and shed her silvery light upon the earth. Thus was the moon born at the will of the Sun Goddess. The moon descended to the earth and became the wife of the morning star, and they brought forth children. These children dwelt and multiplied in the form of the human race. When they died they passed on to take their place in the sky in the form of stars.

The aboriginals say that the stars are the children of the sons and daughters of the morning star and the lady moon, who were created by the Sun Goddess. Bajjara and Arna, the prophets of the Spirit World, said, " You, my children, shall remember to whom you owe your birth, and you shall not seek to change your state like the animals, the birds, the reptiles, the insects, and the fishes. Remember, also, that you are superior to the creatures, and that you and your children and your children's children will all return to the Great All Father, the Eternal Spirit."

The Coming of Mankind

In the long ago, before there were any such human beings as now exist, Central Australia and the surrounding country was peopled by strange creatures—animals, birds, reptiles, and lizards of the same sort as one now sees. These creatures, such as the kangaroo, the wombat, the emu, the eagle-hawk, the goanna, and the carpet-snake, are represented by the tribe story-tellers of the present day as possessed of human intelligence, and as being able to convey and exchange ideas with one another. This was in addition to their possession and exercise of their own animal faculties and activities.

When the Sun Goddess, or Goddess of Birth, moved upon the earth the light and heat that radiated from her produced the forms of animal, bird, reptile, lizard, and fish, but not the form of man. Later on, from her own form, she brought forth into existence the being that to-day is recognized as the Father of All, or the One Great Father or Spirit of Mankind. When the Goddess of Birth beheld her handi-work she was pleased that she had manifested herself upon earth. Then she called the Father of all Spirits, and said, " I give all power to you to complete the work of creation." After saying this the Goddess of Birth took flight into the great regions of space, where she is seen every day, looking down and surveying her works of creation, and sending forth light, heat, and life.

Now the Great Father Spirit had the power of being able to be in every place at the same time. He thought he would endow the works of creation with some greater intelligence in order to assist them in ruling over and caring for the weaker animals, birds, reptiles, and fishes. He was undecided as to what form it should take, so he took a very tiny part of himself, and, looking at it, communed with himself, " Now to give this to the world would reveal myself to the world." After considering the matter he decided that he would take a part, not of himself, but of his intelligence, and place it in the kangaroo or the wombat until such time as would be fitting for the birth of the human being. The reason why the Father of All Spirits did not give this small part of himself to the dwellers on the earth was that it would develop, and would thereby reveal him to the creation, and this would affect his greatness and his holiness and his dignity ; and he had been advised by the Goddess of Birth not to do so.[1]

During this period of the life and existence of animals and birds the intelligence guided and directed the creatures to institute the ceremonies of initiation and the laws and customs that govern marriage. Now these creatures grew great in knowledge and in wisdom, and as time went on the intelligence within them began to expand, and it sought means to manifest itself. The wings of the emu and the eagle-hawk began to shed their feathers ; and the kangaroos, the goannas, the animals, and lizards wondered why their tails began to become shortened as the years went by. In some instances the tail disappeared altogether. The wombat and the blue-tongued lizards lost their tails while they were out in search of food, and they felt rather foolish when they started to return home without what they had considered was a great adornment. They looked so ridiculous that they were subjected to a great deal of ridicule and merriment by a jeering crowd.

But some of the more intelligent creatures realized that they were passing through a wonderful change from one condition of physical structure to another. Some of the fishes found that they could no longer live in the rivers, lakes, and sea at certain times of the year. They therefore

[1] Thus it came about that the Father of All Spirits apportioned part of his intelligence to dwell in animal, bird, reptile, lizard, and fish life until it should manifest itself in some new and definite shapes or forms.

made their habitations on dry land, in company with the lizards and the reptiles. When this change first took place some lizards and reptiles were sitting upon the bank of a river, and when they saw a fish emerge and come up out of the water they ran helter-skelter for refuge. Some climbed trees, while others in their alarm took to the water, although they had never before been in it. The platypus, the rat, and the mountain-devil are, to the aboriginal mind, the most striking evidence of the power of intelligence exerting itself in these strange creatures. These were the only creatures that seemed to take the form of birds and reptiles. Other creatures, the kangaroo, the wombat, the goanna, and the carpet-snake, developed a certain degree of resemblance to the present form of mankind. Some had the head and face of men, while others had the legs and toes, and still others resembled mankind in the form of the chest. The animals, the birds, the reptiles, and the fishes were such a jumbled-up lot of creatures that each sort forgot for a time its own identity. They also began to make remarks about the peculiarity of each other, and spoke of what they considered to be defects.

Now these remarks caused a great deal of resentment, hatred, misery, bloodshed, and death. The creatures began to quarrel, and then to wage war with one another. The owl families were continually in disagreement with the hawk families. Neither the hawk families nor the owl families would listen to the entreaties of the swan families to live in peace with them. The magpie quarrelled with every bird and with the smaller animals, especially the mouse and rat families. The falcon was the greatest terror of the feathered tribes, although he was not so big as the eagle-hawk. He was feared by all for his speed of flight when attacking anyone or even any number. Without warning he would swoop down upon them from his perch on the branch of a tree, or from a ledge or rock upon the cliff or mountain-side.

The Sun Goddess looked down upon her creatures in great pity when she saw how they were attacking and killing and devouring one another. She did not know what to do in order to adjust things properly and bring about a

33

settlement. She summoned the Father of All Spirits into her presence, and said to him, " Have I not endowed thee with all creative power and given thee power over the works of my creation? I alone can give power. I alone can act, and no one can dispute my doings. I walk up and down upon the earth, and the dust and water give forth life—animals, birds, fishes, and insects of every size and form. Some live upon the earth, some in the sea, and some may have to die in order to sustain the lives of others. Some subsist on vegetation, while others live upon other creatures. All living things must find sustenance from the beginning of their existence. And now I behold the results of the plan that you adopted of giving a part of your intelligence to every creature. Tell me why you did this."

The Father of All Spirits said, " O Goddess of Birth and Life, I thought I had conceived a plan by which the earth might be ruled. There was intelligence among the animals, the birds, the reptiles, the lizards, and the fishes, but it was of this earth, and did not go beyond this earth, and could not aspire to higher and nobler things. I knew that I had come direct by thy command and at thy will. I was not begotten of the dust like other forms, but came direct from thee. I cannot create a living form and place my intelligence within its body. I cannot think of form or beauty lest my thoughts produce a form that shall come forth in splendour as thou art. For my thoughts are not my thoughts alone, but are bound up in thine. Thou knowest that I shall not endeavour to produce a form and figure that will represent thee. But when I beheld the many shapes and forms of living things that walked, crawled, swam, and flew I thought that perhaps a small part of my intelligence, if implanted in the kangaroo, the wombat, or the fish, would one day produce that form of intelligence that would rule and assist all other life to accomplish thy great aim. By living in each individual creature it would gain experience of all varieties of life and of form. Then at some time it would come forth in a form separate from and independent of all other forms, and yet retaining a part of the original form. This would make the new creature realize that he belonged to the old order, but was not bounded by it. He would be able to aspire to higher things, even unto thee, O Goddess of Birth."

Then the Goddess of Birth said to the Father of All Spirits, " From this day onward through all the ages thou shalt be the designer, for I have found that thou hast thought rightly, and hast governed wisely all the works of my creation. Thou art supreme ruler of all living forms. Even man shall seek thee, and shall acknowledge thee to be god over all."

The All Father withdrew from the presence of the Sun Goddess, and continued the work entrusted to him. Thus from that day onward through all the changing scenes there existed the conception of a new order of beings with an intelligence derived from that of the Father of All Spirits. He commanded that the winds should take this intelligence and bear it away to the uttermost parts of the earth. As it passed over the north, the south, the east, and the west the mighty winds lashed the waters of the oceans into great rolling billows that thundered upon the rocky coasts. The lightning flashed and rent the mountain-side, and hurled the rocks in fragments before the wind. The kangaroo, the wombat, the emu—in fact, all living creatures—fled. Some hopped, some wriggled, some crawled, and some flew to a great plain to be free from the scattering boughs and the pebbles. Here they found a big cave that had been made ready for this contingency by the Goddess of Birth when first she came to earth. They hurried into it to take shelter from the elements. When they had all entered into the cave the rain descended in torrents, and flooded the whole country. The animals, the birds, the reptiles, the lizards, and the insects all trembled with fear as to what was happening. Never before had they seen such warring of the elements. Then the storm ceased, and after the sun had sunk in the western sky the creatures, both great and small, spent the night within the cave.

Next day not a sound was to be heard upon the earth. Quietness and peace reigned everywhere. For a while no

35

one could muster sufficient courage to venture forth. An old goanna stuck his head out, but quickly withdrew it. The anxious crowd said to him, " What have you seen ? " " Oh," said he, " I have seen a wonderful sight, an awful monster with an eye as big and bright as the moon. But wait a moment, his eye is brighter than the moon, and nearly as bright as the sun." Then, turning to the eagle-hawk, he said, " Will you look and tell us what you see ? " So the eagle-hawk strode toward the entrance of the cave, and looked out. He said, " I saw a form a little larger than the kangaroo. His eyes were not so big as the goanna's, but, oh, they were so bright ! There was power and might in them. They seemed as if they looked right through my whole being. I still tremble from the effect they had on me when I looked at them." Then the eagle-hawk bade the crow have a peep. The crow, feeling a creepy sensation passing all through him, said, " Why do you ask me to look at this being ? Has not the goanna told you that he has big, bright, and brilliant eyes ? Has not the eagle-hawk witnessed that the goanna was right ? Why am I asked to look ? " However, he did attempt to peep outside, but hurriedly withdrew his head. The laughing jack so completely forgot the serious position in which all thought they were that he started to laugh. The crow looked so scared, but he was using such endeavours to appear bold and philosophic that the laughing jack could not refrain from laughing and saying, " O crow, you must have seen a ghost of yourself and been afraid lest your apparition should beckon you to follow it into the Mysterious Land." The crow retorted in anger, " How do you know that I was afraid ? I was never afraid of an enemy, no matter how big and strong he was. You have no right to say such a thing."

Now every one present knew that the crow was the greatest warrior, and feared no one. The laughing jack said, " I have noticed, and so have others, that you did unconsciously duck your head quickly back into the cave as if from a frightful danger." In ordinary circumstances the crow would have attacked the annoying and jeering laughing jack, but in this instance he restrained himself.

Then all the animals, the birds, and the reptiles availed themselves of the opportunity of taking a peep at this strange new being. Some looked with a great deal of interest, curiosity, and reverence, and each saw something that the others had failed to note. They all gathered together to discuss what they had seen, and each had a different account to give of this new Intelligence that had arrived with the rain, the thunder, and the lightning. There was one thing, however, regarding which they were all agreed, and that was the brightness that shone from this formless being. Strange to say, whatever rays of light appeared to the vision of the watcher they were stamped upon his memory and also upon his body, and were plainly visible to those round about. They could not help calling each other's attention to the changes that occurred in their bodies. They became exceedingly afraid, and would not venture forth from the cave, even to hunt for food for themselves or their wives or children. Thus they remained for three days without food or water.

Then one day, when the eagle-hawk could not endure the hunger and thirst any longer, he slew a harmless rat, and drank its blood and ate its flesh. This was the beginning of a great slaughter of the inoffensive and weaker animals and birds that were poorer in intelligence by their stronger and more intellectual brothers.

Now the Intelligence of Mankind knew that if this slaughter continued much longer it would result in the extermination of many of the creatures, so it came to the entrance to the cave, still in its shapeless form, and called on the willy-wagtail [1] to come forth and listen to what it

---

[1] The aboriginals look upon the willy-wagtail as the most intelligent of all living creatures. Some tribes dread to see it near their camp. They will not dare to speak while it is near, and sometimes a camp of from forty to fifty people will remain silent until the bird has gone away. They think that the willy-wagtail will hear every remark they make, and will then fly off and make mischief between them and a neighbouring tribe. Some tribes look upon the bird as being employed by the Evil One to cause strife among men; and others think that he is in touch

had to say. The willy-wagtail, trembling with fear, went to the entrance of the cave. He felt a presence like the gentle touch of a soft breeze about his cheeks and ears. Then he heard a voice whispering to him, " Go back into the cave and tell the multitude of creatures to come forth, and to stand upon the hill-top yonder to the north. Then they shall behold me as I am." The willy-wagtail returned to the cave, and cried out in a loud voice, " Listen unto me, O creatures ! Behold, I have been called by the Intelligence to hear his message and to deliver unto you the words that he has spoken in my ear. At midday, when the Sun Goddess and the Goddess of Birth stand overhead, all males and females, old and young, shall gather together on yonder hill. Then shall we behold the greatness, the power, and the majesty of the Sun Goddess in the birth of the new order and the being of intelligence, who shall rule and be a maker of all other creatures. This is the message, ' Be not afraid. He has not withdrawn his presence. We may go in peace and safety into the woods and forests, and procure food and water.' "

All the elders of the males representing the multitude came forth and gathered food and brought water to supply their families in the cave. Next morning they arose very early, broke their fast, and betook themselves to the hill-top that had been selected for the birth of man, the higher intelligence, the conception of the Sun Goddess. They took with them a supply of food sufficient for two days, and they sat beneath the shade of the trees and the rock ledges, anxiously awaiting the appointed time. They placed sentinels to keep watch in case of any unforeseen event. When the Sun Goddess stood right above them, then old and young, males and females, filled with excitement, rose to their feet. Then a young eagle-hawk that stood upon a rock called out in solemn tones, " Behold, ye creatures ! Look ye to the north ! What do you see ? " The elders replied, " We see

with departed spirits. If the willy-wagtail should hear anyone speak disrespectfully of a departed spirit he will go at once and tell the reviled one, and the spirit will return and haunt the offender. The willy-wagtail is treated with such great respect because he was the first living creature to whom the Intelligence spoke at the beginning of creation.

a pillar like smoke travelling to the west." The eagle-hawk said, " Behold, ye creatures! Turn your eyes to the west! What do you see?" The elders replied, " We see another pillar like smoke travelling south, and the northern pillar seems to be following the western pillar." Once again the eagle-hawk called out in a solemn voice, " O ye creatures, what do your eyes see?" And the elders replied, " We see a third pillar like smoke, and it seems as if it is travelling toward the sunrise. Is it not a manifestation of the power, wisdom, and glory of the Goddess of Birth, the Mother of Life? Let us all stand in silence." Meanwhile, the north wind with its pillar was chasing the west wind in order to overtake and join it. The west wind with its dust-like pillar was chasing the south wind as if to join it. The south wind was chasing the east wind as if eager to join it; while the east wind travelled slowly as if waiting for the other winds and dust-pillars to come up with it. When these dust-pillars first took shape they were about forty miles apart, and they were circling round the hill on which the multitude stood. As they circled they took a spiral course, and came nearer and nearer. Some of the creatures became afraid, but the willy-wagtail said to them, " Fear not, for you shall yet behold your lord and master, who shall become the Father of Mankind when the Goddess of Birth creates him."

Now the pillars of dust were about a mile from the multitude. They rose till they were about a mile above the hill-top. Then they gradually formed themselves into the shape of a huge mushroom. It remained stationary for an hour, and then it gradually descended toward the hill-top. The eagle-hawk jumped down from his place on the rock, and joined the multitude. The stem gradually came down until it touched the spot on the rock where the eagle-hawk had stood. Suddenly the mushroom-like cloud began to take the shape of a water-spout, curving over and over the top, and dropping spray-like water earthward, and dwindling in length until it measured only about twenty feet. Then a thunderbolt shot out of the clear sky down into the centre of the spout, causing a flame of fire. Within this flame of

39

fire there became visible the perfect form of man as he is
to-day. The flame gradually faded away, and left the figure
standing in all its perfection, crowned with the glory of
intelligence. The Sun Goddess remained for one day midway between the zenith and the western horizon, gazing
with a satisfied smile upon her work of conception. This
was the only occasion on which the Sun Goddess rested on
her journey through the sky. She did this in order to shed
a smiling beam of love and approval upon her work, and to
show that man should rule the earth and all that remained
upon the earth and sea. Then man stepped down from the
rock and mingled with the creatures, and conversed with
the kangaroo, the emu, the goanna, the eagle-hawk, and that
most important person the willy-wagtail. Thus did Intelligence make in physical form the acquaintance of his former
companions.

After this the Sun Goddess continued her journey, never
to stop again. Man then began his physical existence side
by side with the animals, the birds, the reptiles, the lizards,
and the insects. There came a time during his sojourn with
these creatures when he became eager to know more about
their ways of living. The first individual he saw was the
peewee,[1] a little bird of form and colour similar to the magpie.
He said to him, " O my friend and companion, you will
recall the time when I lived within you and endeavoured to
develop you into some other form that would become my
everlasting home ; but you refused to expand as my intelligence urged. My intelligence was so great a thing that it
lived in all creatures. Some of them responded a little to my
greatness of thought, but would not go so far that I could
make my permanent home in them. Then the Father of All
Spirits commanded that I should come forth out of all
creatures, and I obeyed him. I spent a long period of existence among the elements, the wind, the rain, and the lightning. From those states I have emerged, and now have the

[1] The peewee (*Grallina cyanoleuca*) is a bird peculiar to Australia. It has a
variety of names, such as ' mud-lark,' ' magpie-lark,' ' little magpie,' ' Murray
magpie,' and ' peewit.'

AN ABORIGINAL FROM THE MUSGRAVE RANGES

Photo Taylor's Collotype Series

40

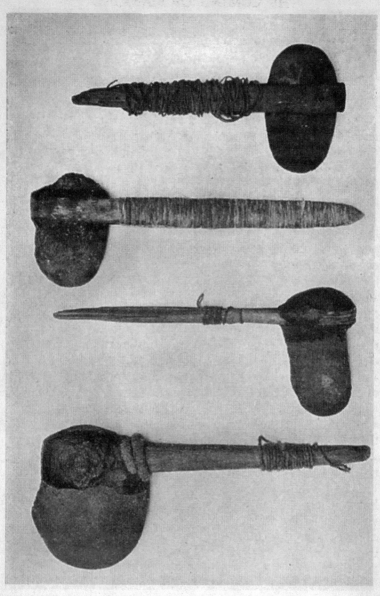

ABORIGINAL STONE AXES, WITH HAFTS

British Museum

48

form and shape in which you behold me. I am anxious to hear of some of your experiences." Then the peewee began to tell his story in the bird language that he uses to-day.

The Peewee's Story

" I sat upon a tree that stood beside a spring of water that flowed continually, summer and winter. I had discovered this spring during the course of my wanderings, and as it was not affected by droughts and was always cool and refreshing I decided to make it my home. One day as I sat gazing around and thinking how beautiful the countryside was I looked down to the ground and saw my footmarks in the soft mud. I flew down and examined the impression, and stood looking at the mud. I took up a beakful of it to examine it. I flew back to the branch of the tree, and placed the mud carefully upon it. Then I sat thinking, thinking, and waiting for an inspiration. I must have sat like this for more than an hour. I looked at the clay that I had placed upon the bough and saw that it had stuck. Suddenly a thought struck me, and I decided to build my home of this clay-mud. As I built I sang, ' O Sun Goddess! My home and abiding place by the cool, refreshing spring of the water of life is a gift from thee.' I stepped into my nest and soon went fast asleep. I woke very early next morning, and went a-hunting. I gathered enough food to last me all day, and then I returned to my home and nest.

" When I arrived I saw to my surprise some one sitting there awaiting my return. It was a beautiful female peewee. I asked her how she came to be there all alone, and how she knew where I lived. She said, ' I was out with the other young girls and maidens gathering insect food, and we became separated in our search for water. I wandered away from the rest of the party, and now here I am.' She seemed to be weary with her journey, so I told her to rest in my home. She thanked me, and slept soundly while I stood upon the branch and kept the mosquitoes from disturbing her. When I looked upon her beautiful face I fell in love

41

with her. She awoke from her sleep, and she was startled to see me standing beside her. She looked around, and she once more realized that she was lost, and that she was in a very trying position with a stranger standing beside her. She began to weep and to sob most bitterly. I tried to cheer her and to comfort her with kind words. Then I promised to take her to her mother and her father and other relatives. So we set out and flew southward until we came to a small flowing stream of water. She recognized this at once as being near to her home. When we arrived at her home she told her mother and father the story of her wanderings, and how she had gone into a strange young man's home, and how kindly she had been treated there. The mother and father thanked me for my kindness to their daughter.

" I bowed my head and flew back to my home beside the spring. After I had lived for three months in my new home I noticed that nearly all living things were busily and happily engaged in mating. I felt lonely, and wished that I might feel the same joy as the animals, the birds, the lizards, and the reptiles. At eventide I heard the magpie singing his love-song to his mate as she sat beside him upon the branch of a tree. I heard the young men bandicoots [1] fighting as to who should be the husband and lord of the young maiden bandicoot. There were other birds and animals whose intelligence seemed to be more advanced, and they sought mates from among the individuals of another species. The emu mated with the goanna tribe, and some of the other bird tribes married into the reptile tribe. The eagle-hawk took a daughter of the crow family as his mate. All this time my heart yearned for the maiden who had slept in my home, for her presence seemed still to linger there. Sometimes when I was resting in my nest, and the gentle breeze from the south fanned my hot cheek, it seemed as if it came from her bosom. Then at night I was startled in my dreams by thinking that I heard her call. On this I rose and began singing a love-song to her, and continued singing until I realized that

[1] This family is the only one among the class of marsupials in which a placenta occurs.

it was only a dream. Then I lay down to sleep. But at intervals during the night I started to my feet because I fancied I heard her calling. Unable to rest, I decided I would spread my wings and fly away south to seek her favour. So one morning, before the sun rose, I started for the south, and flew straight to the home, and alighted about a hundred yards before it.

" Just as the sun appeared over the mountain in the east I sat upright upon a branch of a tree, and, half spreading my wings, pushed out my chest, raised my head upward, and with all the love that pulsed in my heart I pleadingly sang to her, ' I am thinking of making a nest and a home.' Then I stood still for a while, straining my ears in listening for a response. I thought that perhaps she might be asleep. But no, that could not be; no peewee is asleep at this time of the morning. Then a dreadful feeling came over me. I thought I might have come too late. Some young peewee may have claimed her and taken her to another part of the country. This I thought could not be possible when I recalled the look upon her face on that memorable day when she came to my home and I took her safely to her parents and relatives. On that occasion she spoke to me with her eyes, and I saw through the windows of her soul that she loved me. How, then, could she ever forget me and take another whom she did not love? I knew it could not be, and then I raised my head, opened my mouth, and with all the love of my being I sang again, ' I am thinking of making a nest, a home.'

" As soon as I had uttered the last words of my song there came floating upon the morning air the sweet voice of my lady bird answering me, and repeating the words of the song. I was thrilled through my whole being, and was full of joy and excitement at meeting her once more. I sang, ' Let us fly away. My breast swells with joy and love for thee, just like yonder bushes bursting into bloom with sweet-scented flowers.' She replied instantly in the words of my song, but before she had completed the last strain I flew toward her. She heard the rustle of my wings, and she sat

43

shyly awaiting me. I sat down close beside her, and we expanded our wings, spread out our chests, looked upward into the blue sky, and sang together a song of praise to the Sun Goddess, the Mother of All Living Things, who had given us life and sustenance, and who had also endowed every living thing with the greatest of all gifts—the mutual longing for a kindred soul, and the desire to belong to each other and to have children of a like mind.

"Then we sat in silence for a while to allow an interchange of feelings and emotions in a language that no song, or speech, or other medium can express. We sat thus until the sun was half-way up in the eastern sky, and when we awakened from our love-dream we saw the mother and father of my lady bird sitting upon another tree, watching us. We spread our wings and hopped from the bush upon which we had been sitting. We bade farewell to my lady bird's mother and father and turned our faces toward the north, the land of dust-storms and blazing heat. I told the parents of my wife that when they grew old and wished to see their daughter they could come to my home. My wife and I lived very happily, and reared a large family, and our children have migrated to other parts of the country."

After the peewee had finished his story he walked away, and the Intelligence was left to think over what had been told him. Never before had the great Intelligence felt so lonely. The little peewee's story had struck a chord that had aroused in his soul a desire for a companion. He did not wish to choose one from among the multitudes upon the earth, for when he dwelt within the kangaroo, the wombat, the emu, and others they had failed to respond to his dictates and influence. He made up his mind that before he decided to do anything he would consult the willy-wagtail, who might be able to help him. He thought that perhaps among the multitude of beings he might find one that was capable of developing so as to be his fitting companion.

So the Intelligence set off to hunt up the willy-wagtail. When he had found him, he said, "I have heard a most wonderful story of the life of the peewee. These birds will

not marry anyone outside of their kind. Can you tell me
of any marriages where the two who were joined were both
of another kind?" "Oh, yes," said the willy-wagtail, "the
eagle-hawk, the crow, the kangaroo, and the emu all married
outside of their own kind. This is the story of the eagle-
hawk and the crow."

THE EAGLE-HAWK AND THE CROW

"The chief of the crow tribe decided to offer his daughter
as a wife to the only son of the chief of the eagle-hawk tribe.
The swan, the pelican, and the cockatoo families protested
against such a marriage taking place, but the two chiefs were
obstinate, and persisted in having their own way in the
matter. The other bird tribes were afraid to press their
objections, because the eagle family was a very powerful one,
and the crow family was feared more than the eagle family
on account of its intelligence and cunning. The daughters
of the crow family were very handsome, and the eagles were
comely youths, and their one aim was to be married to one
another. Now these beings were half human and half birds
on account of the presence of the Intelligence. They remained in this state for some time, until they ruined matters
by intermarrying. The Sun Goddess decreed that, instead
of their passing into oblivion when they died, they should
return to their first state of being.

"During the period of man's first existence in his human
form the eagle-hawk was the king of the bird tribes. He
gave authority to the falcon to govern his subjects and to see
that all his wishes were carried out. The falcon ruled with
an iron hand, and showed neither sympathy nor pity. He
would suddenly swoop down from the sky upon a culprit
and kill him.

"One day, however, the young eagle-hawk chief took for
his wife the beautiful daughter of the crow. The magpie,
meeting the laughing jack and the killunkillie,[1] said, ' This

---

[1] This is a bird as large as a crow. It partakes of characters of the crow and the
magpie, and receives its name from its cry, *Killunkillee*. It acts as a sentinel for
the kangaroo.

is the end of the eagle-hawk's power. The daughter of the crow will never submit to the commands of the eagle-hawk. The young eagle-hawk will do all he can to break the stubborn will of the crow girl. There is one thing, however—the young girl will be afraid to run away from home because of the vigilance of the falcon. But she will starve herself to death rather than become the slave of the eagle-hawk. While she will endeavour to have her own way, the eagle-hawk will be determined to have his; and the trouble will begin when the crow family go back to their own country.' Many years before the marriage of the eagle-hawk and the crow suggestions had been made that the magpie and the killunkillie tribes should intermarry, but the eagle-hawk tribe refused to allow such marriages to take place.

" One day the young eagle-hawk went out hunting, and when he returned he saw his wife sitting talking with the magpie and the killunkillie. He was very jealous, and he gave strict orders that she was to stay in the camp and remain indoors. His wife resented his orders, so he resorted to other means to subdue her. He was afraid to do anything openly, in case it should come to the ears of the crow family, who would immediately come armed and prepared to fight. So every day when the food was brought the young chief would eat the greater portion, and leave only a very small share for his wife. In this way he was gradually starving her to death. When she had a baby the young chief gave her still less to eat. He knew that her mother-love would not allow the baby to starve, and that she would give most of her food to the little one. The mother became gradually weaker, until one day she was found dead in her camp. The young chief called the peewee, and asked him to go and tell the crow family to come at once, because his wife had been found dead in her camp. He said he thought that probably the magpie or killunkillie tribes had been using their charm-sticks or their pointing-bones in order to kill her.

" When the crow family heard of the death of the young wife they were very sad, and vowed that if she had been done to death by the cruelties of her neighbours they would take vengeance—that from thenceforth every living being would be regarded as an enemy, and that they would slay all such, whether animals, birds, reptiles, lizards, or fishes. When they came within a mile of the home of the eagle-hawk they circled around the camp, crying mournfully, ' Wa, wa, wa.' They did this three times, and then went straight to the place where the dead body lay. Then they began to wail so loudly that their cries could be heard for miles. Every creature that heard the lamentation came and expressed sympathy with the bereaved family. Then the crow family took the dead body of the once beautiful maiden, wrapped it in a shroud of bark and fibre, and placed it in the fork of a tree. They then returned to their country and their home.

" Now the elder brother of the maiden had not attended the funeral. He did not even utter a word or shed a tear, but just sat pondering over the death of the sister whom he had loved most dearly. When the family set out to attend the funeral he instructed them not to say one word about his absence. If the eagle-hawk asked where he was they were to say that he had gone somewhere, but they did not know where. He, the crow, intended to pay a visit to his brother-in-law, the eagle-hawk, as if he were unaware of the death of his sister. He waited until two moons had gone by, and then he set out on his journey to visit his brother-in-law. He went all alone, and took with him one spear and a *wommera*.[1] He had his suspicions that his sister had met her death through the cruelty of her husband, and so he had made up his mind to take the life of his sister's son, who was now being brought up by his father, the eagle-hawk. For the eagle-hawk might at any time marry again and take as his wife the daughter of some other tribe, and so would not be able to give his son all the care and attention that he required.

" The eagle-hawk had made his camp upon a rocky hill. On the eastern side of this there was a plain extending for a mile, and beyond this there was scrub. On the western

[1] An aboriginal name for a throwing-stick. The spelling of this word varies. The many varieties of spelling are the attempts of different writers to imitate the sound of the word.

side the scrub country extended right up to the base of the hill on which the home of the eagle-hawk was. The crow camped out in the scrub country on the eastern side, and approached his brother-in-law's home from across the plain.[1] One morning, very early, as the eagle-hawk sat with his son outside their wurley,[2] roasting some flesh for their breakfast, he noticed a figure emerge from out of the eastern scrub. It moved as if in dire distress, and when about three parts across the plain country it rested as if too weary to proceed. The eagle-hawk recognized the figure as his brother-in-law, the eldest brother of his late wife; and he rose and turned his back [3] and faced the west.

" After the eagle-hawk had turned his back he said to his son, ' I see that your uncle is coming. If you will run your eye directly east across the plain you will see him sitting down to rest his weary feet.' The little boy looked toward the plain with eager eyes. He was glad that his uncle was coming, and he would have run out to meet him, but his father said, ' By his appearance he seems to have travelled a very long distance, and probably he is now hungry.' As the eagle-hawk was speaking the crow rose from the earth and limped toward the camp as if he were lame and footsore with walking. The eagle-hawk saw his poor brother-in-law in distress, and turned to his son, and said, ' My son, will you take the meat from off the coals, and break off the top bough of a mallee?' The boy ran away to the near-by scrub and selected the green, tender tops of the tree, and returned hurriedly to his father, full of excitement, and anxious to serve his uncle. The father took the meat and laid it upon

[1] The eagle-hawk chief decreed that no one should in any circumstances enter into the hunting-ground or dare to approach his home and camping-ground under penalty of death. The crow, however, on account of his relationship with the eagle-hawk, was privileged. Another point to be noted in connexion with this story is that the eagle-hawk, as king of the bird tribes, supplied all the flesh food for a great number of beings, and no one else was allowed to go hunting.

[2] A local name for a native hut. In other localities it is called *mia-mia, humpy,* or *oompi.*

[3] This is a custom adopted by the aboriginals as a sign of honour and respect. To sit or to stand confronting a visitor is considered to betoken rudeness and suspicion and unfriendliness.

the green bough, in order to have everything ready. He then said to his son, ' Go and meet your uncle.'

" The son ran to meet his uncle, and said, ' My poor dear old uncle, will you be pleased to come and take the food we have prepared for you? It is very simple, but it will give you strength after your long and wearisome journey. Come!' So the crow rose and came limping to the camp. He seated himself beside the child, and began to caress him, saying, ' O child of my dear sister, your uncle has travelled a long distance from a strange country to see you before he is called to the Spirit Land. I have taken the first opportunity, my child, to come to see you.' The little boy threw his arms around the neck of his uncle, and asked, ' O Uncle, when shall I see Mother? Where has she gone? Is it a long, long way? Will you take me to her?' The crow said, ' You will soon see your mother, my child.' The child became very pleased, and thanked his uncle. Then he rose and went to sit beside his father.

" Now the eagle-hawk was sitting about fifty paces away when the crow arrived, and he was still facing the west. When the crow had finished his meal he said to his brother-in-law, ' I am very weary after my long journey. I have not slept for three nights, but have walked day and night to come to you. I shall rest now.' The crow walked away to a tree that cast a nice, cool shade beneath it. The little child brought out rugs and placed them upon the ground, and the uncle lay down on them. Soon he fell sound asleep, and the little child sat beside him, watching that nothing should disturb him. The crow slept soundly, and when he woke the sun had sunk in the west. Meantime, the eagle-hawk had been away, seeking for another wife. He had visited the bandicoot family, hoping to find favour with the bandicoot maidens, but he was disappointed. During a conversation he had with the emu and the magpie he had gleaned the knowledge that the bandicoot family were seeking an alliance with the crow family, because they thought that this would be more advantageous than one with the eagle-hawk. The eagle-hawk therefore returned home in a

49

very irritable mood, and decided to make the stay of the crow very unpleasant. Calling his son to him, he said, ' My son, your uncle is footsore and weary after his long journey, and is unable to go hunting to get his food, so he must depend upon our generosity. When I am away you will take only sufficient food to supply your own wants, and when your uncle asks for a share you will say, ' O Uncle, Father has left me only enough of food for myself. Now, Uncle, would you like the son of your dead sister to be in want? Would my mother take from me the sustenance necessary for my strength?'

"At sunrise on the morning of the second day the eagle-hawk was away, visiting the bandicoot family. When the child was having his breakfast the uncle asked him for food. The child gave him the answer that his father had ordered him to give. The poor old uncle bowed his head in grief, and was forced to go and hunt for his own food, although he was very footsore. While he was away the crow decided that next day he would fulfil the object of his visit to the eagle-hawk's camp. He made a special spear with a sharp flint point. Next day he collected a good supply of food. He called the child to him and gave him plenty to eat. The child became very thirsty, and the uncle said, ' Go and get a drink from yonder water-hole.' The child did so, and called from the water-hole, ' O Uncle, can you see me?' The uncle asked, ' Where are you?' and he fixed his spear on to his *wommera*. He then threw the spear and killed the child. The uncle then began dancing around, so that when the father returned he would think that a great number of people had taken part in the killing of the child, and that there had been a fierce fight.

"The eagle-hawk returned just as the sun sank in the west, and the crow told him that a great number of people had passed by, and that he had fought with them and had put them to flight, but that they had slain the child. The eagle-hawk made a vow on the spot that he would not rest

FLINT SPEAR-
HEAD
British Museum

50

day or night until he had slain the murderer of his child. He then returned to his camp, and sat pondering on the death of his son. He rose early the next morning and went back and carefully examined the footprints to see whether he could recognize one particular footprint. He discovered to his amazement and horror that what he had taken to be the footprints of many were the footprints of only one person, and that the person was his brother-in-law, the crow. He was inflamed with a desire to be revenged, for here was the murderer of his son and the one who was about to claim the daughter of the bandicoots for his wife. So he planned to kill the crow. The eagle-hawk returned to his camp, and wrapped the dead body of his child in fibre taken from the mallee-tree and the tea-tree. He then asked the uncle to come and dig a grave. The crow came and started digging, and when he got down about six feet he looked up from the grave and saw the face of the eagle-hawk above him, convulsed with malice and hatred. So he set to work, and very quickly dug a hole into the side of the grave. Then he called out, ' Is the grave deep enough?' Thereupon the father threw down on top of the crow the dead body of the child, and hastily filled in the grave with grass, boughs, and earth. He intended to bury the crow alive with the dead child. As soon as the crow found that he was being covered over by his brother-in-law he began to dig a tunnel leading from the grave into a clump of mallee about a mile away. This work took him all day.

" The eagle-hawk felt very satisfied with his work. He had got rid of the murderer of his child and his hated rival for the hand of the bandicoot maiden. He thought that he would now hasten away to the bandicoot family with the news and that he could ask for the hand of the bandicoot maiden without any fear of opposition. When he had finished telling the bandicoot family the news that the crow was dead the willy-wagtail said, ' Friends, do not be deceived, for as I came across yonder plain a short time ago I heard the familiar voice of the crow calling three times over my head. I looked up into the sky, but could see no one. Again I heard the voice quite plainly saying ' *Waka, waka, wakaroo-oo*.' I again looked, but could not see anything, but I felt a chill running down my back. I ran across the plain as fast as my legs could carry me, but I still heard the voice of the crow all about me. How can he be dead if I heard his voice? And, eagle-hawk, it was the voice of the elder brother of your late wife.' The eagle-hawk became alarmed, and asked the willy-wagtail to go and see that his home, and also the homes of his two brothers, who were staying on the north side of his home, were in good order and able to stand a siege. After the willy-wagtail had done this the eagle-hawk returned home, and the two sat down to rest for the night; but they were unable to rest, for they heard the weird, mournful, dying note of the crow, calling ' *Waka, waka, wa*,' the last word ' *wa* ' being drawn out on such a note that it froze the blood in their bodies.

" At last the willy-wagtail got sufficient courage to look out of the camp. It was a clear night. There was not a cloud in the sky, and the moon was full and was shining brightly. He looked toward the west, and suddenly there was a flash of lightning out of the clear sky, and at the same time the call of the crow broke out on the still night air. Suddenly it dawned upon the eagle-hawk and the willy-wagtail that the crow had adopted the lightning as his totem when he saw the wonder and power of it at the beginning of the creation, and they became afraid. Then the eagle-hawk said to the willy-wagtail, ' Run to the homes of my brothers and see that everything is in order. If the storm destroys my camp I shall seek shelter with you.' The willy-wagtail hurried away, and in about an hour's time he arrived at the camp of the brother of the eagle-hawk. He rested for about half an hour. Then he looked out at the eagle-hawk's camp. A dark cloud stood directly over it, and from the cloud there shot streaks of lightning, and the thunder rolled unceasingly. But above the noise of the thunder there could be heard the wail, '*Wa, waka, wa !*' with the last note drawn out as if some one was in agony.

" All at once a brighter streak of lightning flashed from the clouds in a zigzag fashion upon the camp of the eagle-hawk, and a flame of light sprang up that lit the whole countryside. Then the eagle-hawk started to run to the camp where the willy-wagtail was waiting and shaking with fear. When the eagle-hawk arrived at the camp he dropped at the feet of the willy-wagtail, scared almost to death. The willy-wagtail laid him down gently, and kept putting a moist stick into his mouth until he revived. All the time there came the distressing sounds of the cry of the crow that sent a death-shudder through both of them. They pinched their ears, they plucked the hair from their upper lips, they pushed grass up their nostrils to make them sneeze. All this they did to make sure that they were alive and that they were not dreaming. Then an awful sound greeted their ears, and they were horrified to see that the cloud was changing its course and coming directly toward their camp. The willy-wagtail told the eagle-hawk what was happening, and the eagle-hawk said, ' Go into the next camp and prepare for my coming.' The willy-wagtail dashed out of the camp, and sought a place of shelter. He could still hear the moaning of the crow as he ran. All at once he saw a bright flash of light strike the earth at their last camp. Then he saw the eagle-hawk running as hard as he could.

" When the eagle-hawk arrived at the camp he fell exhausted, and the willy-wagtail revived him with water. Then the eagle-hawk said, ' My sins have found me out. It is the ghost of my brother-in-law whom I buried alive near my first camping-ground. He has come to be revenged. Oh, where shall I fly? How can I atone for the cruelties to which I subjected my wife? Why have I lusted after those who are not of my kind? This has brought destruction to all my hopes. I now have no son.' ' There is only one way out of this curse,' said the willy-wagtail. ' Let us return to the grave and remove the body of your brother-in-law. Perhaps his spirit may be satisfied that you have repented of your evil deeds.' The eagle-hawk

53

said to the willy-wagtail, ' I feel that something is going to happen. A change is coming that will alter the whole course of my life. We will do as you suggest when the storm has passed by.' ' I think,' said the willy-wagtail, ' that the storm intends to follow you until you are worn out in body, mind, and soul. It is the will of the spirit of the crow.'

" As soon as these words were uttered there was heard the awful, deathlike sound of the crow's ' *Waka, waka !* ' which caused the eagle-hawk and the willy-wagtail to shudder, and made their flesh creep. The willy-wagtail said, ' Our fingers, our arms, and our legs seemed to be sundered. We were afraid to move. As the storm approached we lay flat upon the ground, and the voice of the crow ceased. Then our bodies returned to their usual state, and the eagle-hawk said to me, " Go quickly and seek a place where we may shelter." I obeyed, glad to escape the awful ordeal that we were passing through ; and I ran for about half a mile, till I reached the mountains. I took shelter underneath an overhanging boulder, and I watched the storm as it came nearer and nearer to the eagle-hawk's camp. Then I heard the voice of the crow above the roar of the thunder. The strange thing was that sometimes it seemed that the voice had the sound of mockery in it, as if the crow was amused at our vain attempts to escape him. " *Wa-ha-ha !* " The *wa* was drawn out and the *ha* came in quick, sharp, laughing-like notes. Then a streak of lightning, brighter than the two that had destroyed the camps of the eagle-hawk, made the night seem as if it were midday in the places where we were hiding. Then there arose a great flame of fire, ascending from the place where the eagle-hawk hid ; and as I watched the flame began to take form, until it showed the shape of the eagle-hawk's former self. He spread his wings joyously, as if glad to be free from the half-man and half-bird state. He shouted, " *Pillchorke ! Pillchorke !* " and floated majestically, and rose higher and higher, until he was above the thunder, the lightning, the rain, and the storm.

54

" ' When the morning came I heard a voice far away in the sky. Then there came a noise as if a mighty storm were raging ; and the noise came nearer and nearer, until I saw an object come straight down upon the mountain-peak and rest there for a while. This was the eagle-hawk, who had returned to his own surroundings that had been planned by the Goddess of Birth in the beginning, before he had been endowed by the Father of All Spirits with intelligence. Meantime, the crow had not escaped entirely, for, as a result of his visiting the earth in the flashes of lightning, seeking revenge, he was burned and singed just the colour of a dead coal fire. Thus was the crow changed in colour from pure white to black. He was punished, too, because he had slain his nephew, and instead of living half man, half bird, he was brought back to his former state. There were other forms that were brought back to their true selves, and some have still maintained the resemblance of some other species by the marriage that had been performed. The eagle-hawk, before marrying the daughter of the crow, had been allied by marriage with the snake family. Such was the shocking state of marriage customs which allowed animals to marry into the bird and the reptile and the lizard tribes.' "

Then the Human Intelligence sat down to consider all that had been told him by the peewee and the willy-wagtail. After that he went away and lived by himself upon a mountain. After some time he came to the willy-wagtail once more, and inquired for the evidence in support of his story. The willy-wagtail said to the Human Intelligence, " Have you seen the bat family, the platypus, and some of the lizard species ? These were at one time the offspring of the bird tribes. They intermarried with animals and reptiles."[1] The Human Intelligence looked about him, and saw that there was truth in what the willy-wagtail said.

The Intelligence then retired to contemplate in solitude. The years rolled by, and age after age brought various

[1] This story gives an account of the origin of the great custom of totemism. The marriage customs of the aboriginals had their origin from this mythology.

great and wonderful changes. Then once more the Human Intelligence descended from the mountain-top, and made his home amid the animals, the birds, the reptiles, the lizards, and the fishes. He saw and understood their ways, and gained knowledge of their manner of living. All the species married into their own kind, thus returning to the custom originated by the Goddess of Birth. He saw the magpie with his companion constructing a nest and a home. He was fascinated, and he sat day by day watching things as they developed. Then one day, when the nest was complete, he saw that one bird sat in the nest, and he wondered why. Another day, when the nest was vacant, he looked in it and saw what at first he thought was a pebble. This was the first egg that he had seen. Some time after he saw the birds flying toward the nest with something in their beaks. Presently he saw a little head pop up from the nest. This greatly aroused the curiosity of the Human Intelligence, and he watched the actions of the animals, the birds, the reptiles, the lizards, and all living things. He saw that they were giving expression to themselves according to their nature, and that the result of this expression was the reproduction by each of its peculiar kind.

All this made him feel lonely, as there was no living thing that could express its feelings to him. This made him feel that he was alone in the creation. He had been told of the trouble that had arisen at the mating of the eagle-hawk and the crow, and of the displeasure of the Goddess of Birth at these mixed matings. He saw that in the whole creation there was not one being that could become his companion, not one who could understand his feelings. He remembered that when he had lived with the kangaroo, the goanna, the eagle-hawk, and others they could not respond to his feelings and wishes. He cried unto the Goddess of Birth, " O Mother, I am alone in this creation. Is it your will that I should dwell by myself, I who have a mind and soul that came from higher sources and am not like the animals and the birds that came from the earth? Give me a companion, a helpmate, to assist me to fulfil thy will."

Then the Goddess of Birth spake unto the Father of All Spirits and told him to go and speak with the Human Intelligence and say, "You are man. You are greater than any other created thing that walks or crawls upon the earth, or that moves on the water or under the water. No other living things have been given the power to realize their wishes as you have. If you are earnest in your wishes and are pure in heart you have now power to fulfil your desires. Go and view all my creation, and select your companion."

When the night had drawn its curtain across the sky the Human Intelligence slept, and as he slept he saw many strange beings. He saw a form that had a resemblance to his, a shape more beautiful and more attractive than the daughter of the kangaroo, the emu, or the goanna. It seemed to be the Queen, the Goddess of All Living Female Forms, the masterpiece created by the Goddess of Birth. The Intelligence lay down and stretched himself in deep sleep. Suddenly he awoke and found that he had only been dreaming. He made no effort to sleep again, but sat up through the earlier part of the morning until the sun rose. He came out from the scrub where he had been sheltering himself from the darkness and the dew. He walked round, gathering herbs and berries, and by and by he came to an open space within the forest. Here he sat down upon a log and thought over what he had seen in his sleep, but he was unable to recall the vision clearly, and had only a glimmering recollection of what he had seen.

Then he looked about him and saw the kangaroos, the opossums, the snakes, and the birds, with their companions and their young ones. This sight brought back to him his one need and desire; and, as he pondered, the dream came back to him just as he had seen it. He looked about him every morning to see whether some object would meet his vision that would in any way resemble the beautiful form that he saw in his dream. He could not see any animal, bird, reptile, or lizard form that came near to his ideal. Then he thought he would look for his desire among the plants. He found a large gum-tree that had weathered many storms, and had given shelter to birds, and had protected animals and reptiles from the heats of summer. Then he saw a wattle-tree in full blossom, and he stopped to admire it. Then his attention was attracted by the waratah[1] among the flowers. And so he passed on through the whole of the trees, flowers, and shrubs. He thought that if his ideal possessed beauty he would desire nothing else from her ; so finally he chose for his companion a grass yacca-tree. He saw how it grew, and noticed how tall and straight the flower-stalk shot up from among the leaves. He slept by it at night. He watched it grow. By and by he saw the sweet, honey-producing flowers appear on its stem, and he watched its graceful, swaying movement as the passing wind stirred it. Then the Goddess of Birth saw that the Human Intelligence had made his choice, and that his wife should come from among the plants.

One morning when the Human Intelligence awoke from sleep he was surprised to see that the birds, the animals, the lizards, and the reptiles were all congregated around the grass yacca-tree that he had so greatly admired. Sunbeams were playing about it, and all the colours appeared to be separate. By and by, however, the colours were all fused into each other, and only a very brilliant light remained. This light surrounded the grass-tree like a halo, and in this he saw the form of the figure that he had seen in his dream. All the tribes present sang a song of praise to the Goddess of Birth and Creation. Human Intelligence in the shape of a man stepped forth and claimed his companion that had come out from the grass yacca-tree. He took her hand and led her, because she was not yet fully conscious of where she was, and looked as if she were walking in a dream. She remained in this state for a great many years. Man led her from place to place, sheltering

[1] The aboriginal name for a genus of plants bearing flowers of the most brilliant colour. It is regarded as the most characteristic of the Australian flora.

"HE SAW THE FORM OF THE FIGURE THAT HE HAD SEEN
IN HIS DREAM"   58

DANCE AT A CORROBBERY

Note the wurley in the centre of the photograph.

From "The Arunta," by Sir Baldwin Spencer and F. J. Gillen, by permission of Messrs Macmillan & Co., Ltd.

her under rock-ledges, in caves, and under shrubs and bushes. He never ventured far from her side, and his keen eye was always on the alert in case some one should venture to take her from him. The only method of conveying any thought to her was by touching her head gently with the hand and pressing it. Then sometimes she might turn her gaze upon him. He would take her head between his hands and sometimes with difficulty turn it to look toward him. He would then move it in the direction in which he wished her to follow him.

Then he began to teach her to accept various kinds of food. After years of training and education the woman's mind began very slowly to develop. She began to observe and to distinguish animals, birds, reptiles, lizards, fishes, and insects, bushes, trees, rivers, brooks, lakes, and the sea. It was the care that man bestowed on the woman that gave an impetus to his mind and reason. When man first came into existence he lived on and roamed over the plains, and passed an indifferent sort of existence in the vast forest, or sat idly by the bank of a river, watching the kangaroos and other animals coming down to drink. Or he would gaze at the wild waterfowl feeding and floating or diving in the smooth waters. Sometimes he noticed a rippling of the water followed by a splash, as a fish leaped out of the water and fell back again into it. All these sights made impressions on him which helped to enlarge and develop his mind. But his chief desire had been fulfilled. He had been made the protector of another. He had to provide food for her, and to guard her against all danger. This was man's first work. His next work was to teach her to understand what he was saying, and to answer him.

The Birth of the Butterflies

Long ago, before a race of men inhabited Australia, the animals could talk with one another, and they had no experience of death. All through the summer months it was the custom of the different tribes, the animals, the birds, and the reptiles, to gather together on the banks of the river Murray in order to enjoy the cool waters of the river and the shade of the gum-trees. The wise old men of the tribes used to sit and talk, while the younger members enjoyed themselves at play and sports.

One day a young cockatoo fell from a high tree and broke his neck. He lay dead on the ground. All the animals gathered round to try to wake him. They touched him with a spear, but he could not feel. They opened his eyes, but he could not see. The animals were completely mystified, for they did not understand death. Then all the medicine-men tried to awaken the cockatoo, but without success.

A general meeting was called to discuss the matter of the dead bird. First of all the owl, who with his great eyes was supposed to be very wise, was called upon to speak. But the owl was silent. Then the eagle-hawk, the great chief of the birds, was asked to explain this mystery of death. The eagle-hawk took a pebble and threw it out into the river, and all the onlookers saw the pebble strike the water and disappear from sight. Turning to the tribes the eagle-hawk cried, " There is the explanation of the mystery; as the pebble has entered on another existence so has the cockatoo."

This explanation, however, did not satisfy the gathering; so they next asked the crow to speak. Although all of them knew that the crow was very wicked, they also knew he had great knowledge. The crow stepped forward and took up a wit-wit [1] and threw it into the river. The weapon sank, and then gradually rose again to the surface. " There," said the crow, " is the great mystery explained. We all go through another world of experience, and then return."

Now this explanation impressed all the tribes, and the eagle-hawk asked, " Who will volunteer to go through this

[1] A thin and somewhat pliable stick about three feet long, with one end expanded in ovoid form, and pointed. It is thrown at a disc made of bark, and requires a good deal of skill on the part of the performer.

experience and test it, and see if it is possible to return?"
Certain of the animal and reptile tribes offered to make the
test. "Very well," said the eagle-hawk, "but you must
go through the experience of not being sensible to sight,
taste, smell, touch, or hearing, and then return to us in
another form."

When it became winter-time all the creatures that creep
into holes and hollow logs and sleep during the winter
months went away—the goanna, the opossum, the wombat,
and the snake.

In the following spring the tribes gathered together
again to wait the return of those who were trying to solve
the great mystery. At last the goanna, the opossum, the
wombat, and the snake returned, all looking half starved.
When they showed themselves to the gathering the eagle-
hawk said, "You have all returned in the same form as
you went out, although the snake has half changed his
skin."

Still the gathering was anxious to solve the mystery of
death. At last the insect tribe, the moths, the water-bugs,
and the caterpillars, volunteered to try to find a solution
of that mystery. All the others, and especially the laughing
jacks, ridiculed this, because the insects had always been
looked upon as ignorant and stupid. The insects persisted,
so the eagle-hawk gave them permission to try. But the
insects did not crawl away out of sight. The water-bugs
asked to be wrapped in a fine bark and thrown into the
river. Some asked to be put in the bark of trees; and
others to be placed under the ground. "Now," said the
different bugs and caterpillars, "we will return at the
spring-time of the year in another form, and we will meet
you in the mountains." The tribes then dispersed until
the following spring.

All the animals knew by the position of the stars at
night when spring-time was approaching. As it drew near
there was great excitement everywhere. The animals felt
that the mystery would now be solved. The day before
the time fixed for the return of the insects the eagle-hawk

sent out notice, and all the animals, birds, and reptiles
gathered in the mountains to await the great event. That
night the dragonflies, the gnats, and the fireflies came
round the camp-fires as heralds of the wonderful pageant
that was to take place on the morrow. Already the trees,
the shrubs, and the flowers had consented to lend themselves
for the occasion. The dragonfly went from camp to camp
and from tribe to tribe, telling every one what a marvellous
sight it was going to be, to see all the insects returning from
the dead in their new bodies.

At daybreak every animal, bird, and reptile was out to
witness the arrival of the pageant. The wattle put forth
all its wonderful yellow, and the waratah its brilliant red,
and all the other flowers showed their blossoms of varied
colours.

Just as the sun rose over the tops of the hills the dragonflies came up through the entrance of the mountains heading
an array of butterflies. Each species and colour of butterfly
came in order. First the yellow came up and showed themselves. They flew about and rested upon the trees and the
flowers. Then came the red, the blue, the green, and so
right on through all the families.

The animals were delighted. They gave great cries of
admiration. The birds were so pleased that, for the first
time, they broke forth into song. Everything looked its
best. When the last of the butterflies had entered the
mountains they asked the great gathering, " Have we solved
the mystery of death ? Have we returned in another form ?"
And all nature answered back, " You have."

And all this can be seen at the return of every spring-
time.

The Confusion of Tongues

In the long ago, the time of the many dawns and many
sunrises, the sun shone on sea and land, giving life and
energy to animal, bird, reptile, and insect. The sun made
its journey across the sky to the mysterious West. There
was never a cloud of disappointment or sorrow; only

eternal sunshine. Creation smiled, and animal, bird, reptile, and insect were bound together by one common language. The kangaroo and goanna were able to converse and to exchange ideas; so were the eagle-hawk and the platypus, and the wombat and the dragonfly. Each endeavoured to please and to entertain and instruct the other while following his own individual inclinations.

The food of the animals, birds, and reptiles consisted of vegetables and fish. Once every year they would all congregate and have great feastings and corrobberies,[1] and there would be great marriage celebrations. But a time came when they proposed to do something that would change the condition of the whole of the affairs of the race. Some proposed that they should join in marriage the kangaroo with the emu, the dingo with the goanna, the koala with the lyre-bird. While some were in favour of such an arrangement, others were strongly opposed to it. Those in favour were represented by the kangaroos, emus, dingoes, goannas, carpet-snakes, koalas, pelicans, cockatoos, and lyre-birds. Against these were the tortoises, frogs, and crows.

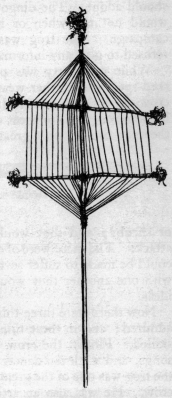

CORROBBERY SYMBOL FROM
NORTH-WEST AUSTRALIA
British Museum

The three last were opposed to the whole of the tribes. The majority felt that they had a powerful antagonist in

[1] Nocturnal assemblies of aboriginals at which there would be revelling and dancing.

the crow, for they knew that his wit and cunning would be sufficient to overcome their brute force. The advocates of the proposal set to work to consider what tactics they should adopt. The dingo inquired of the tortoise, but he would not tell when or how the crow would begin his campaign. The frog was next approached, but he too refused to give any information.

While one party was preparing boomerangs, waddies, reed-spears, and other weapons the three confederates, the crow, the tortoise, and the frog, whose one weapon was their intelligence, used to meet on the top of a mountain, or in the open country on a great plain where there were no trees

WADDY FROM TASMANIA
British Museum

or shrubs; and they would sit and discuss a method of attack. The three were of one mind, that if their opponents could be made to suffer severe hunger and to become angry with one another they would soon be rid of all their silly ideas.

Now there were three things that the whole of the tribes admired; and in these things their opponents were highly skilled. Firstly, the crow was a great composer of native songs, and a clever dancer and impersonator. Secondly, the frog was one of the greatest dancers, surpassing even the crow. He was also an artist, and painted designs on his body that were unique in colour and were much sought after. He possessed a wonderful bass voice which could be heard for miles; and, what was most remarkable, he was a ventriloquist. Thirdly, the tortoise possessed neither voice nor ability. The three decided to make use of their accomplishments, so they invited the animals, the birds, the reptiles, and the insects to a great performance.

The first act was a dance by the tortoise in imitation of the kangaroo. This aroused intense curiosity and wonder. Every animal, bird, reptile, and insect in the place turned out to see the tortoise dance. They were asked to sit in a semicircle, and no one was allowed to cross over, because the crow required the remainder of the circle for his performance. The tortoise and frog retired, and the crow began to sing the song of the kangaroo. Presently a figure approached the front. There was great shouting as the tortoise came creeping slowly toward the audience and, at a sign from the crow, commenced leaping and bounding here and there just like a kangaroo. They whispered among themselves how wonderful it was to see the slow-moving tortoise acting the kangaroo dance. " Hurrah! Hurrah! " they shouted. The dancer was really the frog, who was wearing a *coolamon* [1] on his back and a shield on his chest.

The second dance, the swan dance, was announced, and it was stated that the tortoise would sing the swan song. The tortoise took his stand in front of the audience and apparently commenced to sing, and the crow danced to the song. The animals, birds, and reptiles could not understand how the tortoise could be singing. It was really the cunning frog ventriloquist who was singing. The audience was carried away with enthusiasm by the marvellous performance of the slow-moving, voiceless tortoise. " Hurrah! Hurrah! " they shouted.

For three days and three nights the performance lasted. On the fourth morning every one began to feel hungry, and the kangaroo called out to the pelican, " Get the net; bring the net and go fishing. The people are famishing with hunger." The pelican set out and caught a number of fish, and the crow was unanimously appointed by the various tribes to take charge of the distribution of them. " Come, let us go to yonder point and cook the fish," he said. " You know it is against the rules of the tribe to cook fish where they are caught. But there is not sufficient to go round; try to get some more in yonder bay."

The pelicans dragged with their nets and caught some more fish.

" Come to yonder point. It is unlawful to make a fire

[1] A long, boat-shaped wooden dish for carrying water.

and cook here," the crow kept repeating, until the whole assembly became impatient.

They began to abuse the crow, and the cunning frog supported the crow, but made it appear that the voice came from the kangaroo. Presently it seemed that the kangaroo

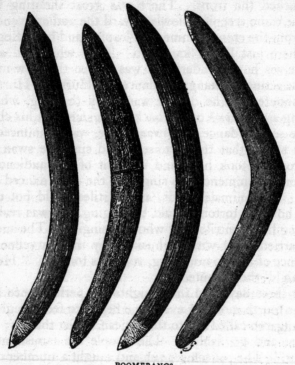

BOOMERANGS

The one on the right is a returning one.

From *Among Cannibals*, by Carl Lumholtz (Murray).

was insulting the emu; then that the goanna had commenced to insult the laughing jack, and the wombat the dingo. They all grew angry with one another. The frog saw his opportunity, and called, " To battle! To battle! "

The tribes were all so angry that they commenced shouting and calling each other ugly names. Each challenged the other to battle, and there was hurling of the spear and the boomerang. There was quite a pandemonium of sound. Only the lyre-birds stood aloof and took no part in using insulting words, but strove to bring about a reconciliation; but no one would listen.

Since the time of this great battle the animals, the birds, the reptiles, and the insects have each adopted a language of its own, but because he took no part in the fight, but tried to maintain peace, the lyre-bird is able to imitate them all.

The Discovery and the Loss of the Secret of Fire

Among the animals, birds, and reptiles that have made a name for themselves and their tribe are the bat, who, with the wonderful boomerang which was given him by the lizard, brought back light and warmth to the tribes; the koala, the great astronomer, philosopher, discoverer, and navigator; the pelican, the great fisherman; and the water-rat, the discoverer of fire. Before this wonderful discovery of fire all food, both flesh and vegetable, was eaten raw, and in cold climates during the winter season the people suffered great misery. The little dingoes, wombats, kangaroos, and bandicoots would always be crying and shivering, as their clothing was not sufficient to keep them warm.

One day the wife of the water-rat said to her husband, " Oh, dear me, I had a most beautiful dream! Do you remember the *billabong*[1] where you used to come and visit me when these lovely water-lilies were blooming? Well, I was sitting there on a log on the bank, thinking of our courting days, when presently out of the clear water there came a dragonfly. It hurried to a water-lily and sat there for a while. It then returned to the spot whence it came, and flew hovering above the surface of the water. Presently a big, clear bubble rose and floated toward the water-lily, and the dragonfly followed it. Then a great many dragonflies came and gently raised the bubble from the water and carried it carefully and placed it upon the water-lily. I sat gazing in

[1] A depression alongside a river which is filled intermittently by the overflow of the river.

wonderment at this strange sight, thinking what it could mean. Like a flash it appeared to me to be the spirit of the water-lily dancing around it and leaping skyward. At that moment the bubble burst. Oh, dear, what a wonderful sight ! A beautiful baby water-rat was lying peacefully in the bosom of the water-lily."

The young water-rat sat for a while, thinking deeply. Presently he rose and kissed his wife, and hurried away to the spot that she had spoken about. When he reached it he walked round the bank several times in search of a suitable place to build a home for his wife. He selected a place near the *billabong*, and began digging under the roots of a large gum-tree. He went on digging until he came to an obstruction. It was a root of the tree. He was annoyed, but, not wishing to abandon a place that meant so much to him and his wife, he began to use his teeth as an implement to cut a way through. While biting and gnawing the root he suddenly kindled a spark with his teeth. Again and again this occurred. After completing his home and furnishing it with soft grass he hastened to his wife and invited her to follow him.

They wended their way silently to their new home. She stepped inside and sat down in her cosy nest. A feeling of rest and comfort crept over her. Soon she quietly fell asleep. When she awoke her husband told her of his wonderful discovery, and showed her how he produced fire, the much-needed blessing. Then he hastened away and told his father, mother, brother, and sister, and they spread the news to other members of the water-rat tribe. They all came and saw the fire, and felt the comforting and strengthening heat that came from it, and the water-rat tribe resolved that they would endeavour to keep the secret to themselves, and not reveal it to the tortoise, waterfowl, kangaroo, dingo, or any other tribe. So the water-rat tribe lived in comfort in all weathers and in all climates.

Now the kangaroo, wombat, goanna, and tortoise could see the light through the weeds, and the turtles would crawl through the grass, sneaking toward the home of the water-rat to find out what it was. But the water-rat was too wise for them, and when he saw them coming he would hide the fire. Then the other tribes asked the hawk tribe to request the eagle-hawk to wrest this secret from the water-rats. The eagle-hawk consented, and on a sunny morning, when there was not a cloud to be seen, he began his mission. Up and up into the blue sky he soared until he appeared a mere speck; finally he disappeared from sight. But he, with his keen eyes, could pierce the distance; he could scan the river and see every object below, and he saw the water-rat producing fire with the stick. Like a bolt from the sky he sped earthward, rending the air as he came with the noise of a mighty wind. Every living thing was spellbound, and even the water-rat was paralysed. The eagle-hawk swooped upon the water-rat and seized him in his mighty claws, then again mounted into the sky, where he hovered. " Give me your secret," he said to the water-rat, " else I will drop you to earth."

Rather than lose his life the water-rat told how fire was produced. Thus was the secret taken from the selfish water-rat tribe and given to the other tribes.

The Moon

At one time the moon was a man. He was a happy-go-lucky fellow, spending much of his time in whistling and singing and laughing. There were occasions, however, when he would have very despondent moods. The reason of this was that he was unable to win the affection of any one of the beautiful girls with whom he associated. In spite of his merry disposition he failed to attract these girls. They would only laugh and make jokes about him because he was so fat, and very dull-witted. Every night he would travel from place to place, always hoping that he would find a wife. But the tribe that saw him set out on his journey would send abroad a message, " Look out, the moon is on his way, seeking a wife. Tell the girls."

One clear, cloudless night the stars were shining brightly, giving tidings of plenty of food, plenty of enjoyment, and plenty of strength to resist the Evil Spirit. The moon was singing merrily as he sauntered along the banks of a river, and he attracted the attention of the two daughters of a widowed mother. Though full of excitement, they sat quietly awaiting his approach. They thought, " This person who is possessed of such a lovely voice must be handsome ! " Presently he came within their range of vision, and lo ! they saw a very fat man, with short legs, and arms that were very thin, and a big head with shining eyes. " What a funny man ! " laughed the girls. They ran to the riverside and leaped into a canoe, and began to paddle across the stream. The moon shouted and called out piteously, begging them to take him across the water. In mid-stream the girls stopped paddling, and called to him, " We have heard of you, and have been told that you are a flirt. All of us have been warned not to have anything to do with you. Swim across the stream." " Oh," said the moon, " I am hungry and weary ; have pity on me. Oh, for the sake of the Pleiades, who have set all girls an example of how to think of others, look at yonder sky. How disappointed they must be to see you treating me thus ! "

Then the sisters remembered how all the aboriginal girls were striving to imitate the beautiful characters of those lovely maidens who now shine from the sky to remind them to do good to friend and foe alike. They thought for a while, and, responding to the spirit call of the Pleiades, they rowed back to the bank, and both leaped ashore. Then they invited the moon to go on board the canoe, and he stepped into it. They said, " We will lend you the canoe, but you must row yourself across the stream." " But," said he, " I am unable to row." " All right," said the good-hearted girls, " we will take you across."

So, plunging into the stream, each grasped a side of the canoe, intending to tow it across. Before they had swum a quarter of the distance the moon began tickling the girls under the arms. They became angry at this proceeding, and told him to cease his rude behaviour. He desisted for a while, but when they had arrived in midstream he once

70

more commenced to tickle them. This time, without more ado, they tipped him into the deep, clear river, and as he sank into the depths they could see his shining face looking at them. The farther he sank the smaller he grew, until only one part of his face could be seen, and then that too gradually diminished, until there was only a small crescent visible. Eventually even that disappeared from view.

The girls went home and told their mother and the whole tribe the story of the flirting moon, and how he had sunk to the bottom of the river. The news was spread all over the country by smoke signals, and when the crow heard it he sent this message throughout the length and breadth of the land:

" The moon will no longer shine constantly. From this time onward you will see him coming out of the Land of Spirits in the west, with only part of his face visible, but increasing in size night after night, until the whole of it is seen. Then he will gradually disappear into the east, and he will be invisible for a season. Then he will appear again as a thin crescent in the west, peeping expectantly, as if ashamed to show his face. Gradually, as he regains confidence, he will show a more ample face. By and by he will look down with a countenance wholly visible, and try with his silvery smile to win the affections of some young girl. In this he will fail, and so he will gradually fade away to hide his disappointment." [1]

The Wonderful Lizard

When the water-rat had shown all the tribes how to make fire [2] by rubbing two sticks together, and by striking one piece of flint against another, each tribe took away a lighted fire-stick. From this another fire was lighted, and the tribes continued to make fires with branches and large logs, lighting one from the other. When travelling from one hunting-ground to another one of the tribe would be chosen to see

---

[1] The aboriginals have observed that the course of the moon round the earth is from west to east, and that the journey takes a month.

[2] See pp. 67-69.

that the fire-stick was carried safely on the journey. Fire was thus kept alight for a long, long while. But one day there was a great storm, accompanied by wind and rain. The people lived on the plain, and as they fled to the mountain for shelter their fires were all extinguished. This calamity befell all the tribes, even the water-rats.

Several generations had passed since the water-rat gave up his secret, and now it had been completely forgotten because of the habit of all to light one stick from another.

Now the eagle-hawk and all the chiefs of the animals, the birds, the reptiles, and the insects were allowed to have two wives, who had to be sisters. All the tribes expected that the eagle-hawk would choose a wife from either the bird or the animal tribes. But every one got a great surprise. He sent his messenger, the falcon, to summon the two beautiful daughters of the snake, who came escorted by their uncles, the brothers of their mother. On the way people stared at them in wonder and astonishment. When they approached the camp of the hawk family, where the chief was sitting in his wurley, he rose up to greet them with outstretched hands.

The uncles said, "O eagle-hawk, chief of the bird tribes, we are proud and honoured that so great a tribe as yours should condescend to choose wives from among the daughters of our tribe. We willingly give them to you. They shall become your servants for ever." The eagle-hawk said not a word, but took their hands, and so received them.

These two sisters were known, and are known to-day, as the maiden snakes. Members of their family were distinguished by the very red colour of their bodies. Red to the aboriginal is symbolical of fiery temper, warm hospitality, and healing effect; the family to which they belonged had all these characteristics.

At the time of this story all food was eaten uncooked. One day the eagle-hawk went out hunting. Just before midday his young wives were basking in the sunshine. They were resting upon some deserted ant-beds that had the

72

appearance of stumps of trees that were thoroughly riddled with tiny holes. Suddenly the heat of the sun, with the heat of their bodies, caused a fire to start in the ant-beds. When they saw a fire burning without smoke, " Oh, wonder of wonders ! " both exclaimed. " What a discovery ! Let us throw sand upon the fire to hide it from the others." From that time onward they jealously guarded the secret. One day the eagle-hawk came home with some food. He divided it equally, but went to sleep before he himself ate. Then the sisters hastened to their ant-bed (which they had turned into a fireplace), and, gently scraping the sand from it, they began to cook their food. When they had finished cooking they covered up the fire, and sat down and ate their meal. Then they returned to their husband, the King of Birds, and one sat on each side of him.

When the eagle-hawk rose he felt hungry and asked that his meal should be served ; so both eagerly waited upon him. While he was eating he said to his wives, " It is strange that I smell cooked food. Have you been favoured with such ? " " Oh, no," both replied. " How do you think that we, your wives, should be honoured above all others with such a long-lost favour ? " " Come, now, my wives," said the eagle-hawk, " have I smelt aright ? Have you had cooked fish ? Where is the portion of food that I gave you ? Let me see it." They replied, " We have eaten the allowance you gave us." But they did not say whether they had eaten it raw or cooked.

The eagle-hawk said nothing more, but flew away to seek more food. Upon his return he divided what he had brought, but this time he did not go to sleep, but sat up and straightway ate his portion. He asked his wives to join him, but both asked to be excused. " Why," said the eagle-hawk, " you have been accustomed to eat as soon as I gave you your food, but of late you eat in secret ! Come, now, my wives, eat." But they still refused. Presently the eagle-hawk said, " I think I will go a-hunting again. Good-bye, wives." He intended to take them by surprise, and so he went but a little way, flying in a circle, and was soon back again. But the sisters were too cunning. They saw through this wile, and were aware that he had become suspicious.

When the eagle-hawk saw that his wives had not eaten during his absence he said, " Eat, my wives; you are both hungry. Eat and be strong." " Not until you bring us some fish," answered the wives.

So the eagle-hawk flew away across the mountain until he came to a *billabong*. There he sat upon a limb of a large gum-tree, with his keen eyes fixed upon the pool. A perch, feeding in the water, rose a little toward the surface. There was a whirr ; the eagle-hawk shot like an arrow upon his prey and struck his talons deep into its flesh. He then hastened back to his wives, who were sunning themselves. When they heard the flapping of the wings of their lord and chief, they rose hurriedly to greet him, and he gave them the food that they so greatly desired, and asked them to have their meal. " But," said his wives, " we have just finished our meal, and we are feeling satisfied. With your kind permission we will go and rest."

Ever since he had thought that he could smell cooked food the eagle-hawk had been uneasy about the conduct of his wives ; he now went away and met the magpie, and spoke to him of his suspicions. " Now what shall we do to find out whether they have really discovered the lost secret of fire? " he asked. " Will you go among the tribes and ask for volunteers who will help me? " So the magpie went, and first of all asked the cockatoo to help. " Oh, yes," said the cockatoo, " I will endeavour to find out where the wives hide the fire." So he set off and spent many days in waiting around and watching for signs of smoke. He said to himself, " If they make a fire I shall see smoke rising." But waiting began to become tedious, so he determined to try the plan of following the wives when they received food from their husband.

On every occasion when the eagle-hawk returned with his spoil he gave his wives their portion of food, and then went to take his rest. When they thought he was sleeping the wives would steal away to cook their food, and the cockatoo would follow through the bush. But his clumsy feet would become entangled in the shrubs, and he had to snip with his beak to cut his way through. The faint sound of this snipping gave warning to the sisters, who would sneak away from their fire and lie quietly among the bushes. The cockatoo would sit for a while, then, thinking that he had waited long enough, he would begin to go forward again. But, as before, his feet would become entangled, and sometimes he would fall down. He became scared, thinking that some one was tripping him.

By and by the cockatoo returned to the magpie, and told him how he had failed. Then the magpie asked the emu to keep watch, thinking that he would see farther than the cockatoo because of his long neck. The emu tried, but he also failed. " Now," said the magpie, " this will never do. The King of Birds, the eagle-hawk, will make a proclamation that anyone who fails in future shall be slain or otherwise punished. We must make a mighty effort. Let us all form a circle round about the wives, and draw in closer and closer until we come upon them. Surely then some one will discover what they do."

So they all agreed to this. There was the magpie, the cockatoo, the butcher-bird, the laughing jack, the emu, the little wren, the willy-wagtail, and a great many others of the bird tribe. They formed into a big circle, and commenced to draw in toward the place where the wives were cooking. The cockatoo, with his clumsy feet tripping him, caused the laughing jack a great deal of amusement. As they got near to the sisters, and could distinguish the smell of flesh cooking, they all looked eagerly before them, straining their eyes, stretching their necks, and tiptoeing. Then the cockatoo slipped and fell. The laughing jack could not contain himself longer, but burst out laughing. At this all saw that it would be useless to try to find out the secret this time, so they sneaked off, feeling very much ashamed of themselves.

Then the birds asked the animal tribe to assist, but they were a greater failure than the birds, because when they came to where they could smell the appetizing food that was roasting their mouths would water, and they would hurry forward, tumbling over twigs and sticks. The sisters would hear them coming, and would cover up their fire and disappear in the grass and bushes.

Then the birds and animals became desperate, and threatened the sisters that if they did not reveal their secret they would be killed. The magpie said, " Why should you keep from the whole of the tribes a much-needed help ? " But the sisters answered, " You forget we are wives of the great bird chief, and you cannot force us to tell."

All recognized the force of this reply. With heads bowed in shame at their defeat they all disappeared, and went to their own wurleys. As the laughing jacks were walking homeward, enjoying jokes at the defeat of the others, they came across a lizard tribe, who had just returned from a hunting expedition with great spoil of game, and were making a wurley in which to camp for the night. The lizards asked the laughing jacks to spend the night with them, and they willingly consented. As they were sitting down and enjoying as much as possible their evening meal one of the members of the family of the little lizards said, " Oh, if we could only have the long-lost fire, what a happy evening we should be spending, with cooked food and light and warmth! " " Well," said a laughing jack, " there is fire, and we must make an effort to take it from the wives of the eagle-hawk. They have the secret. All our smart hunters have tried to wrest the secret from them, but they have failed. We tried all in a body, and formed a large circle round them, but the cockatoo, at the last moment, got his clumsy foot caught in something, and fell. You know how excitable he is. When this happened to him he screeched and howled, and we thought that the Evil One had got him. Of course the noise gave warning of our approach. Now perhaps you may be able to suggest means by which we shall find out their secret."

A little lizard thought deeply during many long hours of the night, and then he went to bed quietly, and slept soundly. In the morning some of the lizards began their

THE LIZARD BOY STEALS THE FIRE FROM THE SNAKE WIVES

"LIKE A FLASH OUT OF SPACE THERE CAME MANY LITTLE MEN"

journey homeward. But this one little lizard expressed a desire to stay with the other tribes and try to help to discover the secret of the fire. So he went out to the place where he had noticed that the two snakes usually spent their time when they were absent from their husband.

After a time the little lizard came back to the camp, and asked the cockatoo, the magpie, and others of their tribe, as well as some of the animal and lizard tribes, that a few picked men of each tribe who were skilled hunters should accompany him. He asked that they should follow his trail at a distance. So they all set off, the lizard about a hundred yards or more in advance, and winding his way in and out of the bushes and shrubs. They went on until they came to a spot where all of them became excited because they could smell something like food cooking.

The little lizard now suggested that he should go on by himself until he reached a certain spot where he thought it likely that the snakes would be. On this part of the journey he crawled flat upon his stomach for a few yards; then he stood upon three legs and held up the fourth one to beckon the others to follow or stop, as the case might be. Then he went forward through bushes and grass, and took another glimpse to see how far away the snakes were. Then he held up one of his hands, and beckoned to them to keep perfectly quiet. Then he took that hand down, and raised the other. He saw the snakes busy cooking their food with fire that was cunningly hid in the deserted ant-bed, and then sitting down behind the ant-bed and enjoying their meal. The lizard crept up cautiously, stopping now and again, and beckoning to the others, first with the right hand, and then with the left. During all this time he carried a grass-tree stick, and when he came near enough he poked this into the ant-bed, and allowed it to remain for a few minutes. Then he withdrew it, and found that it had caught fire. When he saw the grass-tree stick burning he ran away toward the place where the others were waiting, and on his way he set fire to grass and bushes, and soon the country was all ablaze.

The snakes became very angry indeed when they saw that their secret was discovered. They vowed that they would take vengeance upon everything living that came within striking distance, and that they would inflict a wound that would cause death. They also became the most dreaded enemies of the animal, bird, and lizard tribes from the day on which the little lizard stole their secret and spread the news of it all over the country. What made them so angry was that they themselves were deprived of fire, because they were able to use it only when it burned within the ant-bed, and now, since it had been all taken away, they were unable to restore it or to use it.

Now the task that the little lizard undertook on that day was so trying that, although many and many years have passed, he has never recovered from the effects of it. You will see him in any part of the country among the bushes or rocks, crawling, then stopping and raising first one hand and then the other, as if in the act of giving a signal to stop or a sign to come on. This is one of the peculiar habits which he still retains in evidence of that day long ago when his ancestor restored the gift of fire to the whole world.

The Lazy Goannas and what happened to them

This is a story of the Murrumbidgee river tribe. It is said that this locality was the first settled home of the goanna family after they left their temporary home at Shoalhaven and before they migrated to other parts of Australia. When they occupied this country there was no flowing Murrumbidgee river. The only river then was the Murray, which had been formed by the ancient *ponde*, a fish commonly called the Murray cod.

One of the customs observed by the animals, birds, and reptiles was that members of each tribe should marry not in their own tribe, but into some other. In the case of the goanna, a man would have to marry into the magpie family; or sometimes the wife of the goanna was a teal, a little bird like the magpie in appearance, but of smaller size.

At this time of the occupation of the Murrumbidgee

district there lived on the north side of the goanna tribe a great hunting family known as the porcupine tribe. At the south side there lived another well-known family, the emu tribe. They too were hunters, but they did not attain to the same perfection in bushcraft as the porcupines. After the arrival of these tribes from their island home in the Sea of a Thousand Isles the differences in place and climate made a change in the lives of all, and particularly of the goanna family. In their native land they were a very industrious family; they tilled the soil, and grew vegetables and fruit. But after coming to Australia the climate caused them to dislike vegetable food, and an uncontrollable craving for flesh food took possession of them. They became flesh-eaters, and would slay and devour the smaller lizards of their own species. Sometimes it would happen that a young porcupine wandered from the cave of his parents and became lost. Like a little child, he would begin crying. Perhaps a goanna would hear the noise and would recognize it at once as a cry of distress. He would give a call, and the little porcupine would hurry toward the sound, and the goanna would pounce upon the helpless being and devour it.

One thing noticeable when the goannas changed their diet was that they became very lazy, indolent, and dishonest. They would steal food from their neighbours, the porcupines and the emus ; and it seemed strange that for many years these two tribes could not discover the thieves. The goannas were so cunning that they were able to destroy all clues that could lead to their discovery. All the surrounding tribes knew that the goannas were lazy, and they also had a suspicion that they did steal their food, but they were not able to bring home the charge until proof of it happened to come in an unexpected way.

One day the porcupines organized a hunting expedition, and the goannas heard of it. On the day of the hunt the goannas went along to where the porcupines were assembled, armed with their spears and *nulla-nullas*.[1] The chief hunter

[1] See note on p. 86.

of the porcupine tribe was giving instructions. " Ten of
you," he said, " will go north ; ten south ; ten east ; and
ten west. You will all walk straight forward until you

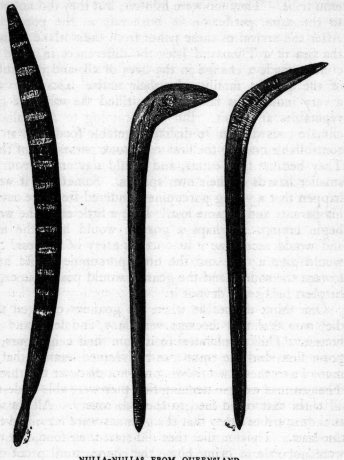

NULLA-NULLAS FROM QUEENSLAND
From *Among Cannibals*, by Carl Lumholtz (Murray).

reach a certain distance, and then you will spread out
and walk back in a circle, gradually coming toward the
centre."

The goannas, who were in hiding and had listened to all

80

that was being said, now came out from their hiding-place, looking as if they were surprised. They apologized for their appearance, and asked where the porcupines were going. The porcupines said, " Oh, that's all right, we are just going to hunt for food."

" Oh," said one of the goannas, " will you allow us to accompany your party? "

" Pardon me," said a porcupine, " but we think that you cannot help us in this matter; you will allow that you are not competent to hunt game and therefore may be a hindrance."

" Yes, we are no hunters of game. We are aware of that, but suppose you allow us to come with you. There is no doubt we shall find honey. I am sure some of you know where there is a store to be got. Admitting that we are unable to hunt, you will allow that you are no tree-climbers. Now you are all very, very fond of honey. Come, let us accompany you."

The porcupines *were* fond of honey. They would give everything they possessed to obtain it; and now here was a proposal made to them by the goannas, who were expert climbers. The offer was such a tempting one that the porcupines could not let it pass. So they consented that the goannas should accompany them. The drive was very successful. Those who were in front and came upon the game first slew the opossums and hung them up on the limb of a tree; those following took them down and carried them on to the appointed meeting-place.

In the meantime the goannas too were busy. As soon as they saw a bee they would follow it until they discovered the hive. They would climb the tree, and in doing so would chop and chop with their stone axes so that the porcupines were under the impression that it must be hard work for the goannas to climb the tree, chopping footsteps as they climbed. But this chopping was only a blind; the goannas were able to climb without cutting steps in the bark of the tree.

Now when the porcupines and the goannas arrived at

the appointed meeting-place with their spoil the porcupines were exhausted with running and catching and carrying the game. Before resting they made a large fire, and began to clean and dress the opossums. After the porcupines had prepared the opossums for cooking the goannas gave them some honey to eat. Then the goannas suggested that the porcupines should lie down and sleep while they cooked the food; they would wake them when it was ready.

The porcupines agreed that this would suit them, and they lay down to sleep. One of the members of the goanna tribe went away to climb a large gum-tree standing on the border of the hunting-ground of the goannas and porcupines. This tree was used as a place of refuge or a vantage-point from which the goannas could view the doings of the porcupines.

While the porcupines were sleeping another goanna was removing obstacles that were in the way leading to this tree, and the rest of the tribe were helping with the cooking of the opossums. Now the cook would place each opossum in the midst of the fire, with tail out so that this would serve as a handle. Sometimes a porcupine would raise himself drowsily and inquire, " Are they cooked? " The goanna would answer, " No; a little while longer," and the porcupine would lie down again. Then another porcupine would repeat the inquiry, " Are they cooked? " and the goanna would again reply, " No; a little while longer." This went on until the question had been put by all the porcupines, and each had received the same answer. At last the porcupines felt that something unusual was happening.

Now the goanna who had been told to keep watch had by this time climbed to the topmost limb of the gum-tree. When he saw that everything was ready, and that there were no porcupines about, he gave the signal for the tribe to bring their spoils. But the cook did not go with the others, for at that particular moment a porcupine half rose in his sleep and asked the usual question. He waited until the porcupine lay down to sleep again, then suddenly rose to his feet, and, taking the opossums by the tails, dashed for the gum-tree. But as he jerked the opossums out of the fire a hot coal fell upon the stomach of a porcupine and burnt him so much that he leaped to his feet, dancing with pain, and jumped upon one of the sticks of the fire. This scattered fire upon the other sleepers, and they were burnt on the legs and other parts of their bodies. They too jumped up, shrieking with pain.

The porcupine who rose first was not very much hurt and he soon came to himself. He looked toward the fire, but saw neither opossums nor cook. He turned sharply round, and saw the cook running as fast as he could with the cooked opossums toward the gum-tree. He shouted, " Look, there goes the goanna with our opossums! " They all seized fire-sticks and gave chase. They overtook the goanna when he was about ten yards from the foot of the gum-tree. One of the porcupines raised a fire-stick and brought it swiftly upon the back of the goanna just as he turned to run round the gum-tree. As he ran round and round the tree, pursued by the porcupines, blow after blow of blazing fire-sticks was delivered at his body, and with each blow there flashed out a blaze of fire. Then one of the porcupines stood still and waited till the goanna came round the tree. There was a flash from the fire-stick as the blow fell upon his head, but still the goanna held on to his spoils. Then in desperation he flung himself upon the trunk of the gum-tree, and climbed and climbed until he reached a hollow, the resting-place of the tribe, where all the goannas had now gathered. They sat down and had a good meal, and when they had finished they stowed away the remainder of the opossums in a safe place.

On the ground below the porcupines were shouting threat after threat, but, strange to say, it did not occur to them to burn down the tree. Time after time they attempted to throw fire-sticks into the hollow, but every time they met with failure, and in sorrow and disgust they went home, vowing to be avenged.

The goanna who had stolen the opossums became very ill; his body was covered with wounds caused by the blazing fire-sticks. When he recovered these marks remained as scars, and they have been handed down to all the goannas as reminders of the theft in the days long ago.

After some months, when the goanna had recovered from his wounds, the tribe went back to their own camping-ground and returned to their usual mode of living.

How the Selfish Goannas lost their Wives

Soon after the events that are recorded in the previous story a great drought visited the country. There was no rain, and all the dams and rock holes became dry. The porcupine and the emu tribes did not know what to do, because among their members there were many aged and infirm. Some were sick, and a great many had little children; so they were in great difficulties. They were not able to move down to the River Murray, where they would have been well and comfortable.

The drought did not affect the goanna tribe, as they had a secret reservoir with a supply of water that would last them for very many years. The cries of the little children, and the distress of the aged and sick, touched the hearts of the wives of the goannas, and they would secretly go among the other tribes and do all they could to supply their wants and relieve their sufferings. One day they asked their husbands to tell them where the great rock hole reservoir was, as they were anxious to supply water to the aged and the sick and the children of the porcupine and emu families. But the selfish goannas refused, and, what was worse, they said to their wives, " Since you are taking such an interest in the needs of others, we will give you only just sufficient water to slake your own thirst."

The wives found that it was useless to plead with their obstinate husbands; but they were determined that, although they had given way to many objections before, and had willingly suffered the indignity of refusals, they would not let this insult pass. So they began to search

84

for the reservoir. They would take up their yam-sticks that their husbands should believe that they were going to dig yams and roots of plants and shrubs. But they would track the footprints of their husbands, which led them to the mountain. At the foot of the mountain they would lose all trace of the footprints, so they would return to the valley and gather a few yams and herbs, and then go to their homes. They would cook the yams in the hot ashes, and then sit down with their husbands and families to eat. Sometimes a goanna would ask his wife where she had been for such an unusually long time. He would say, " I notice a speck of dirt that comes from the mountain. Have you been there?" The wife would reply, " What do you think, you silly? Do you imagine that we go searching for yams on the mountain-top? We find and dig yams in the low, flat country, not on rocky mountains. Now why do you ask such questions?" The goanna, without another word, would lie down upon his opossum-skin.

In the morning, just as the sun rose over the eastern range of mountains, the men of the goanna tribe were out looking for food, and their wives were up too. They had met to discuss what to do in order to discover the secret of the reservoir. One, more thoughtful than the others, said, " It would be a wise plan to go up the mountain and make a *mia-mia*[1] and camp there and make observations. Now who among us has courage? Let us sit a while and think who will go."

So they sat in silence for a few moments, and then one rose. All eyes became fixed on her. She was the wife of the chief. She said, " Sisters, I take the responsibility. I offer to go. I consider it is my duty as wife of a chief. Who will come and help me with my camp necessaries?"

Two young wives stood up, and said, " We will go with you."

So they made haste and rolled up the belongings of the chief's wife, and the three women hurried away to the mountain before the chief and the other goannas returned from

[1] See note on wurley on p. 48.

their hunting. Half-way up the side of the mountain there was a spot which gave a good view of the surrounding valley, and especially of the goanna camping-ground. After making the *mia-mia* the two young women returned home, leaving the chief's wife on the mountain.

In the evening the young chief summoned the goannas to his *mia-mia* and asked them whether anyone had seen his wife, or had any knowledge regarding her disappearance. All expressed great sorrow, and said they had no knowledge of the matter, nor could they suggest any reason why she should leave the camp. They told their chief that they would do all in their power to assist him to recover his wife if she had been taken a captive to some other home.

Then the chief summoned the teal teal,[1] the wives of the goannas. They were closely questioned by the chief and the elders, but they remained standing with their heads bowed, and would not make any reply. The questioners tried by threats to make them speak, but they shook their heads and remained silent. The chief of the goannas then ordered that the wives should return to their *mia-mia*. When the teal teal were safely home the chief said to the men, " I have a suspicion that the emus have come to our home while we were out hunting, and have taken my wife, and have given her to the young chief of the tribe. So to-morrow, before the sun rises beyond the mountain-peak, every one that is able to fight will take with him three *kaikes*, four *waddies*, four *panketyes*, and a *nulla-nulla*,[2] and we will march into their land and seek my wife. Then, if she be not there, we will return and march into the land of the porcupines. So to-night let every one go to his *mia-mia* and wait for the cry, ' Rise at once ! ' "

So every goanna man went straight home to bed and slept soundly. They rose early, and marched into the country of

---

[1] A small duck of the genus *Querquedula*.
[2] *Kaike*, a reed-spear. *Waddy*, a weapon made from part of the stem and root of a certain kind of mallee. This weapon is much sought after by the boys and young men. It is used principally in hunting the kangaroo, wallaby, emu, and wombat when these animals are in motion. *Panketye*, another name for boomerang. *Nulla-nulla*, a battle-club.

the emu. As soon as the goannas had left home the teal
teal rose and met to consider what they should do. One
thought it would be well if the two young women who had
accompanied the chief's wife hurried away and told her that
her absence had caused a stir. So while the chief with his
army was marching into the land of the emus, thinking that
it was they who had captured his wife and made her the wife
of the young emu chief, the young teal teal girls were running to the mountain to tell the chief's wife what was taking
place. She sat quietly and listened to what they had to tell,
and then in reply she said, " Now is our deliverance. We
have been given in marriage to these beings who are not of
our race and kind. I have made a discovery. At the dawn
of day I was fast asleep, and a Tuckonie[1] came into the
mia-mia and sat beside the fire warming himself. Suddenly
I awoke and saw him comfortably seated there. I became
so alarmed that I shrieked with fear ; and he turned his eyes
upon me and said, ' Do not be afraid. I am your friend,
and the friend of all that are in trouble or distress. I and
my companion saw you and the two others come up from
the plain, and some of my brothers have visited your camping-ground and know all about you. You are in search of
a water-hole, and you have been guided by the mind of my
tribe to this spot. You have been sleeping. If you will
follow me when I come again I will show you the opening
on the top of this mountain.' "

When the Tuckonie returned the wife of the chief of the
goannas rose and followed him up the mountain. When
they arrived at the top he bade her sit down and rest. The
little spirit man went away a few paces and gave a call somewhat like the *coo-ee*,[2] and like a flash out of space there came
many little men. Their bodies were striped with red ochre
and white pipeclay. They had white cockatoo feathers deco-
rating their heads and tied round their wrists like bracelets.

[1] These are little men who live in thickly timbered country. The aboriginals
believe that these queer little people visited the camping-grounds and became
acquainted with all the ways of the people.

[2] This is an Australian aboriginal's bush cry to call the attention of a person at
a distance.

In their hands they held their spears, about two feet long. Each one wore a belt of opossum-skin round his waist, and in this belt there were placed three tiny boomerangs and *waddies*. They circled round their leader, eager to receive his instructions. After a little talk they made way for him, and he came out from their midst and walked toward the wife of the goanna and stood beside her. They followed him, and he addressed his bodyguard thus, " Hear, O my brothers ; we have been appointed by the unseen beings that are about—the Spirit of Good, the Spirit of Water, the Spirit of Food, the Spirit of Pleasure, the Spirit of Lightning and Thunder and Wind and Rainstorm, and lastly the Spirit of Sunshine. The goannas have withheld from the tribes that inhabit this country the long-needed water that is locked up in this mountain ; they have used this gift for their own selfish ends, and have refused to share it with the aged and the infirm and the children of other tribes. And, what is more, they have refused to supply the necessities of their own wives. Give this woman the help she requires in order to let loose the water that is contained in the mountain."

The little spirit man turned to the wife of the chief and took her a few paces farther on to a basin-like hole in the rock. He asked her to look into it. She looked and saw sparkling water, clear as crystal. " Drink," he said, and she drank until she was satisfied. " Now," he said, " you must descend, and when you reach the foot of the mountain you will meet two young women. You must ask them to hurry back to their camp and instruct the others that they must all stand on the northern side of the valley toward the porcupine boundary and await your coming."

So she went and did as she had been told. The two young women also hurried back to the camp to deliver their message, and the other teal teal, as they were asked, stood waiting on the northern side of the valley. Meantime the chief's wife stood at the base of the mountain, waiting for further instructions. Presently the Tuckonie stood beside her, and said, " O woman, these good and great spirits have given you the privilege of letting loose the waters that are anxious to be freed from the bonds that have held them prisoner these many, many years. You shall be a blessing to all the animal, bird, reptile, and insect tribes. You must keep this great event in remembrance. Tell your children of the privilege that the Spirit of Water conferred on you. Take this." He handed her a grass-tree stick, and said, " At a given signal thrust it into the mountain-side, and the water shall be let loose."

Again the Tuckonie disappeared. The chief's wife stood there alone, thinking over this strange happening. She pinched her arm and struck her leg to see whether she was asleep. She felt the pinch and the blow. " I am very much awake," she said. " What a wonderful experience ! " Then a voice said, " Thrust the stick into the mountain." She placed the point of the stick against the mountain-side, and pushed hard. It gradually went in farther and farther, until it had gone its whole length. Then the voice of the Tuckonie said, " Now flee for your life to where your sisters are." She sped down the valley as fast as her feet could carry her. When she had gone half the distance a loud noise, as of a mighty wind, broke the still air. It was the sound of the water leaping forth out of its prison and thundering down the valley with the speed of a mighty wind.

The chief's wife arrived among her teal teal sisters, and breathlessly told them that the water from the mountain would be flowing down the valley. While she was speaking they saw dust rising from the hill-side, and the water tearing its way through the valley, and huge trees being uprooted and carried along. They looked with amazement as the water rushed past them on its way to join the Murray River. When it reached the Murray it settled down to be a flowing river. The teal teal came to its bank, and sat in the shade of the trees, watching their children sporting and splashing in the water.

Next day the goannas returned, and were making their way to the camp when they beheld with wonder that a river separated them from their wives and children. They were greatly annoyed. The chief called to the women across the river and asked where this flowing stream of water came from. He was answered by the familiar voice of his wife, " From the rock hole that you and the goannas have kept secret from us and the other tribes, and used for your own selfish purposes. But I, O chief, your wife, discovered your secret, and let loose the water, this great gift and blessing that belongs to all beings. So we, who were your wives, have decided that we shall no longer belong to you. Henceforth our home will be in the trees. And we do not wish to be, and we will not be, your wives."

So this separation came about through the selfishness of the goannas, and since that time the teal teal have refused to become the wives of the goannas. To keep in memory that long, long ago event of the release of the water they make their homes in the limbs or branches of the gum-trees, and they make their nests of mud or clay shaped like the mountain that contained the water. And in these small mountain-shaped homes they lay their eggs, and when these are hatched and the little birds come to see the light and the home the mother in bird-language tells them of the long, long ago when she was in distress, seeking water to quench her thirst, and how a little man helped her in her search and showed her where it was to be found, and promised that their tribe should throughout their generations have a home as a memorial, and rear their children in it.

As for the goannas, because of their rough natures and their stealing from others who endure the difficulties, hardships, and dangers of hunting they are doomed not only to carry upon their bodies the marks received as a punishment for their misdeeds, but to endure a much more grievous punishment for their selfishness to all around them, and more especially to their wives, the teal teal, in that they have lost that great pride of their heart, the wonderful rock hole which contained a lasting supply of clear and refreshing water. And, beyond this, their strictly guarded prize has become a great barrier, separating them from their wives and children for ever. And in sorrow they have wandered to all parts of Australia, and in certain seasons of the year they dig a hole in the ground and bury themselves in it, and weep during the dark, cold wintry nights, until they fall into a deep sleep, which lasts until spring calls them forth to take up their burden of life once more. And, in revenge for the loss of their wives, they rob the nests of the teal teal of their eggs, thinking that by devouring the eggs they may put an end to the existence of their former wives.

What some Aboriginal Carvings mean [1]

At Manly, about six miles from Sydney, there are to be seen aboriginal carvings cut into the flat surface of the rock. Among them there is a figure of a male aboriginal with both arms outstretched and holding in one hand a *waddy*. Another human figure and a form represent a shark. In another group there are four male figures, with a boomerang above the head of one and a fish between the legs of another. And, again, there are two figures, almost oval in shape, and one of the ovals has small circles cut around the edge. All these, as well as the carvings, have a meaning. Each of the objects, whether an animal, bird, reptile, or fish, represents the totem of a tribe.

Tribe Totems.—As in the case of the Manly figure, where a fish is placed between the legs of a person, the fish is the totem of the tribe living in that locality. Before a tribe can occupy a hunting-ground it must select a totem— a fish, animal, bird, or reptile—anything, in fact, that has an existence. It may be sun, moon, wind, lightning, or thunder. Thus, in some instances, one may see a figure representing the sun or a half-moon. Sometimes one notices figures of a kangaroo and an emu, or two other forms. The kangaroo might be the totem of the tribe of the chief, and the emu might be the totem of his wife's tribe.

This totemism plays an important part in the social life

[1] In various parts of Australia there are evidences of the existence of a primitive race which has passed on to the western sky, the Land of Mystery. Many of these evidences consist of figures cut in the surface of vertical or horizontal rocks by the aid of a stone axe.

of the aboriginals. If, for example, a person has committed an offence, or has broken a tribal law, he becomes a fugitive. He may travel to some distant part of the country. He may start from the Gulf of Carpentaria, and, during his journeyings, he may find himself wandering on the banks of the Parramatta. He creeps along stealthily, listening intently for any sound, peering through the dense foliage in every bay or cove to see whether his path is clear, noticing every footprint on the way, reading every mark on the tree-trunks and on the surface of rocks, and scanning every mark to see whether there is hope of protection and

friendship. To be seen would mean death to him. By and by the keen eye of the fugitive catches sight of the figure of his mother's totem. Casting aside all fear, he walks boldly along the beaten track that leads to the camp, and presents himself to the chief. He produces a string of kangaroo teeth, made in bead fashion, and a

NECK ORNAMENT OF KANGAROO TEETH
British Museum

bunch of emu-feathers, and holds them up to view without uttering a word. This is a sign that he belongs to the Kangaroo totem tribe, and that his mother belongs to the Emu totem tribe. He is received into either of these tribes, and becomes one with them, and participates in all their privileges.

At Manly one may notice two figures : a wallaby footprint and a kangaroo, a man figure and a weapon—it may be a boomerang or a *nulla-nulla*. This means that the Wallaby totem tribe occupied that country, and the Kangaroo totem tribe came and did battle with the Wallaby totem tribe and drove them away and took possession. Perhaps the Emu totem tribe is not content. They would like to change their hunting-ground. They have put to flight the Kangaroo totem tribe, and have dispossessed them

92

of their stolen country. The chief orders that his totem be carved upon the same rock; and so matters proceed. From the various figures carved on the surface of one rock one may infer that tribes of different totems shown in the figures occupied that locality.

There are other figures hewn in the rock. The oval with the small circles, referred to above, may represent the sun in its course; in other words, it may show that the aboriginals had knowledge of the earth's motion. There are old men in each tribe who study the stars and their positions in the heavens at night; and at certain times of the year every night at intervals they will give a call, " The earth has already turned."[1] This may be done with the idea of teaching the young generation something regarding astronomy.

[1] The aboriginals appear to have believed that the earth went round, because there is a saying which means, " The earth has turned itself about."

CHAPTER II: ANIMAL MYTHS

The Selfish Owl

LONG, long ago, before there were any human beings, there were birds, animals, and reptiles. Once a year, in the spring-time, these different tribes met and held a great festival for story-telling, dancing, and feasting. The bird tribe were great talkers. The cockatoos cried, " Come and let us prepare ourselves for this great festival." So they retired into the bush, and decorated themselves with leaves and shrubs. When they came out again they began to dance in their decorations before the carpet-snake, the goanna, and the kangaroo and others of the animal tribe. The animal and reptile tribes cheered and praised the dancing of the feathered tribe. This admiration and praise made the feathered tribe very conceited. The cockatoo, who was always a very cheeky fellow, went to the eagle-hawk, the chief of the feathered tribe, and said, " O Father Eagle-hawk, are not we of the feathered tribe greater than the kangaroo, the carpet-snake, the goanna, and all the others?" The eagle-hawk answered, " O my son, cockatoo, of course we are superior to all the other tribes."

Now the other tribes overheard this, and it made them very angry. So, after much wrangling, the feathered tribe challenged the other tribes to fight in order to prove which was the superior. But there was one family, the bat tribe, that stood alone, and would not take any part in the dispute, nor would they consent to join forces with either party in any fighting. The chief of the bat tribe called his family together and told them that they were to stand by, prepared for battle, and when it was seen that one of the combatants was winning they were to join in and help the winning side.

The great conflict began. The animals and the birds were throwing their *waddies* and spears, and others were fighting hand to hand with *nulla-nullas*. When it seemed that the bird tribe would win, since the animal tribes, including the kangaroos with their armies, were being

94

driven back, the chief of the bat tribe commanded his family to join in the fight, saying, " Come, help the eagle-hawk and his tribe! Onward! Slay the kangaroo and his army! " So the bat family stood side by side with

the cockatoos, the laughing jacks, the crows, and the magpies. The bats were experts in the use of the boomerang, and they threw their weapons so quickly that the numerous boome-rangs flying about looked like a huge cloud.

Presently there was a lull in the battle, and the kan-garoo called to his army and spoke words of encourage-ment as they stood awaiting another onset by the enemy. Now when the animals saw their chief and general facing the foe they took courage, and fought bravely, and drove the bird tribe back. As soon as the chief of the bat tribe saw that he had make a mistake he called to his followers to retire from the ranks of the bird tribe, and to go across to the enemy. Thus the bats

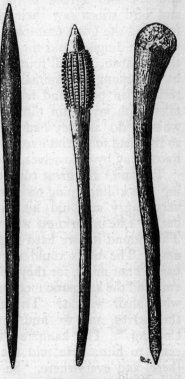

WOODEN SWORD AND CLUBS
From *Among Cannibals*, by Carl Lumholtz (Murray).

joined the animals, and fought against the birds. The tide of war began to swing like a great pendulum. First the animals would be winning, and then the birds; and the bats were constantly changing from one side to the other. At last the kangaroo and the emu came face to face in mortal combat. The kangaroo looked into the eyes of the emu and said, " O emu, why should we be fighting? It causes so much bloodshed, and pain, and misery, and death!" The kangaroo, who is always a kind animal, then asked the emu to shake hands and end the battle. The emu clasped the hand of the kangaroo, and the two agreed to be friends. When the animal and bird tribes saw their chiefs shaking hands they all followed the good example. The cockatoos shook hands with the dingoes, and the laughing jacks shook hands with the wombats, and all round there was a general shaking of hands among the animal, bird, and reptile tribes. This resulted in peace and friendship, and all the tribes were filled with joy. But those of the bat tribe did not know what to do, as they had proved traitors to both parties; so they had to go and live with the wicked owls, who always lived away by themselves, and who delighted in darkness.

The sun,[1] the great ruler of all, had observed this fighting and killing going on among the tribes, and he became very angry and hid his face. Thus the earth became dark. Life in darkness was a great burden to all the tribes. They found it very hard to go about groping in the darkness. The birds could not sing. But the owl and the bat did not mind, for they delighted in the darkness. The emu and the kangaroo met, and the emu said, " O kangaroo, what shall we do? The children are unable to enjoy themselves, and we find it difficult to provide food and clothing." The kangaroo thought deeply, and an idea came to him. He told the emu to build bonfires here, there, and everywhere. So the emu went and asked the crows, pheasants, magpies, and cockatoos to assist in bringing in supplies of wood to keep the fires burning. They continued burning and burning the wood until there was a shortage of fuel.

Once again the emu approached the kangaroo, and explained to him the seriousness of the position. The kangaroo meditated for a while, and then he advised the emu to summon the whole of the tribes to meet and discuss the problem of fuel and light. The emu visited all the

[1] The sun here is male.

camps, and invited every one to attend the great meeting. The whole of the animal, bird, and reptile tribes came and sat in conference in order to find some means of providing light or of bringing back the sunshine. The cockatoos, as usual, did most of the talking, but they were unable to suggest a means of bringing back the light.

There was a little lizard sitting at the feet of the kangaroo, and he spoke up and said, " O kangaroo, the owl and the bat know how to give us the light. I have heard that they are able to bring back the sunlight." So it was decided to send the lizard to ask the owl and the bat to attend the meeting. The little lizard went off, groping in the darkness, to invite the owl and the bat to attend. He found them and said, " O chief of the owls, and chief of the bats, the kangaroo wishes that you should come and attend a meeting. Will you come?" "Oh, yes," said the owl and the bat, " we will come." The little lizard hastened back, his heart filled with joy because he was able to return to the kangaroo with the glad news that the owl and the bat had consented to come to the meeting. When they arrived at the conference the kangaroo asked them if they could give them light or bring back the sunshine. They said that they knew how to bring the light and sunshine, but when the kangaroo asked them to do so they refused.

The curlew and the dingo then howled long and loud for the light. They can be heard even to-day howling for the light. But the owl, who loved the dark and had a wicked heart, refused to give the light, because he said he and his children loved the darkness. Then the curlew called, " O Uncle, you would not refuse your nephew. For the sake of my children and the children of the other tribes, give us the light." Once more the owl refused.

Then there arose a great cry from the animal, bird, and reptile tribes: " O Uncle, give us the light! O Uncle, give us the light!" The cry was so pitiful that it smote the hardened conscience of the bat, and all the wrongs that he had done in the past came up before him. He said to himself, " Now I can atone for all the wrong that I have done." So he shouted, " I will give you the light ! "

All the animals, birds, and reptiles ceased crying, and then the bat asked if anyone had a boomerang. The lizard who had asked the owl and the bat to attend the meeting answered, " I have a boomerang. I will give it to you."

The lizard gave the boomerang to the bat, who then addressed the meeting. " I feel that I am making a great sacrifice. I love the darkness, and my children delight to romp and skip and play in the eternal darkness, but I know that if I make this sacrifice I shall have their approval."

Then he took the boomerang, and with mighty force he hurled it toward the north, and it travelled around the earth, and returned from the south. Again the boomerang was sent on its mission toward the west, and it travelled around the earth and came back from the east. Just as the bat was about to throw the boomerang again the laughing jack said, " Wait a moment, O bat. We do not want an exhibition of boomerang-throwing—we require the light."

" Yes," said the bat, " I know that you are all anxious to have the sunlight, but I am dividing the great darkness. I am going to give you light, and I shall keep the darkness to myself." So again, and with greater force, he hurled the boomerang, this time toward the west, and it travelled around the earth and came back from the east, and while it was still hovering about his head the bat shouted, " Look to the east ! The light is coming ! The light is coming ! " The bird tribe looked, and they became so excited that they began chattering and twittering and whistling at the approach of dawn. Still the bat shouted, " The light is coming ! The light is coming ! " and as soon as the boomerang touched the earth the sun rose. Oh, what joy ! The kangaroos leaped with delight, the dingoes scampered about and turned somersaults, and the laughing jacks laughed with great gladness, even as they do to-day. The native companions ran about and danced, the parrots screeched, and the cockatoos chattered more than ever. Every one was happy except the wicked owl. The bat

98

ABORIGINAL WITH BOOMERANG

Photo Inspector Priest

THE END OF KINIE GER

waited until the sun had set in the western sky, and then he returned to his home in the cave.

When the owl ventures out in the daylight all the feathered tribes fly around seeking an opportunity to peck at him, because he was so selfish in refusing to give them the sunlight; but if the bat comes out at sunset, or on a dull evening before sunset, no bird will ever molest him. They treat him kindly because he was so willing to make amends for the wrong he did, and because, by his act of kindness, he brought back the glorious sunlight on which all creation is so dependent for life and energy.

As for the little messenger, the lizard, he still loves to sit and gaze at the sun, and if you look closely at his neck you will see that he carries there the boomerang which he lent to the bat to divide the darkness from the light.

Why Frogs jump into the Water

The Australian aboriginal has very keen powers of observation. He watches closely the habits, and studies carefully the characteristics, of animals and birds, and, in time, the information gained is woven into the legends of the people. These people delight to give a reason for everything they observe, and to draw a moral lesson from it all. The lesson taught in the legend of the frogs is that man is incomplete apart from woman, and that if men try to stand alone they succumb to fear and fail. The overcoming of fear is the strongest feature in the training and culture of aboriginals.

This is the legend of the frogs.

Once all the male frogs became discontented and left their wives and sisters. Every one went and lived by himself. One night while they were cooking their evening meal they had a strange experience. Each felt a presence come up from the south. They could not see this presence; they could only feel it. Presently a voice asked for some food. The frogs looked, but they could not see anyone. "Yes," said a frog, "I will give you something to eat; but who are you? I cannot see you." "Oh, never mind who I am," said the voice; " later on you will see me. I am tired. I have been travelling all over the world. Give me something to eat." So each frog gave the voice some fish to eat. The frogs could see the fish being moved about and disappearing, but could not see who was eating it.

After the meal was over the voice said, " I am tired. May I sleep here to-night?" " Oh, yes," said a frog. In a very few minutes the frog could hear the sound of snoring.

The frog, however, could not sleep. He jumped up and ran about, crying, " Who are you? Let me see you, and let me feel you." The voice answered, " You will see me coming across the plain to-morrow." In the morning the voice was up before the frog, and moved away from the camp very quietly before the frog could ask any questions. The frog could just hear the voice moving away.

Next evening the frog stood on the high ground near his camp, watching for the voice to return. All he could see was a small whirlwind, a willy-willy,[1] coming across the plain. As it came nearer it circled round the frog's camp. A voice said to the frog, " Here I am again." " But," said the frog, " I cannot see you. I want to see you with my eyes." " Well, then," answered the voice, " you will see me to-morrow night."

Now all the frogs lived by the river-side, close to the water. When the next evening came the frog jumped up to the top of a big log to wait for the coming of the voice. He looked across the plain and saw a huge willy-willy coming. The wind began to blow fiercely, and a hurricane struck the camp. The storm blew round the camp, the big gum-trees swaying under its mighty force. Presently there was a terrific blast of wind, and a voice began, " I am ——" The frog had become so afraid that he did not wait to hear any more, but dived into the river and kept under water until the storm had passed.

The elders among the aboriginals tell this story to their

---

[1] A hurricane that starts on the north coast of Australia and passes along the north-west coast, then turns inland, sometimes depositing very heavy rain ; it usually terminates at the Great Australian Bight.

children. They say that this is the reason why a frog jumps into the water at the slightest sound of wind. "Look, look," they say, " how afraid the frogs have become from living by themselves ! "

Kinie Ger, the Native Cat

In the dim and distant past the faculties of thinking and reasoning dawned slowly. Through the misty ages man beheld countless forms of grotesque beings. Some of these were good, and proved a blessing to mankind, but some were bad, and to this day man is heir to the cruel and evil passions of these bad ones.

Kinie Ger was one who did ruthless and murderous deeds. He had the head, the mouth, the ears, and the body of the native cat of to-day ; but his arms, hands, fingers, legs, feet, and toes were shaped after the human fashion. He had not the power of thought and reason, nor the feelings of love or pity ; but he had the sneaking habit and the love of cruelty found in cats at the present time. He loved to kill even when he had just finished a meal. He delighted to watch the life-blood flowing from the side of his wounded victim. His happiest moments were those when he saw the glistening eyes staring vacantly and the last breath of life leaving the slain.

His fame for cruelty spread far and wide. A wise old kangaroo thought of a plan by which he could prevent this unnaturally cruel being from causing deaths. He selected men of every tribe whose business it should be to educate the young and to warn them not to venture forth alone, whether bent on pleasure or engaged in business. The young people were expected to conform to the instructions given by the elder for the common safety. A bodyguard of warriors was trained and made skilful in the use of the spear and boomerang. Any person who went forth to hunt or to carry a message-stick[1] from place to place could command

[1] A piece of wood, usually about four to eight inches long, and from half an inch to an inch wide, with cuts or impressions on it conveying information from the sender to the receiver.

the services of this bodyguard. But still the killings went on.

One day a conceited, youthful kangaroo, boastfully proud of his strength, and heedless of entreaties and warnings, went forth saying, " I am going westward to gather herbs and berries, and I will return at the setting of the sun to join you all." With mighty leaps he bounded across the plain, and soon disappeared. But at the setting of the sun the proud young kangaroo lay cold and lifeless. A mark upon the body caused great alarm, for it was instantly recognized; and late that evening, when the men were sitting round the camp-fire discussing the death, one of the company whispered, " That wound was the mark of Kinie Ger's spear."

Kinie Ger was one who showed no pity. He wrought his cruel vengeance upon animals and birds alike; he slew lizards and reptiles mercilessly. The animals, the birds, the lizards, and the reptiles met and discussed what means might be taken to prevent these killings. The emu, the kangaroo, the goanna, and the carpet-snake talked together as to how they might capture or slay this cruel enemy. At length the emu volunteered to go forth, spear in hand, to meet the dreaded foe. But at twilight a messenger arrived, overcome with sorrow, to tell how the noble-hearted emu had fought and had fallen a victim to the spear of Kinie Ger.

Among the birds, the owl and the crow had long lived in peace and happiness, for they had married twin sisters. Nothing had appeared to dim their happiness until one bright and sunny day, when the mother owl and the mother crow peeped into the cots where their darling babes slept. What a dreadful sight met their gaze! Each little baby's breast revealed a gaping wound, through which the heart had been torn—again the work of Kinie Ger. With heavy hearts and tearful eyes each mother exclaimed, " O husband mine, thou shalt not eat one morsel of flesh, nor drink one drop to quench thy thirst, nor shalt thou rest thy weary body, until thou hast slain the wicked Kinie Ger."

The owl and the crow thereupon smoke-signalled far and

wide, asking that the water-holes within two days' journey-ing to the north and to the south and to the east should be strictly guarded, but that the well which was half a day's journey toward the rising sun should be left unguarded. No one was to camp near or within this space; nor was anyone to hunt or to walk about it. For a time it was to be regarded as forbidden ground.

The birds, the animals, the lizards, and the reptiles came with sorrowing hearts to express their sympathy, and the elders came to pronounce a benediction. To all the owl in grief and indignation replied, " Forget not, O hands, to wield the trusty spear. Revenge this bloody deed—the killing of two innocent victims by Kinie Ger. Remem-ber, O spear, thy noble mission, and rid us of so vile and wicked a foe. From thy sharpened point and jagged edge shall drip the life-blood of Kinie Ger."

HAND CLUB WITH TEETH
British Museum

This impas-sioned speech aroused the crowd, and they sang the war-songs of their fathers. The crow and the owl danced the war-dance of revenge. Suddenly they stopped, and ran toward the east, bound for the well. The owl ran to the northern side and the crow to the southern side of the well. When they were within a hundred paces of the well they sat down for a while to think and to plan how best to act in order to bring about the death of Kinie Ger. Presently they communicated with each other by signs and gestures. Then they rose and walked to a bush about forty paces from the well. Within this bush they dug a hole deep enough to allow them to stand in it up to the waist. Thus standing, they waited patiently for the arrival of Kinie Ger.

It was a sultry day, and the wind was blowing from the north. A dust-storm raged for an hour, and the throats of the animals and birds were parched and dry, and they were compelled to seek the wells and water-holes for drinks.

When the sun was half-way down the western sky Kinie Ger, in order to slake his thirst, approached the well where the crow and owl lay in ambush. He had his *wommera* and spear in his hand, ready in case anyone should dare to attack him. When he got to the well he stooped down to drink.

This was just what the owl and the crow were waiting for. Each had his spear prepared and fixed upon the *wommera*, and they were quite ready to throw them. As soon as Kinie Ger stooped they discharged their spears with such accurate aim that they entered the vital parts of Kinie Ger and killed him. Then the owl and the crow came forth from their

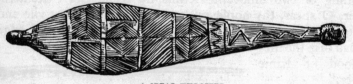

A SPEAR-THROWER
British Museum

place of concealment and drew forth the spears from Kinie Ger's body. They stuck their spears again and again into the lifeless body, and the blood flowed and soaked the ground round about. When the sun had sunk in the west the owl and the crow committed Kinie Ger's body to the flames.

Late that evening, as they sat and watched the body of Kinie Ger burn, they saw that one spark, larger than the rest, rose into the darkened sky. They watched it rise and rise and take a place in the Milky Way. Then they both returned to their anxious wives and told the story of their success.

Next day the animals, the birds, the reptiles, and the lizards came to see the spot where their enemy had been slain. They saw the stain where the life-blood of their enemy had flowed. From that spot they could trace the footprints of some strange and tiny being that seemed to have arisen from out of the life-blood of Kinie Ger. They tracked these footprints anxiously, and they came upon a harmless creature that was as shy as is the native cat to-day.

The Porcupine and the Mountain Devil [1]

The marriages that took place between the animal, the bird, the reptile, the lizard, and the insect tribes were designed to produce children who would be superior to others, and who would thus be able to take a prominent part in the ceremonial rites at the gathering of the tribes. In conformity with this object, the splendid young man of the porcupine tribe, In-Nard-Dooah, chose the beautiful mountain devil girl, Yee-Na-Pah, to be his wife. All the young men of the various tribes paid homage to the beauty and goodness of the youthful Yee-Na-Pah, but she refused to have anything to do with them, since she had given her heart into the keeping of the handsome In-Nard-Dooah.

So one night when the moon [2] was shining and lighting up the whole earth and sky with his silvery light every creature, male and female, old and young, in the country came to witness the marriage of these two. The moon spake to the youthful pair, and pointed out to them their duties to their tribes, to themselves, and to their neighbours. He hoped that they would bring forth children who would be the mould in which human intelligence should be formed and from which it should be given forth. He said, "My son and my daughter, you have both decided to assume the great responsibility of bringing others into being. Thou, son of the animal and bird, and thou, fair daughter of the bird and reptile, I wish you both to be blessed

[1] This story was told by a Cooper river tracker, a member of the Arunta tribe.
[2] The moon here is male.

WAR SPEAR
British Museum

with many children. Hearken to my words. Be not divided in thought or in feeling. In-Nard-Dooah, thou shalt do well to observe my word always. Be meek and be pleasing to thy wife. Thou shalt approve her wishes and desires, whatever they are. Yee-Na-Pah, thou shalt not allow any bitter feeling to be in thy heart against thy husband. Remember that as your minds are so shall your bodies be. Your bodies and your minds shall be mirrored in your children's. Do not think evil thoughts. Remember, Yee-Na-Pah, that you are like a stream of water which flows on and on and gives life and growth as it flows. As your relations are to each other, so shall your children be affected, and what they receive from you they will pass on as dowry to the next generation."

While the moon was speaking the animal, the bird, the reptile, the lizard, and the insect tribes bowed their heads and prostrated themselves reverently. Then they rose and stood silently for one hour. Then the kangaroo broke the silence, and said that it was time they proceeded with the marriage ceremony. The willy-wagtail hastened away and lighted a fire. Into this he placed sticks that were about four feet long and three inches thick. When these had caught fire he distributed them among the relatives of the porcupine and the mountain devil tribes. Then they all marched, carrying their fire-sticks, to a spot that had been selected as the future home of In-Nard-Dooah and Yee-Na-Pah.

When the young porcupine and mountain devil had been married for about three months the husband said to his wife, " Come, let us take a journey toward the east, the place of the cool, refreshing south wind." His wife replied that she was willing to go. So they set out on their journey. As they walked along they became happier and happier, and they were contented to be without companions. Whenever Yee-Na-Pah saw a beautiful flower and admired it In-Nard-Dooah would compliment his wife upon her taste. They continued on their journey in love and happiness until they came to a very dead country, not at all like the country that Yee-Na-Pah had come from. The evenings were chilly,

ABORIGINAL THROWING SPEAR WITH WOMMERA

Photo Powell

106

ENTRANCE TO ELLENSBROOK CAVE, WESTERN AUSTRALIA

This cave is of phenomenal length; it extends over a great distance to the sea,
and many native legends are connected with it.

Photo B. H. Woodward, sometime Curator of Perth Museum

and the nights and the early hours of the morning were extremely cold. Yee-Na-Pah would call to her husband, " Oh, my husband, I am cold and shivering. Will you arise and light a fire ? " In-Nard-Dooah would rise quickly from his bed, and hurriedly gather grass and wood, and make a fire near his wife's feet.

Soon Yee-Na-Pah began to wish that they had never undertaken this journey. She would say to her husband, " Let us return to our own country, to your people and to mine. You must have noticed that the yams in this country are not nearly so sweet or so nice as in ours. The climate is not so warm, the air is not so pure, and the travelling is very rough."

Then In-Nard-Dooah thought they would stop travelling. He set about making a comfortable home to keep out the cold air. He searched round for yams and other kinds of food. He placed his gatherings before his wife and tried to coax her to eat, but she always complained that things did not taste the same as those in her own country. By and by In-Nard-Dooah began to become impatient with Yee-Na-Pah. One day he said to her, " I am going on a journey to yonder mountain. From it I shall be able to view the surrounding country and select a suitable home that will find favour in your sight. You must remain here until I return, which will be in about four days' time." Then his wife said, " It is not right that you should leave me all alone for four days. Will you put off your journey for another day ? " The husband answered, " I cannot delay for another day. I must set out almost at once." Then Yee-Na-Pah said, " If you leave me I shall not remain until you return." Her husband replied sternly, " You will do whatever I command you to do. I am your lord and master." Yee-Na-Pah replied, " You have no right to think of yourself as my master. You are simply my companion, my protector, and provider." Once again the husband replied, " I am your lord and master." Then for the first time the beautiful spirit of Yee-Na-Pah was ruffled, and evil passion rose uppermost. She wept bitterly with rage and hatred. She vowed that she would leave the place as soon as she was able to do so.

In-Nard-Dooah took his spear and boomerang, and walked rapidly toward the south. All that afternoon Yee-Na-Pah allowed her evil passions to dominate her. In the morning of the next day Yee-Na-Pah gave birth to five boys and five girls. She was a very proud mother as she gazed lovingly upon her offspring. Then she decided that on the next day she would set out on a journey that would take her away from her husband. In the morning she said to her children, " Come, we must hasten away to the mountain that lies toward the sun." The five boys walked on one side of her, and the five girls walked on the other. They continued their journey for the whole of that day, and at night they rested under a bush. They rose early next morning and resumed their journey.

Now on the fifth day In-Nard-Dooah returned from his expedition. He was sorely troubled to find that his wife had disappeared. He sat down and pondered over the harsh words he had said to her before he had gone away. Then he thought of the youths who had tried to win the affections of Yee-Na-Pah. Could it be possible that one of them had tracked them to their home, and had witnessed In-Nard-Dooah's departure, and had taken advantage of it? Yee-Na-Pah, he thought, would not require much persuading to leave her husband. Thus brooding, In-Nard-Dooah grew jealous, and allowed wicked thoughts to pervade his whole being. He vowed that he would follow their tracks and slay his wife and her companion.

So he arose early on the following morning. He broke his fast, and as the sun rose over the eastern mountains he went to the camp recently vacated by his wife, to see if he could find any clue as to whether she had gone alone or with a companion. He saw her tracks very distinctly upon the earth. To his amazement on each side of her there were five indistinct tracks. He stood for a while, thinking very hard, and at last the solution of the problem of the track marks dawned on him. He strode forward eagerly, noting the tracks as he went along. Side by side were the marks of the mother and her offspring. As he went along he decided that when he came near to his wife he would lie in ambush, and see if she had any companion with her. Presently he saw her. He watched and watched, but he could see no stranger in her company. He noticed her as she sat by the fire in the evening, cooking food for herself and the children. He kept watch on her for some days.

One evening he crawled very near to her camp, and sat watching her from a porcupine bush. This he did every night for a month. He knew that he had done wrong in leaving his wife, but he was not willing to tell her so. During the time he sat in the porcupine bush he was so given over to evil thoughts that, although the sharp points of the grass began to stick in his flesh and to cling to his body, he would not leave his hiding-place. He watched because he thought that the others who had loved his wife might come to her. He still imagined that some one was accompanying her, and he kept himself hidden from view. He noticed that the sparks from the fire were constantly settling upon his wife, but she was so engrossed with her thoughts that she took no notice of them. She, on her part, imagined that her husband had left her, and had sought other fair maidens. By and by every spark that rested on the body of Yee-Na-Pah left a mark that remained.

Her husband could bear this no longer, so one fine morning he walked toward her, and said, " Yee-Na-Pah, what are you doing here all alone with these children? I am In-Nard-Dooah, your husband." Yee-Na-Pah looked at her husband, and she said, " What have you been doing to your body?" In-Nard-Dooah replied, " I have been sitting among those spear-pointed grasses. And as I sat I was so engrossed with my evil thoughts concerning you that the grass points stuck into me, and there they have remained. But, my dear Yee-Na-Pah, what have you been doing to yourself? What are those marks over your body?" "Oh," said Yee-Na-Pah, "I sat by the fire, brooding over your unkindness to me. The sparks and the ashes alighted on my body, and, as I did not trouble to brush them off, they have left marks. I am now going to continue my journey onward." " But," said In-Nard-Dooah, " let us talk things over and see if we can come to an understanding for the sake of the children." " No," said Yee-Na-Pah, " I do not wish to be your wife again. I hate you." In-Nard-Dooah pleaded with his wife to let him return. After a while Yee-Na-Pah appeared to consent, and she said to her husband, " You may travel with us to yonder mountain. In that mountain there is a cave which I would very much like to explore."

Now Yee-Na-Pah had once dreamed about this cave. She thought that a monster dwelt within it. No one had ever ventured to enter it. So she planned that if she could entice her husband into the cave she would get the monster to kill him, and thus she would be able to have her liberty again, and seek for another husband. So the husband, the wife, and the children journeyed toward the cave. When they arrived Yee-Na-Pah was glad to see that the cave appeared to be exactly as she had dreamed. They entered the cave. The darkness within it could almost be felt. Yee-Na-Pah travelled along until she came to a place at which, according to her dream, there was a passage that led upward through the mountain to the open air. She went along this passage, and after a great deal of travelling arrived at the top of the mountain and passed out into the fresh air and the sunshine. Poor In-Nard-Dooah groped and groped about. He had not had any dream that would have guided him through the passage-ways.

By and by he found a passage that appeared to lead him upward. He passed along this, and presently he came to the end of it. He started to dig his way upward. He dug and dug until he made a way through the mountain into the outer air. He sat for a while in the opening in order to breathe the fresh air and to rest after all his exertion. He wondered what had become of his wife. He was quite unaware of her evil intentions toward him. He put his head out of the opening in order to gain some knowledge about his surroundings, and he found that he was in a very peculiar position. He looked down and saw a steep precipice. He had dug himself right under the top edge of an overhanging cliff. He saw that he could not get out that way. So he went back into the hole, and started to dig a passage that would lead him into the face of the cliff. When he looked out again he still saw the precipice. " Oh, what a funny world this is ! " he thought. " I wonder how I am going to get down into the valley." He went back into his hole again, and sat thinking. By and by he came to the edge of the hole, and took a look down to the valley in the distance. " Yes," he said, " I think I can do it." Then he rolled himself into a ball and started his journey down the face of the cliff into the valley below, where he made his home.

This high mountain, with its steep, jagged sides, has from that day to this been a barrier between In-Nard-Dooah and Yee-Na-Pah. They have never tried to renew their association, and the disfigurement which arose from their evil thoughts and disobedience to the moon's advice is plainly visible to-day on their repulsive-looking bodies.

The Green Frog [1]

This is the story of the green frog, who came into existence through the agency of a spirit of water. Water-spirit, or the spirit of water, is the most mutable spirit of all, because in it and through it there is a continual change from one form of existence to another. It receives something into it, and gives this out entirely different in form or in nature, or in both. This is how the green frog came to be with us.

On the western slope of the Blue Mountains there was a stream of pure, clear water flowing down the mountain-

---

[1] This is one of several stories of a strange being that came into existence. The aboriginals believe that there are many spirits existing in the elements—the wind-spirit, the rain-spirit, the hail-spirit, the sunlight-spirit, and the cloud-spirit. Besides these there are spirits that take the form of trees, bushes, shrubs, and rocks. Everything that exists is supposed to partake in some life apart from itself.

side.   That stream at the present day is a tributary of the great Murray River.

In some of these mountain rills one may note the murmuring and gurgling song of the water-spirits.   The spirits dwell in the form of tiny bubbles that cling closely together in the limpid pools and make the surface look as white as snow.   In one of these clusters of tiny bubbles there dwelt a spirit that peeped out of its many clear, crystal-like windows.   Thinking that it would be good to be free in some form and shape and to play a useful part in the lives of others, the bubble-spirit sat and watched the little fishes sporting and swimming, darting here and there in the clear waters of the pool.   It would watch some of the strange, tiny objects struggling in the water and then bursting forth and taking wing and flying or skimming over the water, away to the reeds and rushes and the flowers that grew upon the bank.   " Oh," it thought, " what a wonderful life to live—to go where you will and to come back when you please ! "

Then the spirit began to think how pleasant it would be to leap forth and feel refreshed by the coolness of the stream ; to touch the tender leaves of the water-lily ; or to ride upon the swaying stem of the reed as it was rocked by the gentle east wind or touched by the warm breath of the sun god ; to become enthralled with the song of the little water-bird ; and sit in wonderment at the merry laughter of the laughing jack, while the forms of these birds were reflected in the clear water as they sat upon the overhanging branch of a large gum-tree.   Oh, what a wonderful transformation it would be to become part of the material world!

As the bright sun shone in the clear sky above, sending beams of light and warmth that gave strength and motion, suddenly the bubble-cluster began, by a wish of the spirit, to become a material living being.   Progress at first was slow, but it gradually developed into a green frog, and began a series of experiences in a new life.   The first thing that the spirit tried to do as a frog was to produce a sound.   Then he began to imitate the various sounds that he had heard in Spirit Land. By and by he became an adept. He lived in this watercourse for a while. The birds would come in the hot summer days to drink from the clear, cool, and refreshing stream. They would then fly up to the branches of near-by trees and pour forth their songs of gratitude. Perhaps in the early hours of a summer morning all the feathered tribe would sing their anthems, sending forth a variety of notes, all blending in sweet harmony. "Oh, could I join in such wondrous melody!" said the green frog, who by this time was known by the bird and reptile and animal tribes as "Son of the clear-running stream of water."

The lyre-bird gave this account of how it was that the green frog received his name. Said he, "I saw a bubble on the pool at the place where we go to drink. I was just a few paces away from the bubble when I saw it floating upon the water, and was attracted toward it. There seemed to be a spirit within it calling on me to release it. But I would not do so. As I sat upon the bank, resting, I began to sing. I sang the song of the crow and the peewee. Then I sang the song of the magpie, and between my songs I imitated the liquid notes of the song of a running stream. All this time I kept my eyes upon the bubbles that were lying peacefully on the clear, limpid water. As I watched a spirit from the Unknown whispered in my ear, ' Sing on. Thy wonderful song doth give life to a spirit within a body that is taking shape.' So I sang the same song, and repeated it again and again. The hot sun gave glow of health and strength to all life upon the water as well as beneath it; and little fishes darted swiftly here and there. Then the bubble disappeared, and nothing was visible until after a little time I was amazed to see a strange living form looking straight at me. I went toward it and stood upon the bank, and felt bewildered.

" I could not recall having seen any shape like it. Then I sang to it. I projected my voice to the opposite side of the bank, and the form turned and looked in that direction. Then I cast my voice quickly all round the bank, and the

113

form turned quickly round and then stopped, as if puzzled. I became very interested in this strange form. In course of time I would pay him a visit after the sun rose high in the heavens, and I would stand upon the bank and sing him the songs of our tribes, and make sounds like the streams running down the hillside. He tried hard to imitate me, and by and by he could make a deep, guttural sound. Then he succeeded in making a variety of sounds. After this I began to ask him questions as to where he came from. I said, 'No one has told of your coming. Tell me, from whence are you?' He said, 'My home is in the running streams. There I live.' I said, 'Then I shall call you Son of the clear-running stream of water.' This was his name then, but now he is called the green frog."

The green frog said that he would like to be able to sing like the magpie and laugh like the laughing jack. The lyre-bird consented to try to educate him. He came every morning and gave lessons to his eager pupil. And after a while he was able to sing a few songs to the lyre-bird. Then the lyre-bird did not come so often to see his pupil. When several moons had come and gone the lyre-bird thought that he would once more pay him a visit. As he came down the valley he could hear, as he thought, the sweet song of his brother. He wondered what his brother was doing at the pool, so he came cautiously down, dodging round the shrubs and bushes, so that his brother would not see him until he was right upon him. When he got to the edge of the bank he looked about, but saw no brother of his. Then he wondered, "Perhaps my brother is playing a joke upon me." And presently the thought struck him, "Perhaps it is the cunning green frog that is joking." So he called, "Green frog!" And the answer came from away up the gully from whence the lyre-bird had come. Again he called: "Green frog!" And the voice answered, "I am coming, I am coming!" seeming nearer and nearer until it sounded right down in the pool of water.

The lyre-bird looked very much amazed, and stood,

pleased that his lessons had been so well learned. He said to the green frog, " I should like to know how many songs you can sing, and how many voices or sounds you can imitate." So the green frog sang like the magpie and the butcher-bird, laughed like the laughing jack, and imitated the sound of the running stream as it gurgled over pebbles, and the splash of the water as it leaped over rocks. When he had finished the lyre-bird complimented him on his wonderful achievements. He said that the green frog was better in the art of ventriloquism than he himself, his teacher, was. And this statement caused the green frog to swell with pride, and to think within himself that he would seek other audiences and impress them with his accomplishments.

Before he did so he settled down and began to practise in earnest. He would make the sound of a magpie's voice at a certain supposed spot in such a manner that his audience would imagine the speaker was at that spot; and when they looked there they found that the bird was at an entirely different place.

Again, he would make the sound of water being disturbed by the sporting water-rats, and would imitate the soft south wind rustling among the gum-trees and moaning through the long, wiry leaves of the she-oak. Presently there would be heard the sound of a mighty storm, with rumbling thunder and breaking boughs, as if the wind were tearing up the huge gum-trees; and then the rain and hail would come as if lashed by the furious wind. All this was imitation on the part of the green frog.

Then the green frog thought that he would go and gain experience of the outside world, and he mentioned his wish to the lyre-bird, who told him that the world was large, and that there were many and many kinds of beings with strange habits and strange languages.

Now, during the time that the green frog was showing off his accomplishments there came, unknown to him, the swift and the falcon to this pool of water to rest and refresh their wearied bodies. They sat enraptured by the wonderful songs that appeared to come from the silent nowhere, until quite by accident they made the discovery that these beautiful songs came from a strange being lying in the leaf of a water-lily. They saw him and heard him speaking to the lyre-bird, who had just arrived. They leaped from their perch, and, as if carried on the mighty wings of the storm, sped through the country, telling the various tribes of a being who could do wonderful things. The animal, bird, reptile, and insect tribes became very curious, and asked if they could be allowed to pay the green frog a visit.

The falcon and swift returned and perched upon the same branches that they had occupied a few days before, and waited for the lyre-bird to appear. Presently he arrived, and they spoke to him, telling him that the various tribes wished to come and be entertained by the visitor. " Well," said the lyre-bird, " if you will wait a moment I will speak to him. I think he may be resting among the reeds yonder." So the lyre-bird, swift, and falcon sat down on the bank of the pool and patiently waited for the green frog.

Now the green frog was sleeping soundly, and in this state he was enjoying himself with the people of his race in the Spirit Land. When he woke he was greatly disappointed. He came out from among the reeds and went to his usual spot. There he saw the lyre-bird with two strangers, the swift and the falcon. The lyre-bird spoke to him, and said that a great many people, as numerous as the reeds that grow in the water of the pool in which he lived, had heard of his wonderful accomplishment, and were anxious to receive an invitation to see and hear him perform. These people included the animal, bird, lizard, snake, and insect tribes. He asked if they might be invited. " Oh, yes," said the green frog. " I would like to meet them. Will you ask them to come next full moon? "

When the swift and the falcon heard this answer they were eager to set off. But the lyre-bird asked them first to think

116

how they would deliver the message. It was arranged that the swift should fly northward twenty miles, then travel in a spiral, widening outward; when he had reached forty miles he should then fly westward sixty miles. The falcon should fly northward forty miles and fly in the same manner eastward twenty miles. They were to continue to travel thus until they had informed every tribe of the invitation of the green frog.

As soon as the instructions had been given the swift was off like lightning, cleaving the air as he went with the speed of a hurricane. When he reached the twenty-mile limit in a straight line he began to fly in a spiral outward, working his way toward the north, and giving the invitation from the green frog as he went. Then the falcon leaped into the air, and rose until he was invisible. He shot forth, like an arrow from a bowstring pulled by a mighty archer, away to the north. He began to fly in an ever-widening spiral, until he and the swift met. Then he rose upward in a small circle till he reached a certain height. He then shot forward in a straight line toward the east. They continued thus until they had completed their journey and given the message that the green frog desired that the tribes would be at his home at the next full moon.

After the swift and the falcon had fulfilled their mission they came back to where the green frog lived, and became his servants. They held themselves in readiness to carry any messages that he wished to be delivered before the great entertainment began. On the appointed day the great army of birds, the kangaroo with all his family, the animal tribe, the eagle-hawk and his family and tribe, the snake, the reptile, and the insect tribes all came to see this strange being who could sing their songs when heard once, and could mimic any peculiar gesture of an individual or a tribe. As evening approached they were all seated on the bank, waiting. Then they heard all around them some very wonderful songs. They sat the whole night entranced, and when the sun rose the green frog was still performing his wonderful feats. In the still air the guests imagined they heard the noise of a mighty wind; in the clear sky they fancied they saw the flash of lightning, and that they heard the thunder roar and the sound of rain and hail lashed by the fury of a mighty wind. It was so natural that they all scattered, and ran to seek shelter. Suddenly the sound of the storm ceased, and they all looked about and saw a clear sky, which had been there all the while. They looked at the trees and saw that they had not been disturbed. Then they heard the sound of a cataract of falling water. They looked about, but saw no waterfall, and they were greatly bewildered. They all shouted, "Hurrah! Hurrah!"

After a few days' entertainment the animals, the birds, the reptiles, and the insects all went away to their homes, and for many days afterward they spoke to each other of the wonderful things they had seen and heard. By this time the spirit of the running stream gave a beautiful wife to the green frog. One day he was entertaining his wife with his wonderful voice. He sang and sang, and as he sang his pride became greater and greater, until he attempted to do something beyond his powers and strained his voice. The next minute the only sound he could make was a croak. To-day he can only croak, and he will never more be able to sing the song of the birds or imitate any of the sounds round about him.

How the Tortoise got his Shell

Long, long ago all the bush birds and animals lived in a big, deep valley that was hemmed in on every side by high, rough hills. Food had become very scarce, and all the birds and animals held a special meeting to discuss how it could be procured. They all talked and talked, but they came to no decision as to how to obtain more food. At last the tortoise rose to speak, and all the animals laughed. Everybody made fun of the tortoise, for he was so slow and ungainly; and everybody looked upon him as a fool, because he was always either asleep or sleepy. However, the tortoise proposed that the big eagle-hawk, the fierce

118

AN OLD FOOTBRIDGE AT BUSSELTON, WESTERN AUSTRALIA,
BUILT BY THE ABORIGINALS
Photo B. H. Woodward, sometime Curator of Perth Museum   118

THE MISCHIEVOUS CROW COMPELLING THE TUCKONIE TO
ASSIST HIM IN MAKING THE TREE GROW

king of birds, who was a great hunter, should fly over the ranges and find food. "Oh, yes," said the big eagle-hawk; and away he flew.

When the eagle-hawk had gone a long way over on the other side of the ranges he saw a beautiful country full of all kinds of food, but he saw no birds or animals there, except one little willy-wagtail. So the eagle-hawk said to the little willy-wagtail, "May I fetch my brothers and sisters, who are starving, into this beautiful country of yours?" "Oh, yes," said the willy-wagtail, "but you must wrestle with me first."

Of course, the big, strong eagle-hawk thought this was easy, but the cunning little willy-wagtail had placed some sharp fish-bones like spikes in the ground where he proposed that they should wrestle. When they began to wrestle the willy-wagtail was very quick and nimble, and hopped and jumped about just as he does to-day. Suddenly the willy-wagtail tripped up the eagle-hawk, who fell among the sharp spikes and was pinned to the ground, where he was at the mercy of the willy-wagtail, who at once pecked him to death.

Meantime, all the other birds and animals over the ranges waited for the eagle-hawk to return. By and by they became tired of waiting, and they sent out the kite-hawk. But the kite-hawk met the same fate as the eagle-hawk. Then the magpie, the wombat, the dingo, and others were sent out in turn, but the wicked little willy-wagtail tripped them all on to his spikes, and then pecked them to death. All the birds and animals became very much alarmed, because none returned.

At last the position became serious, for food had to be found somewhere. Then the old tortoise volunteered to go. He went away, crawling slowly and painfully, over the ranges and into the land of the willy-wagtail. As usual the willy-wagtail invited his visitor to wrestle. "Oh, yes, willingly," replied the tortoise, "but just wait a while." The tortoise went into the bush, and cut a *coolamon* and a thick strip of bark out of a gum-tree. The tortoise placed the *coolamon* on his back, and he tied on the thick sheet of bark as a breastplate; then he went to wrestle with the willy-wagtail.

The quick, lively willy-wagtail hopped round and soon tripped up the slow old tortoise, who, when he fell on the spikes, was protected by the *coolamon*. Again and again the willy-wagtail threw the tortoise, but he was always saved either by the *coolamon* on his back or by his bark breastplate. After a while the willy-wagtail became exhausted, and then the tortoise was able to catch and kill the cunning little bird.

Of course the tortoise let all the birds and animals know as quickly as he could where there was plenty of food. What the eagle-hawk, the dingo, the kangaroo, and all the other animals failed to accomplish by main force the slow-moving old tortoise achieved through wisdom and cunning, and to this day he is allowed to carry the *coolamon* and the breastplate as a memorial of a great victory in overcoming a cunning and wicked enemy. He is to be seen during the long years of his lifetime seeking no applause, but humbly bearing his shield of service.

The Mischievous Crow and the Good he did [1]

According to the Narrinyeri legend, the crow set out from the north of Queensland on his travels, and struck the Darling River. He followed its course, and by and by he reached the Murray.

After staying there for some time he made the acquaintance of the eagle-hawk. One characteristic of the crow was his habit of addressing every person by the name of

---

[1] Many races have traditions regarding the origin of evil. To many of these peoples the spirit of evil presents himself as a serpent with all the fascination and cunning of that creature. Sometimes he comes in the guise of an angel. Among some of the Australian tribes it is the crow that plays the chief part in the story of the introduction of evil. Although the crow is an embodiment of all that is mischievous and evil, yet he has taught the aboriginals many great and good things. Chief among these is the immortality of the soul. Many stories of the crow are current among the various tribes. The one here narrated is a tradition of the Narrinyeri tribe.

ronggi,[1] meaning ' brother-in-law.' Now by becoming a brother-in-law to a man by marrying his sister one is assured of that man's hospitality and protection.

When the crow arrived at the home of the eagle-hawk he addressed him as " brother-in-law." Then the eagle-hawk questioned the crow as to how it came about that he was his brother-in-law. The crow explained that far back in the ages, long before any of the people then living were in existence, a crow girl married into the eagle-hawk tribe. " Oh, then," said the eagle-hawk, " come and stay with me, and after you have slept and eaten sufficient to strengthen your body you shall continue your journey." Thus invited, the crow made his home with the eagle-hawk. After spending two weeks with his host the crow said, " O my brother-in-law, I shall leave you now and go on my way." The eagle-hawk replied, " Go on your way, brother-in-law of mine, while the day is as yet young."

Then the crow set out on his journey. Soon he began to limp on his way. The eagle-hawk watched him as he gradually disappeared in the distance. When the crow was satisfied that he was beyond the sight of the eagle-hawk he ceased to limp. His lameness was only a sham, a make-believe that there was something the matter with his leg that caused difficulty in walking. As he was endowed with the spirit of evil he was carried from place to place on the dark wing of the Evil One. In a moment of time he had been transported from the Murray to Lake Victoria. The speed at which he travelled was so great that when he arrived at his destination he stood for a moment, dazed by the shock.

As he stood thus and tried to collect his thoughts, one

[1] The crow here claims the relationship of *ronggi* on the statement, whether true or not, that a girl of his tribe had married into the eagle-hawk tribe long before. The usual use of the word is illustrated in the following facts. In the Tararorn clan and the Rangulinyeri clan of the Narrinyeri tribe, on the shores of Lake Alexandrina, a man calls his sister's son *ronggi*—*i.e.*, " brother-in-law "—and this is reciprocal. These facts show how cautious one requires to be in investigating the meaning and usage of aboriginal terms in even closely allied tribes. When a man calls another man " brother-in-law " he can claim that man's hospitality and protection.

of the elders of the pelicans, who was sitting alone, meditating, was startled by a noise as of a mighty wind. He jumped to his feet, and gazed round with wide, staring eyes to see where the sound came from. He saw the crow standing not more than ten paces away. The pelican did not know whether to run away, he was so frightened. He was about to flee when the crow spoke. He said, " Brother-in-law, I am exceedingly sorry that I came to you so suddenly. Will you forgive me? " The pelican stared with wide-open mouth; he had not expected to hear the stranger address him as " brother-in-law." When he got over his surprise he said to the crow, " O stranger, why do you so address me? I have not seen you before, neither have I heard my elders speak of you." The crow, in reply, said, " Brother-in-law, before your great-grandfather was born a brother of my family married one of the sisters of your family. In the land of the north my race, the race who speak my language, have a tradition that the pelicans are my brothers-in-law. See, read for yourself a record of our relationship."

The crow held out a message-stick which, by its appearance, seemed to be ancient. The pelican did not take the message-stick because he was not able to read the various curves, angles, and dots; and he did not like to show his ignorance. So he said, " O brother-in-law, I accept what you say, and believe that we are brothers-in-law. Come, follow me, and I will take you to my home and the camping-ground of my race." So the pelican led the way, followed by the crow, who began to limp behind, and to make a noise, as if in pain. The pelican turned round and saw the poor old crow limping, and inquired, " What is the matter, brother-in-law? When did you hurt yourself? "

The crow now related an imaginary incident. " O my brother-in-law, I was coming down from the great mountain yonder, and when walking in the plain country I fell in with the emu tribe. They would not invite me to their home, but began to show that they were not related to me by taking up their *kaikes* and *waddies* and boomerangs and challenging me to do battle. I responded, and took hold of my shield to defend myself. The emu threw a spear, and I caught it upon my shield. Then he threw a boomerang, and it struck the shield and broke in halves. One piece fell away from me, and the other half struck me on the ankle. That is why I limp. When I threw my spear, behold, I saw the tribe of emus coming out to do battle with me, and of course I thought the best thing for me to do was to escape by running. So I ran and ran. That is how I came upon you so suddenly."

"But," said the pelican, "where were the emus? I did not see them."

"I do not suppose you would see them," replied the crow, "for I ran like the wind, so fast that they were not able to come near me."

Then the pelican said, "Come, it is only a little way now and you will soon be at our wurleys. There you shall have food; you can lie down and rest and we will attend to your wounds. Will you sit here for a while? My wurley is there, beside the bank of the lagoon. I will go before and explain to my people that our brother-in-law has come from the north."

The crow sat down, and the pelican went to his camp and saw the elders of his tribe, and told them that a stranger had arrived, and had made himself known, and had claimed relationship with them. The elders were anxious to meet this stranger who professed to be their brother-in-law. "Go," they said to the pelican, "and ask him to partake of our hospitality, and we will do all we can to make him happy and well, so that he may be able to continue his journey." So the pelican went and asked the crow to come, for all things were ready. When they arrived at the camp all the elders of the pelican tribe came forward and made their salutations, saying, "Brother-in-law, you shall rest a while with us."

The crow sat down just outside a wurley which one of the pelicans had given up for his accommodation during his stay. To show their appreciation of his visit other members of the tribe were offering him for food choice portions of Murray cod, cat-fish, and lobster. These delicacies were placed upon plates of gum-tree bark.

The crow was so hungry that he ate all the food that was placed before him. Then he turned to his host, and said, " Brother-in-law, with your permission I will lie down and sleep. My body is feeling tired with the long journey." The pelican rose and took him into the wurley, and showed him where to sleep, and said, " Sleep well." With this last remark the pelican left the crow to himself.

The crow slept soundly, and when he awoke, about an hour or two before midday, the sun was well up in the heavens. Now it was unusual for the crow to sleep so long and so soundly, and to wake so late. He sat up in bed and looked round him, wondering why he had made such a mistake as to sleep so soundly and so long. This worried him greatly. Then he began to think those evil thoughts that he was so accustomed to. " Perhaps the old pelican, my host, has used witchcraft," he thought. " He must have placed a charmed hair-rope[1] around this wurley."

The more the crow thought of these things the more he became convinced that he was right, and he vowed that he would be revenged. He was so accustomed to do evil to other people that when anything unusual happened to him he always thought that some one was trying to do him an injury. So he came out of the wurley, and just by the doorway, about three yards away, there was a fire ; and by the fireside he saw various portions of food in bark plates. He sat down and broke his fast, and continued sitting beside the fire, brooding over the cause of his sleeping late. Then, rising to his feet, he looked about him to see if there was anyone at home. The wurleys were all empty. There was not a pelican about. Then he began walking round the camping-ground in a circle several times, widening out in a spiral. Each time he crossed the tracks of the pelicans he noticed that they were all leading in one direction, and that

[1] A *thumie*. This charmed hair-rope is regarded as the only thing that will cause deep sleep. (See pp. 190–201.)

was toward a large lagoon. He followed the tracks until he came upon the pelicans. They were all sitting down. There, upon the bank, were the old pelicans and their wives. The youths and maidens, and the younger male and female pelicans, were enjoying themselves in the water, while the elders were making and mending their nets, and preparing to go a-fishing.

The crow sat in hiding, watching and taking in everything the pelicans did, and planning to do them some injury for the imagined wrong done to him. Suddenly he saw a pelican running as fast as he could from the opposite side of the lagoon toward the other pelicans, who were busily engaged with their nets. The other pelicans rose to their feet, with their nets in their hands, and hurried toward him. The younger pelicans did the same, ceasing their sporting in the water, and following their elders. Then this one pelican led the others to the opposite side of the lagoon, where they waded into the water and spread their nets, capturing the fishes, Murray cod, mud-fish, and such like.

Presently there was a sound of babies crying. The crow, leaving his hiding-place, searched for the cause of the noise. He looked into every bush. He saw no sign. He peeped into hollow logs, thinking perhaps the mothers might have placed their babies there; but there was nothing visible. Again he heard the crying sound, which seemed to come from everywhere around him. Then he ran round in a circle until he returned to his starting-point. After that he ran in an ever-widening spiral. Suddenly he stopped. The voices of the crying babies seemed to be above his head. He looked up, and there, just beyond his reach, were the baby pelicans, placed between the forks of the branches of a huge gum-tree. Their mothers, who were sisters, had placed their babies upon this gum-tree because the trunk was smooth. They did not notice, however, that there was a hole leading from the foot to half-way up the tree where they had placed the babies. Around the base of this gum-tree was tied a net to catch them and prevent them from being injured if they should fall.

125

The crow stood a while, thinking deeply. " Now is my opportunity," thought he. " I shall steal the babies, and give them to the swamp-hawk. I am sure he will be glad to have these young pelicans. What a nice, tender meal they will make for him ! " Such were the wicked thoughts that passed through the mind of the evil crow. Then he made efforts to take the young pelicans down, but failed in every attempt. So he decided to cut down the tree. He hastened away to the camp and found an axe. He hurried back and attempted to cut down the tree on which the baby pelicans were, but the axe belonged to the pelicans, and it refused to cut the tree down. He tried again and again, but to no purpose. So he cursed the axe, saying, " O you useless, good-for-nothing axe ! You have the resemblance of an axe, but you are deceptive."

" Oh, oh," said the axe, " do you think I am going to obey your wicked command, and respond to every stroke you give with me to cut down the tree on which are the babies of my masters, whom I obey ? I am not your servant. Oh, you cruel, wicked old crow, I will not obey you. I am the servant of the pelicans, and I obey them only."

So the crow threw the axe to the ground and cursed it, saying, " I can do very well without you. I shall use some other means. I shall set fire to the tree, so that it will fall to the ground."

Again the crow ran to the camping-ground, and brought along a fire-stick. He placed a heap of dry wood round the trunk of the gum-tree. Among this he put some dry grass, and applied the fire-stick to it. But the fire-stick refused to burn the dry grass and wood ; so the crow fanned the fire-stick to make a flame. Still the fire-stick refused to set the grass alight. The crow grew angry, and said, " And do you, too, O fire-stick, like the axe, refuse to do what it is your business to do ? "

" Yes," said the fire-stick, " I am the servant of the good and inoffensive pelicans. They do not seek to harm anyone. They have given you hospitality, and now for the good they have done you you seek to do them an injury. I am the

126

servant of the pelicans, and take my orders from them only."

The heat of the fire left the stick, which became only a dead, black coal in the crow's hands. He did not know what to do ; the axe refused to cut the tree, and the fire-stick would not burn the wood.

" Now let me think a while," said the crow. " Oh, I have it ! I will sing the Tuckonie tree-song." [1] So the crow began to sing the tree-song. Suddenly, from out of somewhere, the little Tuckonie appeared, each with a tiny boomerang. They danced round to the song, singing, " O thou tree of all trees, grow upward and upward, ever sky-ward." Every time the crow came to the word ' upward ' the little Tuckonie would leap upward, and act as if they were pulling and pushing an imaginary something upward. Every time this was done the tree, as it were, leapt skyward. It grew and grew, until the pelican babies looked so small that they were indistinguishable. The crow laughed to him-self, feeling pleased that he had accomplished something great, since he had placed the babies far beyond the reach of their parents. He said to himself, " What I was unable to accomplish with the axe and the fire-stick I was able to do with the song of the forest, assisted by the Tuckonie."

The crow thought that he had been able to be revenged on the pelicans for a wrong, little dreaming that he had done them a great service. For on that very day Mr and Mrs Carpet-snake arrived in a canoe made from the trunk of a tree. They had just been sunning themselves on the bank of the river, and Mr Carpet-snake, feeling a bit hungry, had gone in search of food. Wending his way through the bush, he had come to the camping-ground of the pelicans. He began searching in each wurley, thinking he would find at least a young baby pelican ; but the mothers had safe-guarded their children, fearing that they might be visited by their enemies, the carpet-snakes.

When the carpet-snake came to the tree he was amazed

---

[1] One of the magic songs which the people of the forest sing to the little trees in order to make them grow into big trees. It is a song foreign to the pelicans.

to find that the tree had grown much larger, and that to reach, in length, from the hole half-way to the fork would require a hundred or more carpet-snakes. So the snake looked about and saw the crow, gazing up and laughing, " *Caw, caw!* Well done! I have had my revenge! What a blow to the mothers! Won't they weep! What a great sorrow will be theirs when they find that they are unable to rescue their babies!"

" Hello!" said the carpet-snake. " You seem happy over the growth of this tree. This is the tree where we get our meals. Every new moon somebody leaves a baby here while gathering mussels in the lagoon, or picking wild herbs for food. This new moon it is different. There are babies belonging to the pelicans about. I can smell them. My spirit tells me that food is there."

" Oh, yes," said the crow. " There are six little pelican babies up there. The tree was a small one; but I sang the forest song, and this caused it to grow up so high that the parents of the babies will be unable to rescue them."

" Oh, you interfering and wicked old crow! You are always making trouble of some kind. First you are doing an injury to the parents, which, however, does not concern me. But, secondly, you have taken my food or removed it so that I am unable to procure it. Oh, you nasty thing!"

" Wait a moment," said the crow, " and let me think. Perhaps I shall be able to cause the tree to come back to its former size."

So the crow thought and thought, but he could not think of a way, or find a song or any witchcraft that would cause the tree to return to its former state. " No," said he. " I am unable to call up the little magic workers who caused the tree to grow. They are tiny little men, but they have the wonderful power of causing the trees to grow. I cannot understand why they will not respond to my wish."

The crow did not know that the Tuckonie were little spirits who came to do good, and not evil. They came at the song of the crow, and caused the gum-tree to grow, because the little fairy Good Spirit knew that the carpet-snake would be on his way to this particular tree. She therefore sent the Tuckonie along, so that while the crow sang they should dance round and make the tree grow, and thus place the children beyond the reach of the carpet-snake.

Now the little Tuckonie had received their instructions. They knew that something important would happen. Their mission so far was ended, but they were allowed to witness from the unseen world the wonderful deliverance of the babies of the pelicans.

By and by the pelican mothers began to feel anxious about their babies, so they hastened back from the fishing-ground to the place where they had left them. When they arrived there they saw that the tree had grown far larger than the other trees, and that they were unable to see or speak to their babies. They could hear them crying, however, and this made the mothers so sad that in their grief they beat their heads with yam-sticks, and cut their bodies with flint knives, causing deep flesh wounds. In desperation they sent up a long, shrieking wail, which could be heard all round the lagoon. This had the effect of bringing all the members of the pelican tribe to their help. They saw that they could not do anything for the children and their mothers. So they all sat round the huge tree and wept and wept, until all the other tribes, the goanna, the emu, the kangaroo, the opossum, and the magpie, heard them lamenting and joined in the wailing.

After they had mourned thus for an hour the kangaroo called for volunteers. The goanna and the opossum responded, and said they would attempt to climb the tree. Now when the tree began to grow in height it grew also in thickness. Just below the fork of the trunk there was a growth like a bracket. This had grown also, and to such an extent that it was impossible for anyone to climb past it.

The goanna was the first to start climbing. Up and up he went; then he wound his way round and up the tree until he arrived half-way to the fork and saw that the obstacle had become much larger since the tree had begun to grow. He came down to the ground and told the pelicans

129

and the others that the difficulty was greater than they had imagined. He said, " Give me an axe to help me to cut my way past the obstacle that you see growing there." They gave the goanna an axe, and he climbed up and up. He reached the obstacle, and tried to get beyond it by cutting his way, but he failed. He descended to the earth the second time, feeling greatly disappointed. The goanna told the pelicans that he did not think they would be able to rescue the babies, but perhaps the opossum would be able to climb the tree and overcome the difficulty.

So the opossum ran up the trunk until he reached the obstacle. He tried to pass the obstruction, but failed. Sad and disappointed in spirit, he descended to the earth, and told of the one difficulty that prevented them from bringing the babies safely to their mothers. The kangaroo, opossum, goanna, and magpie began to weep with the pelican tribe.

The little blue wren, with his two wives, had heard the outcry, and they came quietly along from shrub to shrub, and from bush to bush, until they were able to hear and see what was causing the trouble. Without uttering a word to the weeping crowd the wren spoke to his wives, " O my two dear little wives, I cannot bear to hear the great, strong pelicans, kangaroos, goannas, and others cry. Nor can I bear to think that such big people should be so helpless to save the babies. Now both of you will stay in this bush. Do not allow yourselves to be seen. I shall go along and ask my cousin, the woodpecker, to come and secure the babies. No one can climb the trees as he can."

With that the blue wren hurried away through the great gum-trees. It was a big undertaking for so small a bird, but he was spurred on by the spirit that makes small people do great and noble deeds. This spirit carried the wren on wings like those of the mighty eagle. He sped on his way through the boughs of the huge gum-trees in search of the wonderful climber.

Presently the blue wren stopped suddenly, because he heard a familiar voice near at hand. He wondered from which tree the sound was coming. Two trees farther on he

CLIMBING WITH THE AID OF A PORTION OF THE STEM OF
THE CALAMUS

No tree is too high or too smooth for the aboriginal to climb in
this manner.

From "Among Cannibals," by Carl Lumholtz (Murray)   130

THE WICKED CROW CARRIES OFF THE ADDER WIFE

saw the woodpecker approaching him. He said timidly,
" O woodpecker, will you come and rescue the babies of the
pelicans that are up in the tree? The goanna tried, but failed.
The opossum climbed up a good way, but could go no farther.
He had to give up the attempt and come down, a most disappointed person. Oh, come! The mothers of the babies
are sisters. They will break their hearts with weeping."

So the woodpecker told the wren to return and tell the
pelicans that he was coming to rescue their babies.

The blue wren, his little heart filled to overflowing with
gladness, came to the pelican tribe, and, in comforting
words, told them that the woodpecker was coming and
would restore the babies to their mothers. Every one,
therefore—the pelicans, magpies, kangaroos, opossums, and
goannas—was anxiously awaiting the presence of this wonderful climber. The woodpecker arrived, unobserved by
anyone. He said to the little wren, " Bring the kangaroo
to me. I would like to say a few words to him." So the
wren went to the kangaroo, and whispered into his ear,
" Kangaroo, the woodpecker would like to have a word with
you before he begins to climb the tree. Will you hurry to
his side? "

So the kangaroo made a couple of bounds, and in a
moment was at the side of the woodpecker. The woodpecker told the kangaroo that every one must stand away
from the foot of the tree, and that no one was to speak or
whisper or look up, but that all should bow their heads and
close their eyes, so that no one should see him go up or
return. The kangaroo told those present the wish of the
woodpecker, and all promised to do all that they were
asked.

When all those present had sat down on the ground and
bowed their heads and closed their eyes the woodpecker
began to ascend. He climbed over the obstacle and tied
one baby upon his back with a rope made from the fibre of
the tea-tree, and came to the ground with it, and placed it
in charge of the kangaroo. He ascended a second time,
and brought down another. He climbed the tree six times

131

in all, and rescued the six babies, and delivered them all to the kangaroo.

The pelicans and the mothers of the pelican babies still kept their eyes closed, and did not know whether he had succeeded in saving their babies or not until the kangaroo told them that they could open their eyes and look. They were all hesitating to open their eyes in case they should not see the children beside them. But the mothers, who were very anxious, opened their eyes and saw their babies sitting on the ground. They shouted for joy, and rushed forward to embrace their children. When they looked round to thank the saviour of the babies they could not find him. He was far away, for he did not wish to be made a hero.

When the kangaroo saw that all the excitement was over, and that the babies were once more in the safe keeping of their mothers, he said to those present, " Now some enemy has been concerned in this matter. It should be the duty of everybody here to find out who caused the tree, by some witchcraft, to grow to such a height in so short a time. Can any one of you call to mind anything that aroused your suspicions? Before you leave for your homes I would plead with you to give this your most serious consideration."

Up jumped the little blue wren. He said, " When I and my two wives were enjoying our customary outing we were attracted by your crying. So I suggested that we should come and inquire into the cause. We cautiously wound our way from bush to bush until we came in full view of the big tree. You were all looking up eagerly, so we also looked up, and saw the goanna making an effort to reach a certain spot. Then we saw the opossum, and we also heard the babies crying up in the tree. We came a little nearer, and we heard the sad news that it would not be possible to rescue the children. Our hearts were greatly moved. I said, ' Come, my wives, let us go to yonder bush and discuss the matter.' So we moved away to the scrub. When we arrived at the spot there was, to our surprise, a stranger there, a person we had neither seen nor heard of before. He looked such a wicked person, and he was in conversation with the carpet-snake. I heard this stranger warning the snake not to say anything about this incident to anyone, lest it should come to the knowledge of the pelicans, who had given him such a nice bed to lie on, and such good, appetizing food, for it means death to break the laws of hospitality. The snake replied, ' Well, you had better run for your life, and not stop until you reach Mypolonga.' So the stranger, without another word, ran away. Now let us go to the carpet-snake and surround his wurley, and ask what explanation he is able to give about the magical art that made the tree grow."

They all arose with one accord, and the kangaroo said, " Now then, little wren, you and your wives will please lead the way in search of the snake." The little blue wren led them on until he came to where the carpet-snake and his wife were camping. They formed a circle round them, and the kangaroo called to the snake to come forth, because they would like to have a few words with him. So the snake came out of his wurley, and, confronting the kangaroo, said, " It is not customary for you, as representative of the animal tribe, to approach me, of the reptile tribe. It was your duty, according to custom, to have asked the goanna to seek me and ask me to attend any conference that might be held with other tribes. You have not only broken one law, but you have, by your impudence, broken also the law of relationship. You, a hairy tribe, have the effrontery to address a scaly tribe! You, who belong to the hairy tribe, break the law by asking one of the feathered tribe to accompany you to find me. This violation of a strict law, you, O kangaroo, must answer for. One thing more. The feathered tribe are more nearly related to me than to you. You are not related to them in any way whatsoever."

The kindly and wise kangaroo listened patiently to the angry carpet-snake. After a few moments of silence he said to the snake, " I am well aware that a law of all races draws a line of distinction, and I am also acquainted with the importance of that law. There is no one in this company that endeavours to maintain and observe it more carefully than I and my tribe do ; but, as you know, and as all those present know, there is one thing to which all law, custom, and tradition give way, and that is that when a child is in danger or requires assistance, then law, creed, and caste vanish."

When the kangaroo had finished his reply to the carpet-snake the audience cried, "Well done! We all agree with you, O kangaroo." Then, turning again to the carpet-snake, the kangaroo said, "You have heard the voice of the various tribes on this matter—animal, bird, and reptile. Does it not clearly show that you, as a family of the reptile tribe, stand alone? Come, now, let us be friends. Join us in our effort to find the person who did this cowardly act to innocent and helpless babies. Remember, O carpet-snake, that you have children of your own. Some day you and your wife may be in a similar position to the pelicans, when you will require the assistance of others. Think not so much of yourself, O snake, but of the love and helplessness of weaker creatures."

The carpet-snake approached the kangaroo with bowed head, and said, "O kangaroo, I admit that I was hasty in my reply. I am also sorry for accusing you of breaking the law, customs, and traditions of our race. Will you forgive me?"

The carpet-snake then told them that the person who worked this magic of causing the tree to grow so rapidly was none other than the mischievous crow, who was sheltered and fed on the previous night by the pelican family.

"But," said one of the pelicans, stepping forward, "how can it be that the crow claimed relationship with our tribe? He addressed us as ' brother-in-law,' and how is it possible that one who has married our sister should stoop so low as to do such a despicable deed? It cannot be, O snake. Be careful, lest you may with a sore heart repent the day you accused an innocent person."

"Friends," said the carpet-snake, in a more sympathetic tone and with much feeling, "I am very sorry that I was beside myself when I used such an expression. I ask the kangaroo to forgive me. I come of an ancient race, and we

134

have in caves and on trees carvings and drawings from time immemorial of the family trees of all tribes. The person who was your guest last night is not your brother-in-law. He is a deceiver. He is of the Evil One."

" Then," said the pelicans, " we have been deceived, and have fallen victims to his cunning devices. Come, let us follow him and destroy him from the face of the earth."

" Pardon me, pelicans," said the kangaroo, " let us not be too rash in vowing vengeance upon this Evil One. He will soon exhaust the evils that are within him. His own evil designs may come back upon himself, and may make him repent or cause his destruction. The only way open to us is to send the falcon along to warn the other tribes to be on their guard against him."

After every one present had departed to their homes the pelicans consulted together, and decided that they would no longer place their offspring upon shrubs or trees. From that day till now they have kept their vow. They leave their babies on the ground—that is, they lay their eggs upon the ground. They will never again take the risk of placing their progeny upon trees.

The falcon now went in search of the crow. As he flew up in the clear sky his experienced eyes took in every living object below. At one time he thought he saw the crow, and he steadied himself in mid-air to catch another glimpse, but the object disappeared as suddenly as it had come. He flew round and round in a gradually widening spiral, feeling sure that it was the crow that he had seen. He then flew round, and kept coming toward the centre, but he saw no further sign of the crow. Then he flew to the nearest cliff, and sat and rested in order to prepare himself for the next morning's scouting. He spent the night upon a branch of a tree on the side of the cliff. The night was clear and still, and he fell into a deep sleep. Presently he felt a light touch upon his shoulder, and he looked up and saw the owl sitting beside him. The visitor whispered into his ear very softly indeed, fearing that the clear night air would carry the sound to some prying folk. He said, " There is a stranger in these parts. I saw him in the twilight, just as I and my neighbour the bat peeped out of our cave in the deep valley yonder. He was acting rather suspiciously. His very walk and action seemed to us as if he were being followed by some one; or it may have been his own evil conscience."

Just then the bat put in an appearance. He sat down on a branch a little above the falcon, and grasped it by a hook on his wing, and allowed himself to hang head downward alongside of the falcon. He said, " I saw a stranger. It seemed from his actions as if he had done something wrong. Not very long ago, when I was up in the valley, I saw something. I thought at first that it was my friend the owl, who is sitting on the other side of you. Then something went up into the sky with wonderful quickness, and when it reached a certain height it shot forward like a meteor, leaving a shower of light behind. I became so afraid that I hastened to my cave and stayed there a while. When I thought all danger was past I came out to seek the owl in order to warn him of this unknown stranger, this dreadful enemy, this wicked monster, making his way down the Murray. I saw you sitting here, and also saw the owl sitting beside you, so I came myself to tell you what was happening." The falcon said, " I am commanded by my king, the King of Birds, to capture this stranger who is causing trouble and sorrow among the tribes."

By this time the crow was on his way down the Murray. He met the swamp-hawk, who was resting on the limb of a dried gum-tree, and bemoaning his failure to capture a kangaroo-rat. " Oh," said the crow, " now I come to think of it, are you not my brother-in-law?" " Well, I don't know what relationship exists between us. You are a perfect stranger to me and to these parts," replied the swamp-hawk. " So I am," said the crow, " without a doubt. This is the first time that I or any of my family has come to this country. But will you allow me to ask you one question? Is not your totem the *pellati*?"[1] " Yes," said the swamp-hawk, " how

[1] The *pellati*, the totem of the swamp-hawk, is an edible grub found in a species of banksia.

come you, a stranger, to know that?" The crow answered,
" That is one of the secret records of our race, the race I
belong to, the crow tribe, so you are my brother-in-law."

" All right," said the swamp-hawk. " Let us be friends.
Now will you sit here while I go to see whether I shall be
able to catch a rat?"

" Oh, yes," said the crow. But as soon as the swamp-
hawk had left him he hastened away into the scrub, and
made a place similar to the hiding-place of a rat. He took
the spikes from the back of a porcupine and stuck them
into the ground of this apparent home of the kangaroo-rat.
He came back, and in the distance he saw the swamp-hawk,
so he beckoned him to come quietly. The crow led the
way, and they came to the trap that he had laid. The crow
pointed before him, and whispered, " There, in those grasses,
rests the rat. Go steadily and quietly."

The swamp-hawk sneaked up until he came near the
place. Then the crow, making signs, said, " Jump on to
the hiding-place, and you will secure the rat."

So the swamp-hawk jumped right on top of what appeared to be the resting-place of the rat, but, instead of
alighting on the rat, he landed on the spikes of the porcupine, which stuck into his feet.

" Oh, oh," cried the swamp-hawk, writhing in pain, and
looking round to see where the deceiver was. There was
not a sign of him. The swamp-hawk sat down and groaned
with pain. He was unable to remove the spikes from his
feet. He called loud and long, but no one heard his cries.
He called again and again, until he became exhausted with
intense suffering, and laid himself down to die.

Now the magpie on his way home noticed the swamp-
hawk lying on the ground and struggling unsuccessfully to
rise. So he came and attended to him, and supplied him
with food until he was well. His wounds healed with the
spikes still in his feet, and so ever since he has been able to
take hold of his prey more effectively. Before this injury
the swamp-hawk would hold his prey with difficulty, because it would struggle and struggle until often it freed

itself. But now his claws are armed with something from which no animal can escape, and instead of the swamp-hawk looking upon the crow as an enemy he looks upon him as a friend.

Following on his evil course, the crow met with another victim, the wife of the death adder. She was lying outside her home one beautiful sunny morning, bathing herself in the sunlight. The death adders were an inoffensive people. If anyone did them an injury they would suffer rather than retaliate.

" Now," thought the mischievous crow, " what a lot of surprises there will be! I shall place this *wirrie* [1] in her body." So he crept up toward her, stealthily looking about him to see that no one was watching him. He came close up to her, and, after looking to see if she really was asleep, he touched her gently upon her forehead. She did not move. He thrust the *wirrie* into her tail, and jumped up and ran away. He crouched behind a bush to watch what the effect would be, but she lay quite still, without moving. The point of the stick had entered her tail, causing terrible pain, and she had fainted. The crow once more approached his victim, and tried to rouse her by shaking her, but he was unsuccessful—she was entirely unconscious.

Suddenly, from above, the falcon pounced down upon him. The crow struggled to free himself, but the falcon held him fast, and said to him, " You have been causing great trouble and anxiety among the various tribes by your mischievous deeds, and now you shall give an account of your wickedness."

During the struggle between the falcon and the crow the other members of the death adder family arrived from their hunting, and saw their poor relative lying, as they thought, dead. They began to wail. Their cry went forth, and was carried by the winds into the valleys, and up to the hill-tops.

---

[1] A stick which has been inserted into the body of a dead person and allowed to remain there until the body is decomposed. It absorbs poison from the putrid products, and if it should puncture the flesh of a healthy person it will probably cause fatal blood-poisoning. (See pp. 189–190.)

Birds, animals, and reptiles heard it. They recognized the call of the adders, and hastened to see what had happened. They gathered round the body, and they too wept with grief for the harmless adder, and were anxious to know the cause of her death. The falcon said that the crow had stabbed her with a *wirrie*. They shouted, " Away with him! Bury him alive! He must be buried in the same grave as his victim!"

So they raised the body of the adder, and placed it on a stretcher, and conveyed it to a gully near by. They all marched in procession with the crow, and were led by the emu and the kangaroo. The wombats dug the grave, and when it was sufficiently deep they prepared the body carefully, and wrapped it in tea-tree bark for burial, and told the crow to get into the grave. He hesitated, but then leaped into the grave. When he touched the bottom he disappeared suddenly and mysteriously. A wombat jumped into the grave to see whether there was an opening in the side. To his great astonishment there was a tunnel leading south. The wombats were great tunnel-makers, so he knew by sight what its direction would be, and how far the distance was to its next opening upward on the surface of the earth. He shouted to those above, " Away toward Salt Creek!"

In an instant the falcon was on the wing and on his way through the air, toward Tintinara, in the south-east. Seeing no sign of the crow, he continued his journey past Kingston, right on to Mount Benson. Here he perched, and with his far-seeing eye viewed the surrounding country, but not a sign could he see of the crow.

Becoming restless and anxious, he flew upward into the sky, until he became a mere speck. Then he circled round and round, gradually going farther outward, until he had covered many hundreds of miles. Still there was no sign of the crow, nor could anyone give the falcon information as to his whereabouts.

All this while the crow had discovered a great many underground tunnels, and he considered that it would be safer for him to stay in these passages for a time until the falcon

139

thought he was dead. The life underground, however, was so uninteresting and became so monotonous and so tiresome that he decided that he would come out during the night and enjoy the fresh air. He continued to do this for some time, and then he said to himself, " I shall take advantage of the early morning before the sun rises, and I will enjoy myself before the falcon is up and on his watch."

So he did this from one new moon to the following new moon. Finally he said within himself, " I shall come out all day and take the risk," and once more he enjoyed the bright and beautiful days that came and went. He also boldly began his usual routine of living, going about in search of his victims.

When the falcon began his spiral flight at Mount Benson, he saw the adder family in a state of great excitement. He alighted among the adders and inquired what all the excitement was about; so they told him that the apparently dead adder had come to life, for she had come out of the unconscious state into which she had been put by the poison stick. The wound was healing rapidly. The *wirrie* had grown into her flesh, and all birds and animals were sore afraid to come near her or to touch her, and they would not allow her to touch them, because she had a dreadful sting.[1] Thus from that day on the creatures that were once despised and cuffed and kicked about were equipped with a weapon that caused death to anyone who was unfortunate enough to be stung by it.

After this the falcon took to his wings and flew by way of Tintinara to the Murray River, and then beyond Mobilong, to the place where he was to report to the eagle-hawk about the doings of the crow. The eagle-hawk was sitting on a huge dry gum-tree, awaiting his arrival. The falcon came and took a seat beside him, and said, " O eagle-hawk, the harmless adder has fallen a victim to the mischievous crow, and now the family are endowed against their will with a sting that causes death."

[1] The death adder, called also the deaf adder (*Acanthophis antarctica*), is a venomous snake. The so-called ' sting ' at the end of the tail is harmless.

" Up and away ! " said the eagle-hawk, " and prevent him from causing injury to the other members of the reptile tribe."

Again the falcon was on the wing, hastening toward Tatiara and Tintinara, stopping now and again when he came near the goannas and lizards, and warning them to avoid the crow. " Do not speak to him," he said. " Whether he feigns hunger or thirst or illness, do not assist him. Keep a great distance between yourselves and him."

When the falcon inquired of the goanna, " Where are the other members of your tribe ? " the goanna said, " The crow invited them into the underground passages. With tearful eyes and a heart almost broken I have pleaded with my tribe not to be so foolish as to listen to the flattery of the cunning and mischief-making crow. All the lizard family, and two snake families, the carpet and the diamond, gave heed to my warning, and have refused the invitation. The rest of the snake families are already the guests of the crow in the caves."

Now when the crow took the snakes into the beautiful caves he prepared a great feast, and the snakes sat down. Then the crow, addressing the snakes, said, " Will you allow me to retire for a while ? I have to attend to an important matter." The snakes replied that they would try to make themselves comfortable while awaiting his return ; so the crow hastened out of the caves into the sunlight, and flew into the air, circling round as he ascended, until he thought that he was out of reach of the hawk family. Then he looked down from his high position, and tried to locate the home of the adders. When he had found the spot he saw an excited assembly below. Like a bolt from the sky he descended into their midst, and beheld a sight that gave him great pleasure, for there, upon the tail of one of the adders, was something that should fulfil the purpose for which it was intended—the sting. He turned to the adders that were congregated around him, and said, " Have I not spoken the desire of my heart ? Grow, O poisoned pointing-bone, into the flesh of the adder. You must become part of the adder. All the hatred of your soul shall enter the sting, and it shall become the sting of death. Have I not desired, too, that it shall not only remain in your individual self, but that you shall transfer it to your children, and they shall pass it on to their children through all the generations to come?"

Suddenly, before an eyelid could wink, the crow seized the adder and carried her into the cave. There the snakes were fast asleep. They had eaten and eaten until they had gorged themselves. They were lying in a state of stupor, and were dreaming of feasting, and beholding beautiful visions. The crow tried to rouse them, but there was no response. He looked into their faces, and noticed that they seemed to be smiling and looking happy and contented. He again tried to rouse them, but failed. He was baffled. He had brought the adder with him to show them what an effective weapon she possessed. So a thought struck him. He said to himself, " Now if they are in a happy, sleeping state I shall make this cave ring. I must go and ask the laughing jacks to help. They are such happy-go-lucky chaps, they will fill this cave with laughter."

So the crow went out, and he discovered the laughing jacks down by Reedy Creek. He told them that the snakes had been feasting, and had eaten so much that they had fallen into a state of stupor, but that, notwithstanding this condition, they had smiling faces, and seemed to be happy. " Now," said he, " there is an opportunity for you to put that wonderful laugh of yours to some good purpose in waking up the snakes." "Well," said the elder of the laughing jacks, " I know that our laugh is infectious. When we laugh we bring life and pleasure to weary, broken-hearted ones. Our laugh makes pleasant the passage to the land beyond. We will go. Lead the way!"

The snakes heard the infectious laughter of the laughing jacks in their dreams. They all threw up their heads, opened their mouths, and laughed so heartily that they woke themselves up. Hastily the crow asked the laughing jacks to retire, so they left the cave and went back to their homes. Then the snakes, who were now wide awake, asked the crow

142

for what purpose they had been invited to the cave. " Oh,"
said the crow, " I have something to show you, something
that it would be well for you to have in your possession.
Look ! " And he presented the adder to them, and asked
whether any of them noticed a change in that individual.
The snakes looked and looked at her and remarked to the
crow, " Only that we see a *wirrie* grown to her body. Of
what advantage is that ? " " Wait a moment," said the
crow; " you shall witness this day one of the greatest sights
of the age."

He had hidden a wombat in a crevice of the rock, and he
now called him forth. The wombat came out, and the crow
ordered him to tread upon the adder. As soon as the wombat made the attempt the adder swung her tail and struck
the wombat in one of his forelegs, making a wound. The
crow said, " Watch, and see the effect." Presently they saw
the poor wombat's body quiver, and then he fell to the
ground dead. " There ! " said the crow, " wouldn't you
all like to have a weapon like that ? You may have it in
your mouth. Will you permit me to present you with these
weapons ? Place them in your upper jaw, and rest in this
cave until they become fixed and grow so that they become
part of you." " Yes," said the snakes.

So the crow performed this operation upon the snakes,
and that is how they came to possess the deadly fangs, the
gift of the evil crow. When the time arrived for the snakes
to leave their hiding-place the crow thought it would be
safer for him to seek other climes, so he journeyed to Mount
Gambier, and lived there for a while.

Now the snakes, with their new gift of killing, began to
seek victims on which to try the effect of it. The kangaroos,
wombats, emus, and smaller animals were being killed by
the snakes and the adders. So they called a meeting to discuss the great danger of the whole race being wiped out
unless something were done to prevent it. At this meeting
of the animals the wombat said to the kangaroo, " I think,
from what I have gathered, that the reptile family is divided
against itself. The lizards are prepared to fight against the

snakes at any time. They are not good friends with them since they were guests of the crow at the cave. I think it would be wise, therefore, to invite the goanna and the sleepy or blue-tongued lizard here, and listen to what they would suggest."

"Good," said the kangaroo. "Bandicoot! Will you oblige me by carrying a message from me to the goanna and the lizard?"

"Yes," said the bandicoot. "When would you like me to go?"

The kangaroo replied, "At this very moment. Take this message-stick, and bring me a reply."

Carralinga	come here to-morrow and take	Nowwanjung.

A MESSAGE-STICK, WITH INTERPRETATION OF INSCRIPTION
From *Among Cannibals*, by Carl Lumholtz (Murray).

The bandicoot set off at once on his errand. When he came to the home of the goanna tribe he asked one who was lying in the shade of a tree, "Where can I see your chief?" He was told to go to a large gum-tree that had fallen some years before, and was quite dry, and had a hollow on the south side of its trunk. So the bandicoot went along until he arrived at his destination. He knocked at the open door. Presently a little goanna peeped out, and asked what he wanted. "Oh," said the bandicoot, holding out the stick. "I have brought this from the kangaroo to deliver to the chief of the goannas."

The little goanna took the message-stick to his father, who was sitting pondering over the grave dangers that were confronting the tribes in the deadly bite of the snakes and the sting of the adder. He was examining the herb that was recommended by their medicine-man, who said that it would counteract the poison of the snakes. When the stick was brought in he laid aside his work and read on the stick the message from his dear old friend the kangaroo. When he had done so he hastily cut on a stick beside him the message, " I and my family accept your invitation to a conference at which we shall discuss the awful danger that confronts us. Let us meet at an appointed place." The message-stick was delivered to the bandicoot, who ran until he arrived safely at the home of his lord and chief, the kangaroo.

After reading the message the kangaroo gave instructions that they must leave at dawn next day, and journey to the appointed meeting-ground. There was a great gathering there : animals, birds, reptiles, and insects. The goanna told the animals, birds, and reptiles that the only remedy was to join forces and wage war against the snakes. He said, "I have discovered a herb that will counteract the effect of the poison for my tribe. I was out the other day, and met my cousin the brown snake. I asked him where I could procure food for my children. In reply he spoke an angry word. That was more than I could stand, so I grappled with him, and we fought furiously. He bit me on the shoulder, and I felt the bite smarting very much. I ran away and plucked some of the herb that I now hold in my hand, and began to chew and swallow it. The effect was instantaneous. The pain disappeared like magic, and I seemed to gain greater strength. I returned, and there was the snake, lying quietly beside a shrub. He was surprised to see me alive. At first he thought he saw my ghost returning to haunt him. But I spoke and said, ' O my enemy, and the enemy of my whole tribe, I am no spirit. I am myself, the one who fought with you half an hour ago. Come, let us do battle ! ' With that we grappled with each other. I took him by the throat and gripped him firmly. As I said, the herb gave me double strength, so that I was able to strangle him to death. But there is this about the herb ; what cures me will not cure you. So I think that if we all join forces and declare war against them they will become friendly or be exterminated. It will be for them to choose."

They agreed that they would send for one of the snakes. Away went the frilled lizard to ask the tiger-snake to represent that tribe. The tiger-snake listened to what the goanna said. " O tiger-snake," said he, " tell your family that the animals, birds, and your cousins the reptile families have vowed to join forces in order to exterminate you. Go! Think it over."

The tiger-snake returned to his family and gave them the message; but they could not agree among themselves regarding what to do.

And such is the position to-day. The old goannas are always at war with the snakes, and are their most hated foes. Another enemy of the snake is the little, short, stumpy blue-tongued lizard. This lizard will attack a snake five or six times its length or size. The reason why the lizards, such as the goanna and the blue-tongued lizard, bear such hatred toward the snakes is that before the snakes acquired their poisonous fangs they were harmless and unable to defend themselves against their enemies, and the goanna and the frilled and blue-tongued lizards stood up for them and fought their battles, and provided food and shelter for them during the cold weather in winter. Sometimes the laughing jack and some of the hawk family would engage in sporting and hunting expeditions, and would delight to capture and destroy the harmless and inoffensive snakes. At these times the little lizard used to act as sentinel to the snake family, and when danger threatened he would give the alarm to the frilled lizards, who would come forth to fight.

At this time, when all these events were taking place, the crow was sitting on what is known to-day as Mount Gambier, weeping. He reviewed his past life, and felt deeply sorry for the wrongs he had done, and he wept for forgiveness. As he looked upon his past life he felt that everything had been a failure, and that no good had come out of it. But presently, as if from nowhere, came the form of the little blue wren, and he said to the crow, " O Evil One, good may come of wrongdoing. When the little pelicans were the victims of your cunning and witchcraft it awoke in me the

146

spirit to think of others and to feel for them. I hastened and brought along the woodpecker, and begged him to deliver the little pelicans."

When the crow again looked round he saw before him another form, the little robin red-breast. " Cheer up, O crow," said the robin, " your mission has been productive of some good. What if you gave to the adder and snakes the sting of death? It has caused much sorrow and many deaths, but we have now found a way of avoiding death through the discovery of the virtue of herbs."

In the twinkling of an eye the robin disappeared. A dark cloud overshadowed the mountain on which the crow sat. From out the dark cloud lightning flashed, and the thunder seemed to rend the mountain-top. Rain and hail poured down, and the wind blew with fury, tearing huge limbs from the trees. " This is dreadful," said the crow. Suddenly, as if by magic, the storm passed over. The sun shone brightly; flowering plants shot up everywhere and decorated the mountain; and in the valley below the flowers formed everywhere a sea of colour. " Well," said the crow, " I have done some good, although I intended only evil." A light touch upon his shoulder caused him to turn. He beheld a form. It beckoned to him, and said, " Come up. A place awaits you in the heavens."

Now if you will look at the sky to-night you will see the crow, no longer a symbol of darkness and evil, but a shining star, fulfilling the mission for which he was created.

Whowie [1]

Whowie was the most dreadful creature in existence. In form he was like the goanna, only a great deal larger. His length would be somewhere about twenty feet. The strangest thing about this creature was that he possessed six legs, three on each side of the body, somewhat like the goanna's legs; he also had a tail. He had an enormous head shaped like the head of a frog. Now this creature was

---

[1] This story is told by an aboriginal of a River Murray tribe.

very treacherous, and would attack and devour anything that came in his way. The people in those far-off, bygone days would flee in terror from him. He was not swift in his movements, but very slow. Sometimes he would come across a camping-ground where the people were fast asleep, and, without making a noise to betray his presence, he would swallow first one and then another, perhaps a mother and child together; and what he could not swallow he would take in his mouth to his den. He would devour from thirty to sixty people at a meal.

The home of the whowie was in the Riverina district, and it was in and about this locality that he lived and hunted. His chief abode was in a cave on the banks of the Murray River, and this cave extended underground for many miles. During the hot summer days he would bask in the sunshine upon the bank of the river or on the sand. By his tramping about on the sand great heaps were piled up. These exist till this day. This was the beginning of the formation of the sandhills in the Riverina district.

Now this dreadful creature was taking great toll of the people. The water-rat tribe were among the greatest sufferers, so they held a meeting among themselves to decide what they should do for safety. The chief of the water-rats said to his fellows, " We are a very small race, and we are dwindling rapidly. Soon there will be none of us left unless we remove to some distant country. To stay here means that we shall all be eaten up, and none left to represent our race. So I leave it to you to decide what we shall do." Thereupon he sat down beside a log, waiting for his subjects to make suggestions. From among the assembly there arose an elder with a long, flowing beard. He began to address the others of his race, " O my children, I am far gone in years, and it would be out of the question for me to think of taking a long journey elsewhere. Furthermore, I have spent many happy days wandering up and down the Murray, and living in the surrounding country. In those delightful days we had plenty to eat. We gathered many mussels from the river. Fish was plentiful. So it is to-day, but we dare

THE WHOWIE RETURNING WITH VICTIMS TO HIS LAIR

148

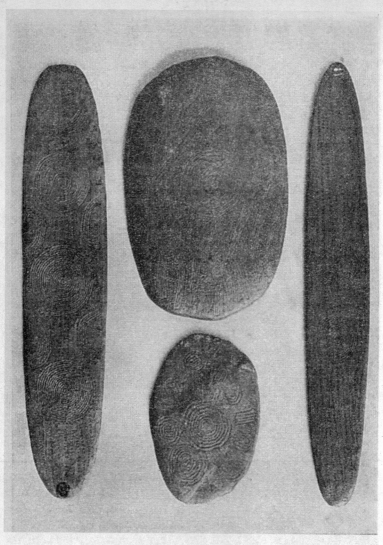

CHURINGA OF WOOD, WITH TOTEMIC MARKINGS

The aboriginal attaches great importance to the *churinga*. He believes that it equips him with creative power and gives him the protection of his ancestors.

British Museum

not go to the river-side to catch them for fear of our great enemy, the whowie. So, as I do not feel inclined to leave, let us think of some other means by which we shall be free from this great danger without an overwhelming loss to ourselves. We must endeavour to secure the assistance of three or more of the other tribes."

After the elder had spoken the chief ordered that they should build many fires immediately after the rising of the sun. So they retired to rest that night, and while some were sleeping others kept guard, in order to give the warning if the whowie should appear in their camp. During the watching hours some of the water-rats would keep watch for a time, then these would be relieved in order that they might sleep. This is how they kept guard while the family slept. These relays of watches were continued throughout the night.

After the sun rose every water-rat busied himself with collecting materials and making fires in various places. When the surrounding tribes saw the many smoke-signals they knew that these were messages of distress and calls for help, and they sent up smoke-signals that they were willing and anxious to give whatever help was required, and that they would arrive about sunrise on the following morning. So all the water-rats set to work and hunted and captured as many fish as possible, and some gathered bags of mussels. Some of these mussels were roasted upon the live coals, and others were baked in ovens dug in the earth. The water-rats were very busy that day, some of them in preparing for the many tribes that would arrive in the morning, and others in spying out the country to discover the whereabouts of the whowie, and whether he was at large, hunting food, or basking in the sunshine. But that day he was nowhere to be seen, so some of the bolder of the water-rats journeyed to the cave of the whowie by the bank of the river, and went quite close to the entrance of it, searching for footprints. After a careful survey they were convinced that the footprints led into the cave. Now it would take the whowie a whole week to come to the end of the cave, because it was such a

149

long one. There were no other openings but the one on the river-bank.

On the following morning, just at the time appointed, people came from all directions, some marching with spears and *nulla-nullas*, and some with stone axes. The animals, birds, reptiles, kangaroos, opossums, platypuses, eagle-hawks, crows, magpies, cockatoos, and all the feathered tribes, also the lizard and reptile tribes, were represented in full force.

When the scouts of the water-rats returned to camp and told the others of the result of their scouting—that they felt sure that the whowie had entered his home in the cave, and that it would take him a week to reach the end of it—the water-rats and their guests spent the day and night in entertaining one another with dancing, and singing, and story-telling, feeling that they were safe. Next day, after this rejoicing, they set about preparing the attack on their great enemy, the whowie. Now everybody gathered sticks, and made them up in small bundles, just large enough to be carried into the cave, because they would have to carry them for a long distance inside. The people of the various tribes went about the work in earnest, beginning in the early hours of the morning, and carrying on till late at night. This was kept up until they thought that the whowie would have reached the end of the cave. Then they stacked the bundles about half-way along the cave, and they piled up a great heap at the entrance. Then they set fire to the heaps, and when the wood began to burn it caused enough smoke to fill the cave. This made things rather uncomfortable for the whowie, so he began to force his way toward the entrance, battling with the heat and smoke. By and by he realized his dangerous position, and began to roar like an angry beast, as if in deadly combat with some mighty foe. This struggling lasted for six days. On the seventh day the whowie came out of the entrance, blinded and dazed and stupid. When he got right out of the cave the animals, birds, and reptiles began to attack him in earnest, with spears, stone axes, and *nulla-nullas*. They beat him all over the body, and caused great wounds, from which blood flowed freely. With the beating and the great loss of blood he fell to the ground, dying.

And now, when the gentle night winds are blowing into the cave, you will hear, as it were, the sighing of the whowie as he lay dying. And when the little aboriginal girls and boys are naughty and disobedient their mothers will say, " Look out, the whowie is listening," and the children will crouch up against their mother's breast for safety, looking round with wide, staring eyes, and expecting to see that dread dragon, the whowie of the Riverina.

The Flood and its Results

There was a time when the animals, birds, and reptiles multiplied so rapidly that the country in which they lived could not support them in comfort; they were continually bumping against one another or treading upon each other's toes, with the result that some ugly words were spoken. So they decided among themselves that something must be done, some understanding must be come to in order to avoid bloodshed and to benefit all. They therefore agreed to have a meeting of representatives of the various tribes.

The animals decided that they would send along the kangaroo as their chief, and that the wise koala should accompany him as their advocate and his adviser. The bird tribes agreed to send their chief, the eagle-hawk, with the crow as advocate and adviser. The reptile tribes were represented by their chief, the goanna, accompanied by the tiger-snake as advocate and adviser.

When the chiefs and the advocates first met they agreed that the conference should take place on the Blue Mountain.

The first business at the opening meeting was to arrange which representatives should be given the first opportunity of stating their claims and grievances, and of making suggestions to overcome the difficulties. The animals and the birds, with one consent, gave preference to the reptile representatives. So the goanna and the carpet-snake were invited to speak.

The goanna rose and addressed the kangaroo and the eagle-hawk and their advisers, saying, " The only way out of the difficulty would be for the bird tribes to consent to a suggestion that my adviser will make, and I will ask him for it now." Then, turning to the tiger-snake, he said, " Will you kindly proceed to make your statement? Remember, you are supported by the whole of the tribes of your race, a fact which we are proud to recognize."

So the tiger-snake rose and began his speech, " O representatives of the animals and birds, I have been thinking deeply on the whole situation, and I would suggest that one or both of the tribes which you represent should go into some other country. Both of you are better fitted to travel than we are. You, the birds, have two legs, and the majority of you, the animals, have four legs to support your body so that it does not drag along the ground when travelling. These legs that you are blessed with are fitted to carry you with great speed and for long distances. They also enable you to overcome obstacles on your path. Now, O kangaroo and O koala, does not my proposal appeal to you? May I have the honour of your approval now, or shall I leave the matter for your consideration? "

Then the tiger-snake turned to the eagle-hawk and the crow, and said, " O chief of the bird tribe, to you and your family has been given the blessing of the Gods, the power of speech and language, the gift of expressing your thoughts, and thus of exchanging ideas. With this gift you are not only a blessing to your own family, but you are a blessing to the animals and to my family. You have delighted us with your songs of cheer in the morning, as well as your love-songs at twilight. Then, again, you and your families are blessed by the Gods of Flight. You are able to change your abode in a moment of time. You take delight in your swiftness ; you travel like the wind ; you can rise above the storm. But we of the poor reptile family are unable to change our abode as quickly as the animals can, and far less quickly than you can. Consider us, and allow me to ask that you will take your flight to some other clime. I am

152

sure you will agree with me that you will not entertain the idea of fighting a battle for mastery. Let us not have to settle this matter by trial of strength. You are aware that we are gifted with the sting of death, but we are anxious to avoid any clash of hatred between the tribes represented here to-day. I leave it to you till we meet again. Remember! Let us refrain from force of arms."

The kangaroo rose at this stage. He said, " Friends, representatives of the bird and reptile families, I have much pleasure in introducing the platypus. He is present here this day because he belongs to a class that has a majority in numbers. His family outnumbers the whole of my race and your family, O bird tribe, and your family, O reptile tribe. Now, O reptiles and O birds, can you not suggest that we should come to terms with them or ask them to take some means to prevent their rapid increase? Just look on either side of this range of mountains—platypuses in great numbers are to be seen everywhere! "

The crow, the advocate of the bird tribe and adviser to the eagle-hawk, rose without asking permission from his chief, and moved that the conference should adjourn till next day. So, with one consent, they rose, and the meeting closed for the day.

When the tribes met on the second day the kangaroo instructed the koala not to think too much about the animals, but to concentrate his thoughts upon how to settle the great question of the day, and also to think out ways of helping the platypus family.

There were present at the meeting the chief of the animal tribe, the kangaroo, with the koala; the chief of the birds, the eagle-hawk, with the crow; and the chief of the reptiles, the goanna, with the tiger-snake. The tiger-snake rose and said that before going any farther he would like to have a definite reply as to whether the bird tribe would be willing to accept his suggestion that they should migrate. The crow leaped forward, and in his croaking voice said that they considered that the animals should be made to take their way to some other country. He said, " Was it not the adventurous spirit of the koala that brought us from the Sea of the Thousand Islands? How is it that such a great mind is not able to grasp this problem and find a solution of it? Has he lost the spirit of his fathers and become weak in mind and body?"

Then the crow, working himself up into a mischievous mood, and looking the koala in the eyes, taunted him thus: "O koala, your mind was great in the long, long past when your family bridged the mighty ocean. Where is that mind now? Come, think of a way out of this difficulty! Did your thinking power reside in your tail, which you lost?"

These remarks stung the koala to anger, and he rose to his feet and was about to say some unpleasant words to the crow when the kindly kangaroo intervened and prevented a quarrel. Then the snake rose, and said, "We have not come here to stir up strife. I would like to ask the crow to take back the unkind words he spoke to the koala. We are all thankful that the koala brought us from lands far away. To him we owe our great brotherhood of families. Come, let us not quarrel."

Now there was a tribe or family connected with the reptiles that possessed the knowledge of rain-making. Their totem was the elements—lightning, thunder, rain, hail, and wind. These people were becoming important. They resolved that they would not consult anyone, but would act as they pleased. They were the frilled lizard family. So while the conference was progressing they sent representatives to various parts of the country with instructions that on the days and evenings of the week preceding the new moon every lizard was to begin singing the storm song, and when the time arrived they were to take their flint knives and cut the body and cause the blood to flow, and then were to smear the body with fat and red ochre and daub the face with pipe-clay. They were to begin chanting their prayer song, pleading that the Great Spirit of the lightning, thunder, rain, hail, and wind would grant this, their humble request. They sang, "Come, O lightning; come, O thunder and wind;

come with all your force and destroy the platypus family. They have become too numerous."

They repeatedly sang their song of the storm until the last few days and evenings before the appearance of the new moon. Then great clouds began to mantle the clear sky, and out of the black clouds the lightning flashed and rent the sky and earth, and struck terror into the hearts of the animals, birds, and reptiles. The thunder roared in reply to the angry lightning-flashes, and the winds came hurrying and tearing the limbs from the huge, towering gum-trees, uprooting smaller trees and shrubs, strewing them along its path, and driving the rain and hail into every hiding-place of the animals, birds, and reptiles.

When the bird tribes saw what was coming they took wing, mounting upon the wind, and soaring up and up until they were far beyond cloud and storm. The animals struggled hither and thither in the blinding storm, seeking shelter, travelling up and up, and dodging behind trees and rocks and boulders on the mountain-side, until they reached the summit, where they sought safety. Thus the conference ended in desolation and death.

It rained and rained. The valleys and the low-lying country were deluged. Nearly all life was destroyed in the great flood. But the cunning frilled lizards, while their medicine-men were singing their storm song, had sought the mountain-tops, and there had built homes to protect themselves against the storm.

When the storm ceased and the floods had abated and the sun shone the kangaroo looked about him and called the others of his tribe, the wombat, opossum, and koala, and instructed them to go in haste and scour the country, and find out whether the platypus family[1] was safe, or how many of them had survived the awful storm. So the wombat, opossum, and koala ran down the mountain-side into the valleys, visiting water-holes, *billabongs*, creeks, and rivers in order to find out whether the platypuses were safe. An

---

[1] The platypuses are very slow of movement, and in a flood they would be more easily overtaken than any other tribe.

awful and distressing sight met their gaze. There, upon
the broken branches of the gum-trees, and among the rocks
on the hillsides and in the valleys, were the dead and mangled
bodies of the poor platypuses. Not a living one could they
discover. So they came back to the kangaroo and told him
the sad news, whereupon he and his tribe began to bewail
the loss of the platypuses, and the reptile tribes that were
hidden among the rock ledges and caves heard the noise
and came out to see what the outcry meant. The frilled
lizard, that was hidden away comfortably upon the mountain-
top, came out of his snug home, and inquired, " Why weep,
O kangaroo? Have you suffered great loss among your
family and tribe? " " No," said the kangaroo, " I would
not feel it so much had some of my tribe and family been
lost in this flood. I am so sorrowful because the platypus
family is no more."

After three years had passed the bird tribes returned to
their homes. Some came to live upon the lakes and rivers,
lagoons and *billabongs*. Others made their homes in the
dense forest, and some went into the desert country. Sometimes the emu would become sad when thinking of the poor
platypuses, and he would make a long journey, seeking the
cormorant, in order to inquire of him if he had heard or seen
anything that might have given rise to some talk that he had
heard that a number of platypuses had been seen somewhere.
The cormorant said, " Yes, that reminds me. I and my
wife were living for a while beyond the Blue Mountain.
Half-way between the mountain and the shore there is a
stream flowing on to the Eastern Sea. On the bank of the
stream I have noticed the tracks of several platypuses. One
night I was lying down, thinking where I should go fishing
in order to provide food for my wife, who was at that time
looking after the children. Presently we noticed that, just
beneath the tree in which we lodged, there was a large pool
of water, and we heard a sucking noise like that which the
platypuses made when they were feeding. I rose from my
perch and flew to the pool to see whether I could come
across any traces of the platypuses. I saw none, but what

I did see made my heart jump. There, along the bank, was the impression of the beak of a platypus. I rose, and flew back and watched the stream, thinking that perhaps a platypus would come out to feed. But none came, nor have any come out since. Perhaps they have gone to some other stream."

With the little information that he had gathered the emu went home, thinking seriously. He lay, tossing from side to side, all through the night. In the early hours of the morning he rose and made his way to the kangaroo.

When the kangaroo saw the emu coming he went out to meet him. After the usual salutations the kangaroo placed his right hand across his stomach and closed his fingers, as if gripping his stomach. He then placed his closed hand upon the stomach of the emu, which is a sign of " With all good feelings of pity and love I receive you. You are welcome to all my food and all the comfort of my home." The emu nodded his head and said, " Is that so? " and he accompanied the kangaroo to his home, and sat down and partook of the food that was offered him.

After finishing his meal the emu began to relate what the cormorant had told him. It seemed that there must be some truth in it, because there were others who had seen the footprints and the impression of the platypus's bill near the same locality. So the kindly kangaroo sat silent for a few moments, as if offering a prayer to the spirit of their being. None of the tribes could understand why the platypuses would not show themselves. But, on account of the flood coming during the conference, the platypuses were under the impression that the animals, birds, and reptiles had become their enemies, and that they had caused the great flood to come in order to wipe them off the face of the earth. That was why they moved about only at night. The kangaroo asked the emu if he would summon the various tribes to a meeting to organize a select party to explore all the rivers, lakes, water-holes, and *billabongs*, and try to discover these few remaining platypuses. The emu said that he would gladly do anything that would help them to get in touch with the platypuses. The emu took his departure, and asked all the tribes to meet the kangaroo at a certain spot on a day fixed.

In the meantime the carpet-snake had made up his mind that he would discover the whereabouts of the platypuses. So one day he wandered along the steep valley until he came to the stream where it was said the platypuses had been seen. He went to sleep, and slept all that afternoon, a few yards away from the pool that the cormorant had described to the emu. After sunset, when darkness covered the valley, the snake crept stealthily to the bank and peered into the pool during all that night, but he saw no platypuses. Then in the morning, after the sun rose, he made his way farther down the stream, and came to a pool of water, and went to sleep a few yards away from it. By and by he rose, and crawled to the edge of the pool, and peered into the water. Again he met with failure—he saw no platypuses. Then, in disappointment and disgust, he made up his mind that he would return home. When crawling on his way through a dense valley he came to an ideal spot surrounded by ferns and convolvulus. There was a pool of water, clear as crystal, and in the middle of this pool there was an island covered with ferns. As the carpet-snake was admiring this little island, thinking what a beautiful home it would be for the platypuses, his keen eyes noticed a hole beneath the surface of the clear water which, by its shape and formation, could belong to no other than a platypus. He crept as fast as he could through the dense undergrowth of plants, up over the mountain-tops, and down the other side away from the mountain and into the plain country of the west, until he arrived at the home of the emu. Exhausted, he threw himself down at the door of the *mia-mia* of the emu and lay there as if dead. The emu and his family rushed out to see this visitor. When they looked they saw the almost dead body of the carpet-snake. They lifted him up and took him into a spare *mia-mia* and gave him water to drink, and waited until he had recovered from his exhaustion. Then the emu inquired, "What is your mission?" The carpet-snake

158

said, " Oh, I think I have made a great discovery. I have
found the home of the platypus. Now hasten as fast as you
can. Tell the kindly kangaroo he need not worry much
longer. The lost ones are found ; I have seen their home.
I shall wait here and rest a while until you return with the
kangaroo. Then I shall take him to the home of the
platypus."

So the emu selected one of the young men of his family
who was a great runner. He told him to run and not to
stop until he found the kangaroo. The emu ran with great
speed, and covered a great deal of country. He ran round
and round in a circle that widened and widened until it
was a hundred miles in diameter. With ever-increasing
speed he hastened on, urged by the thought that he had
been chosen to convey a message of great importance. At
length he arrived at the camping-ground of the kangaroo
family. Without delay he was taken to the chief, who was
anxiously awaiting news of the platypuses. The emu said,
" O kangaroo, I have pleasant news for you. The platypuses are found. The carpet-snake has brought us the
tidings, and I was sent by my chief to tell you, and to be
at your service should you require me."

The kangaroo was so overjoyed that he shed tears of
gladness. Such a great burden had been lifted from his
mind. He said, " Wait, my child emu, until I have recovered myself. I have been thinking much of the platypuses, fearing that they had been completely swept off the
face of the earth and were no more. Now will you rest a
while, and take food to renew your strength for your journey?
In the meantime I will think out some plan to go and meet
the other tribes—the animals, the birds, and the reptiles."

So the emu sat down and heartily enjoyed a meal of berries
and sweet, tender grass, freshly picked in a glade especially
set aside for the use of the elders of the kangaroo tribe.
The emu could not help exclaiming, " What lovely berries,
and what tender grass, and how sweet and appetizing !
I feel tempted to eat and eat until I have gorged myself.
I should like always to be sent by my chief to carry messages

to you, so that I might partake of such nice food." After his meal the emu, as was the usual custom, without further talking, said, " I am ready to do your bidding, O kangaroo. What do you command?"

The kangaroo gave the emu a stick with his sign on it, and with curves and angles denoting localities and representing messages to all peoples of the animal, the bird, and the reptile tribes that he would like to meet them in conference, to discuss the future of the platypus. He said, " I am afraid we shall have a difficult problem to deal with when we come into touch with the platypuses. Something within me tells me that it is so." After expressing himself thus to the emu, he said, " Go, my son, and prepare the bird and reptile tribes to meet me in conference."

With that the emu leaped forward on his mission. Again he ran in a spiral course, ever widening, and meeting the various tribes, until he had completed his duty. Then he returned by a direct course to his tribe. He ran with great speed until he reached his home, and delivered his message to his tribe thus, " All tribes have agreed to meet the kangaroo, and to arrange and decide upon some definite way of assisting and encouraging the platypus to resume his traditional rights and occupy once again his social position."

Until the conference was held no one was allowed to go near the home of the platypuses, lest they should think that the animals or birds or reptiles were trying to do them further injury. The time that elapsed between the issue of the instructions by the kangaroo and the holding of the conference was twelve moons. At the beginning of the first week of the new moon after the period fixed preparations were being made for the conference. Every tribe, with its respective families, journeyed to the Blue Mountain. There was one huge camping-ground, made of boughs, with *mia-mias* made of boughs and grass. The kangaroo family, the wallabies, the tree or climbing kangaroos, and the opossums had their *mia-mia* on the north side. The birds—the emus, eagle-hawks, crows, and other members of that family—

160

camped on the west side. The reptile tribe occupied the south side. The insect tribe camped on the east side.

The larger tribes did not recognize the insect tribe. They looked upon them as a very inferior race, and did not consult them or invite them to any of their great meetings. This was the first occasion on which this course was not followed, for the kangaroo, since the flood, had thought that all life, whether animal, bird, reptile, or insect, was one in life and death, and that, although insects differed greatly in structure and in their manner of living, the mystery of life and death was common to all. Some insects lived to a great age, while the lives of others were only of short duration : but all were subject to the same troubles. The kangaroo thought that the insect tribes might help them to understand life and death and other problems. So for these reasons the insect tribes were invited to this important gathering.

The kangaroo gave notice to the others that at the first week of the new moon the conference would begin. In the meantime all the tribes must consult their family trees and the traditions of the race from which they sprang in order to gather sufficient knowledge to find out how nearly they might be related to the platypus, and what claim he had on them for assistance. The emu, the pelican, the swan, the eagle-hawk, the parrot, the lyre-bird, and the various kinds of ducks were all busily engaged in looking into their traditions and consulting the drawings and carvings on the rocks and trees. The reptile tribes were similarly engaged in order to see what relationship existed between them and the platypus. So also were the animal tribes.

The first to discover traces of relationship were the bird tribes. "Why is it," said the black ducks, "that the platypus has the beak of a bird, resembling so closely that of our cousin the duck ? " For this reason the birds swore allegiance and promised help and protection to the platypus. Then a solemn-looking pelican said, " The platypuses must be related to us because they lay eggs." " So they do," said the cockatoos and the laughing jacks. " The only difference is that their egg is more like the eggs of the reptile family." "That does not matter," said the native companion. "It's an egg all the same."

The laughing jack was in a mischievous mood, and when he heard the dull native companion speaking he said, "Just fancy the native companion having something to say! He looks so ridiculous with his bald head and thin, long, wiry legs. It makes me laugh, *koo ka koo ka koo ka*!" "Be quiet," said the snappy magpie. "We are not here to make jokes and say funny things to each other. We are here for something more serious than that." "Come now," said the crow. "Let us get on with our business." "It is a pity," said the emu, "that the platypus does not dress himself in feathers. I am sure that he would make a nice bird." "*Koo ka koo ka*!" said the laughing jacks. "What a ridiculous bird he would make, with those short and funny webbed feet of his! Just fancy your grandson and granddaughter, O emu, with four short, clumsy feet and that funny tail, jogging along beside you! Oh, what funny relatives to have! The whole tribe of animals would look on it as a joke, and the reptiles would laugh you to scorn." "Now," said the magpie, "if you do not stop your impudent talk I shall have to put you out." The emu gave orders that they should not discuss the subject now, but wait until the general meeting should take place.

On the southern portion of the great camping-ground the reptiles were earnestly searching the traditions of their race, to find out what relationship they had with the platypus. The carpet-snake said, "I must admit that he resembles the animals and birds more closely than he does the reptiles. There is no likeness whatever to us, except in the laying of eggs."

"And that is not much to go on, is it?" said the goanna, addressing the sleepy lizard, who was at this time yawning and showing his blue tongue.

Just at that moment the impudent frilled lizard threw a pebble right into the open mouth of the sleepy lizard, who coughed and coughed until he ejected the pebble from his throat. The goanna ordered the frilled lizard to retire, and said that if he began his nonsense again he would instruct the tiger-snake to destroy the whole of the frilled lizard family, as they had already been the cause of the great flood, in which many families had perished, and that he, the goanna, and others of the reptile family would see that this sort of thing did not occur again.

So the frilled lizard wandered away. He said he would not take any more interest in tracing his relationship to the platypus. He sulked and brooded over being ordered away from the conference. His whole being was filled with hatred, and he bears the ugly frown of anger to-day in the spiky frill of whiskers on each side of his face. The more he thought of the humiliation imposed upon him by the goanna the uglier he became.

The goanna instructed the other members of his tribe to keep an eye upon the wicked frilled lizard, to prevent him from causing further trouble. By this time the animal tribe had decided that they were certainly related to the platypus family. The kangaroo advised the koala, the opossum, and the rat not to put forward any suggestion, but to let the others make their claims and see how much resemblance they could find between themselves and the platypus, and how far back they could trace their relationship.

The kangaroo called a general meeting for the day before the full moon. When all were assembled he asked that no one should speak out of turn; that no reflections should be made against any tribe or person; and that each should consider the interest that was at stake—the building up of a race that was in its decline. He said, " The platypus comes of a very ancient race. Not only so, but he belongs to a very learned and cultured people. I feel sure that although he has not made himself heard upon this question before, he will be able to throw much light on the subject. Now I should like the carpet-snake to go and ask the remaining platypuses that are to be found at the little island in the lake to attend. To-night, being the night of the full moon, we shall discuss the question and hear what the platypus has to say."

Amid great applause the carpet-snake rose and set out on his journey to ask the platypuses to attend the meeting. The carpet-snake wound his way down the mountain-side until he arrived at the foot, where he rested a while, and lay down to take a short nap until the sun should be well over the western mountain. As darkness gradually approached he hastened to the lake in which he had seen the home of the platypuses, and he eagerly waited, gazing intently into the clear water for a sign of life, but nothing revealed itself. Presently he could hear the voice of some one speaking as if addressing a great audience. It was the elder of the platypuses addressing the younger members of his tribe, and advising them that they should make up their minds and send travellers north, south, east, and west in search of their people or tribe. " It will be a great calamity," he said, " if we should fail to discover some of our race."

The carpet-snake, without waiting to hear anything further, glided across the clear stream to the island, and, with a soft, sweet voice, said, " Brother platypus, I have been sent by the animal, the bird, the reptile, and the insect tribes to ask you to stay and enjoy yourselves among us until such time as you see fit to leave us. We are all anxious to have you. Come, rise and follow me."

Without questioning the carpet-snake, the platypuses rose and followed, until they arrived at the top of the Blue Mountain. Then the carpet-snake said, " Rest here a while until I return ; I go forward to prepare the tribes to receive you." So the carpet-snake came to the gathering-place of the tribes. He saw that all the tribes were grouped in a large circle, waiting to receive the platypuses. Then he returned to the platypuses and said, " Come, friends. All are ready to receive you." The platypuses followed the carpet-snake, who led them toward the gathering.

The owl announced their arrival. All heads were bowed, and on each there was placed the pipeclay cap that is used in mourning. All eyes were closed. A pathway was made leading into the centre of the large gathering, and a circle was formed in the midst of this gathering so as to leave a clear, open space for the visitors. When they took their seats they also bowed their heads, and clay caps were placed on them by the wombats. This was a sign that all were sharing in the great loss suffered by the platypuses. They remained thus till midnight. Then all the tribes rose to their feet and went to their homes, while the platypuses remained where they were, surrounded by the elders of the animal, bird, and reptile tribes, who had provided them with coverings from the fibre of the bark of the trees. The platypuses slept soundly till morning, and then a *mia-mia* was built round them to protect them against the heat of the sun.

In the late afternoon the kangaroo came to see the platypuses alone. He placed his arm round the neck of the elder of the platypuses, and wept bitterly. He said, " I am sorry, O platypus, that you have suffered. I am your friend. We have met in order that you should choose the most beautiful daughter of any among us; either a bird from the emu girls, or the swans, or the pelicans, or some of the beautiful daughters of the parrots or cockatoos; or one of the reptile girls, the snakes, or lizards; or you may choose from my family. Are you willing? We give you the opportunity of making a free choice." When the kangaroo had said this he left their *mia-mia* to allow them to consider the question.

Just after sunset everybody, instead of retiring to rest as was their custom, attended the conference. This arrangement was intended to give every encouragement to the platypuses, because they come out only at night, and are not accustomed to daylight. The audience gathered in a large circle around the platypuses. When all were seated, and silence reigned, the elder of the platypus tribe arose and addressed the audience thus: " Animals, birds, and reptiles, there was a time in the long, long ago when I was closely akin to the reptile family; then, as the years went on, I became related to the animals, and later on to the birds. That was a very long time ago; but I can still claim relationship with my great friend the kangaroo. In fact, I can call him ' brother ' without fear of contradiction; for we are one flesh, and belong to the hairy or fur family. I do not wish to say more until I have heard the bird and reptile families express their opinions."

Having said this, the platypus called the emu by the name of "Theen-who-ween" and sat down. Every one looked amazed at hearing this name which sounded so ancient. The crow looked at the magpie. The owl gazed as if he were trying to recall some carving or painting in a cave somewhere in the mountain and to remember the name he saw. Then he looked upon the platypus, and, turning to his friend the night-jar, said, "We are in the presence of a learned man. He speaks a dead language belonging to past generations. That name is not in our records, neither is it known to the animals or reptiles. This will show how far back the platypus can go."

The emu rose and, addressing himself first to the animals and reptiles, expressed his pleasure at being able to meet and converse with the remaining few of what was considered a great race, in numbers as well as in knowledge and wisdom. He said he was rather startled when he heard the platypus calling him by such an ancient name. He was always called by the name "Pinyali," but this morning he had been called "Theen-who-wheen." This showed that the platypuses came of a very ancient tribe, and that their knowledge would be a great help to all the tribes present. He said, "I will not say much, only I am pleased that, on an occasion like this, which is considered sacred to our race, the tribes are allowed to discuss and inquire into relationships."

So the emu availed himself of this opportunity to inquire directly of the platypus, "What is your totem? Who are your flesh?"[1] The platypus replied, "The bandicoot. This is the tribe to which I should be allied. But allow me, O emu, to ask to whom do you belong? To what tribe are you allied? Who are your flesh?" "We belong to the snake family," replied the emu. Then the platypus said to the emu, "Once upon a time your family and mine were

[1] Compare this usage with Genesis ii, 24, and elsewhere in Hebrew and other literature.

166

brothers, but since then you have embraced another belief and religion." " Yes," said the emu, " we have different religions and beliefs, because this suits your purpose and mine." The platypus said, " What benefit do we platy-puses gain by your change of religion ? " The emu replied, " It makes it possible for you to marry into my family."

This matter of law which was stated by the emu placed the platypus in a dilemma. There seemed to be no way out of it. So he said, " Give me time to consider the question, and after the conference I will give you a reply. I shall interview my uncle, the bandicoot, and find what he thinks of it." " That is not the case," said the emu. " The bandi-coot is my uncle, and is no longer a relative of yours." " Then," said the platypus, " if things have so changed since the flood, I do not wish to become a relative of either of you: Let us ask the audience whether it is possible to agree to bring this matter up at the next conference. I should like to have all the fur tribes there, and all the snakes and lizards, and the feathered tribes."

The behaviour of the platypus made the emu angry, and he would have forced him to accept his terms but for the kindly kangaroo, who intervened and advised the platypuses to steal away at night and make for the north. A daughter of the bandicoot tribe heard the kangaroo advise the platy-puses to go away unseen by anyone. She told her family, and they waited in the way where the platypuses should pass. When they saw them passing they called out, " Will you come with us to the home of the bandicoot? We of the hairy tribe are sympathetic with you. Come and spend a few moons with us. We are living away down near the water-pool from which you came." The platypuses agreed. They made their home with the bandicoots, and made love to the bandicoot daughters. When they married they took their young wives with them to the north. There, in their adopted country, they lived happily.

But there was one of the hairy tribes, the water-rat tribe, that became jealous of the platypuses for taking the girls that should, by the law of the country, have become wives

167

to them. So the young water-rats followed the trail of the platypuses as far as to their homes. When the platypuses went in search of food at night the young water-rats attacked them. There was a great battle. The opponents fought in the water, grappling with each other. The platypuses called out to their wives, " Bring our spears, we are in danger." So the girl bandicoots ran in haste to the rescue of their husbands. Each had a spear in her hand, which she used with fatal effect upon the jealous water-rats. Then the platypuses with their wives returned to their homes in the bank of the river.

Although the platypus tried to break away from the bird tribe he is ever reminded that this is impossible, for his wife lays eggs and he still retains the bird's or duck's bill. He has tried hard to separate himself and his family from the birds. He has succeeded in getting rid of the feathers which the emu reminded him he wore long, long ago ; and he tried to sever his connexion with the animals, but in this also he has failed. He still belongs to the kangaroo and opossum tribe. He tried hard to make a great gulf between himself and the kindly kangaroo, who looked upon him with pity, but the more he tried the greater the difficulty became ; so now he makes no further effort, but contents himself to be neither a bird, reptile, nor kangaroo, but a plain platypus. He no longer seeks the companionship of the animal, bird, or reptile families, but lives happily with his wife in the river or *billabong*.

He sings to the god of food, " Give me more grubs as the water ripples, and make for me bread of the *nardoo* seed. Do this as often as the sun rises ; and I shall gather in the shade of night the food thou shalt throw into the water, my hunting-place, because I am hiding all day, fearing that some one may call up the lightning, the thunder, and the rain."

How Spencer's Gulf came into Existence

The people of the Narrangga tribe who lived long, long ago on Yorke's Peninsula had a story that has been handed down through the ages. It is a tale of a strange and wonderful being who lived when there was no Spencer's Gulf, but only marshy country reaching into the interior of Australia. It was a bone of this being that was the means of bringing the Gulf into existence.

At the lagoons in the marshes there lived various families. At one there were the duck families—the black duck, teal, and wood duck. At another lagoon fifty miles away there lived the shag families—the big black shag and the small black shag, the big white-breasted and the black-backed shags, and the small white-breasted and all the Gulf family of shags, in which there were many individuals. The snipe family was also well represented. The swan family frequented another lagoon. Each water-bird family lived on a lagoon by itself.

About a mile or two away from this lagoon there lived the land birds—the cockatoos, the laughing jacks, the emus, the hawks, the magpies, the crows, and birds of the forest. Along with the land birds there also lived the opossum, the wallaby, the kangaroo, the kangaroo-rat, and the native cat. These all lived side by side, and took shelter under the same gum-tree. The reptiles and the lizards also lived in one home, but they slept apart, the snakes by themselves and the lizards by themselves.

Now all these families lived in harmony. The duck family would invite the lizard family to visit them at their lagoon. Perhaps the blue-tongued and the Jew lizards and the goannas would accept the invitation. The shag family might invite the kangaroo family to come to visit them. And at the beautiful shag lagoon one could see the blue, grey, and black kangaroo and the kangaroo-rat enjoying themselves. In this manner lived all the folk on this chain of lagoons and marshes. There were no family or other boundaries until one day some one suggested rather foolishly that each kind of family should live alone and not associate with the other kinds of families. This proposal was favourably received. For instance, the pelican said, " I do not think that it is advisable that the duck family should invite the lizard family to visit them, or that the shag family should entertain the kangaroo family; but birds should invite birds, animals invite animals, and reptiles invite reptiles." So the bird tribes made a proclamation prohibiting the animals and reptiles from coming to their lagoons.

Then the kangaroo, who was the chief of the animal tribe, and who was respected and admired by all the tribes, came to discuss the matter with the occupiers of the lagoons. He pleaded that it would be in the best interests of all to allow free access to the lagoons for the purpose of procuring water. He said that water was necessary for the existence of all. The owners consented that the lagoons should be visited only for the purposes of obtaining drinking water; and so peace was maintained for a great number of years.

Then the cockatoo said to the other birds, " Just fancy allowing the frilled lizard and the blue-tongued lizard to come down into the water and pollute it with their presence!" " Yes," said the magpie, "and I hate to see the hedgehog and the wombat drinking side by side with the beautiful parrot girls." So at last the pride of the bird tribes prevailed, and they refused to allow the animals, reptiles, and lizards to come to the lagoon to drink.

There then began a great warfare between the birds and the animals, lizards, and reptiles. Although the animals were fighting for a good cause the kangaroos, emus, and willy-wagtails took no part in the combats. They were grieved at the continual fighting. The elders of the kangaroos often sat and discussed things, in order to find a way of bringing about a settlement. "Now," said the emu, " if something were done to deprive the selfish ones of their possessions I am sure that they would become more considerate and friendly." " But to do that," said the kangaroo, " would cause a great deal of bloodshed, although I am sure the loss of some of their possessions would make them more friendly." The willy-wagtail suggested that they should endeavour to make the sea flow into the lagoons and marshes. He thought that if they could do this the problem might be solved. So the kangaroo, the emu, and the willy-wagtail camped together. They determined to think out a scheme. At the end of a week, however, they were still unable to think of how to make the sea flow into the lagoons and marshes.

One day the kangaroo, the emu, and the willy-wagtail were sitting on the seashore between Cape Spencer and Port Lincoln. The emu wandered away from his companions, and found a leg-bone of a huge kangaroo. He carried it back to where they had slept the night before, and put it down near the entrance to their camp. The kangaroo and the willy-wagtail soon arrived. They saw the bone, and asked where it had come from. The emu then told them of his find of the previous day. The kangaroo asked where he had found the bone, and the emu promised to show him the place next day. They went to bed, but they were so tired with thinking of how to let the sea flow into the lagoons that they all passed a very restless night.

In the morning they discussed matters. The willy-wagtail spoke first. "Oh ! " he said, " I had such a bad dream ! I dreamed I stood upon an island that was round in shape, and without a mountain or hill upon it. The sea was all round me. Suddenly a great wave rose up, and came rolling and tumbling toward the island. I was scared. I ran this way and that way, but the waves were now all tumbling over the island. I threw up my arms in despair. I do not know what kept the sea from passing over and flooding the island and drowning me. I have not yet got over the effects of that awful dream, so I should be glad not to speak of it any more."

"Oh ! " said the emu, " I dreamed that where the lagoons now are was a dry, dusty, and parched country. Desolation was everywhere. Animals, birds, and reptiles were lying dead all round." Then the emu and the willy-wagtail said to the kangaroo, "Perhaps you will tell us of your night's experience." " I neither dreamed nor saw a vision," said the kangaroo. " All through the night one thing was present before my mind, and that one thing was the leg-bone. Come, let us go forth and search for the other bones."

The emu led the kangaroo and the willy-wagtail to the spot, and they dug and dug until they found the other bones. The bones were lying pointing in a straight line toward Port Augusta. The kangaroo took up the bone that the emu had discovered and probed the ground with it. He did not know that the bone was a magic one. But as soon as he used it the earth opened itself. The kangaroo started to walk toward Port Augusta, and as he advanced he probed the ground with his magic bone. The sea broke through, and came tumbling and rolling along in the track cut by the kangaroo-bone. It flowed into the lagoons and marshes, which completely disappeared. Ever since that memorable time, when the kangaroo made Spencer's Gulf with the aid of his magic bone, birds have displayed no selfishness.

CHAPTER III: RELIGION

The Belief in a Great Spirit

THE aboriginals of Australia build no places of worship, nor do they erect altars for the offering of sacrifice. Notwithstanding this lack of ceremonial religion, they believe in a Great Spirit, and in the son of this Great Spirit.

There arose among the aboriginals a great teacher, Nurunderi. He was a chosen one of the Great Spirit. He spoke to the people thus : " Children, there is a Great Spirit above whose dwelling-place is heaven. It is his will that you should know him as the whole spirit of whom you are parts. He is your provider and protector. It has been my pleasure to give you the privilege to sojourn a while in a bodily state to fulfil my great plan. Remember, children, your life is like a day; and during the short period you are on earth you are to educate yourselves by self-control, and to realize that all of you are parts of me. Live as children of your Great Father. Control your appetites and your desires. Never allow yourselves to become slaves to your appetites or desires. Never allow your minds to suffer pain or fear, in case you become selfish, for selfishness causes misery to yourself, your wife, your children, your relatives, and those with whom you live. Selfishness is not of the Great Spirit. Cultivate everything good. Be moderate in eating and in pleasure. Be generous to others. Cultivate a healthy state of mind and body. Be guided by pure morals. Show kindness to others, remembering that they also are a part of that Great Spirit from whom you came."

This knowledge develops the soul, which is a part of the whole spirit, till it is fit to become companion to the Great Spirit. To this end the children are placed in the hands of the elders of the tribes to be educated.[1]

When the course of education has been completed all the members of the tribe assemble at a sacred spot reserved for

[1] See pp. 19–21.

the purpose, and an elder, in the presence of the whole assembly, declares that the boys and girls are ' men ' and ' women.' Then all the men of the congregation stand up, and the women sit with their heads bowed. The men turn their faces to the setting sun, and point to it with spear and *nulla-nulla*, and shout, " Well done, girls and boys, you have fought the battle of life and have conquered; manhood and womanhood is perfected in you; the Great Spirit is pleased, and he is now awaiting your presence in the Home of the Spirits."

The Land of Perfection

On the Plain of Nullarbor there existed a wonderful and beautiful country. From legendary accounts it had the appearance of a city surrounded by four white walls, which varied in height from five hundred to a thousand feet. The distance from one corner of the city to the other was a day's journey—about forty miles from sunrise to sunset. Along the top of each wall there were domes and spires. The outside of the walls was composed of white quartz stone, and the inside was formed of a sky-blue stone resembling slate. The country within the walls was mountainous, and many of the hills were cone-shaped. In one mountain there was an underground reservoir with an outlet on the top. The clear, cool water spouted up through this opening, and trickled down the side of the mountain into the valley. Many shrubs and ferns grew on the hillsides, and in the valley and on the plain there were large gum-trees and plants with beautiful flowers. The ground was covered with a soft carpet of green grass. The flowers and the grass had the ordered appearance of a well-laid-out garden.

Now the only inhabitants of this beautiful country who were allowed to enjoy peace free from all danger were the birds, the insects, and the fish. The birds, the insects, and the plants breathed their life into the air. All living things obtained their livelihood from the pure air, and each to the other breathed into their bodies life and strength. Thus in the Land of Perfection there was no need for one creature

TOTEMIC DESIGNS PAINTED ON THE BACKS OF INITIATES DURING THE ENGWURA CEREMONY

From "The Arunta," by Sir Baldwin Spencer and F. J. Gillen, by permission of Messrs Macmillan & Co., Ltd.

A MEDICINE-MAN

*From "The Arunta," by Sir Baldwin Spencer and F. J. Gillen,
by permission of Messrs Macmillan & Co., Ltd.*

184

to prey upon another in order to live. Neither the bird nor the fish needed to hunt the insect. So all lived in happiness and harmony. The most remarkable thing about this country was that no one had knowledge of it, or was even conscious of its existence until he became ill or diseased in body, mind, or soul.

The soul, being the one controlling power in man, seeks a resting-place, and so would lead the body onward into a land where all was peaceful harmony, there to enjoy its pleasures for ever. But before a soul could find entrance into that Land of Perfect Bliss it must pass along a narrow ledge of rock. On one side of this ledge was a perpendicular wall, one thousand feet high, with a perfectly smooth face. Not a single living thing could climb up its surface. At one spot, about half-way along the ledge, there was a recess in the face of the wall in which one could take shelter if danger should approach. On the other side of the ledge was a chasm—deep, dark, and unfathomable. The darkness was so dense that any who fell into the chasm floated about until a good spirit from the Perfect Land came forth to rescue the unfortunate one and carry him to a point on the ledge where the danger was not so great.

Another danger to contend with was a rolling stone, circle-shaped and resembling a grindstone. In size it was about six feet in diameter, and in thickness it was about equal to the width of the ledge.

Beyond the ledge, upon the boundary line of the Perfect Land, were two cone-shaped crystals, that stood about two hundred feet high and measured about six hundred feet round the base. Round these two crystals were coiled two snakes, so one may gather some idea of the length of these monsters—Biggarroo, the wombat snake, and Goonnear, the carpet-snake. Biggarroo is the good snake, and Goonnear the evil snake. Biggarroo is a great physician. The Father Spirit entrusted him with healing virtue for the human race.

When anyone, whether male or female, old or young, is troubled in mind or diseased in body, and goes forth with a seeking soul urged by a compelling force and an over-powering attraction, the soul's instinct guides him in his search for that land over mountains, hills, and valleys, through dense forests, and over dusty plains. The weary pilgrim soul is recognized by all nature. To show their sympathy the trees cast their shadows straight along his path, and so help to cool the fevered body and to protect it from the blazing sun. The flowers too, with their fragrance, refresh and revive the fainting soul.

When the sick and stricken soul arrives at the border of this Perfect Land he is bewildered, and wonders what to do. He feels the compelling force urging him onward. Before his vision lies a narrow pathway, bounded on the one side by the towering, smooth-faced wall, and on the other by the deep, yawning chasm. He hesitates, and fears to advance a single step. Then the soul begins to plead, " O my brother, my partner in life ! From yonder land where you and I weathered many of life's tempestuous storms it is now only a few more steps, and then we pass beyond the veil into the Land of Perfect Bliss where we shall find joy, rest, and life. Oh, come, my brother, with me. I am in pain and agony when I see you hesitate. When you place your feet upon this ledge you must go on until you reach the recess half-way along. In it there is refuge, safe and secure, while the stone passes by. After it has passed we will continue our pilgrimage to the Perfect Land. Then shall we behold Biggarroo and Goonnear. Biggarroo, the friend and physician, will make you whole again in body, mind, and soul, and fitted for the Land of Perfection."

A sick man journeyed along the road. Guided by the dictates of his soul, he walked onward with undaunted courage until he reached the recess. Here he waited for the stone to pass by. It came rumbling along, and passed by right on to the end of the ledge.

Then the soul aroused the man from his unconsciousness into activity. " O my brother self," said he, " just a little way, and then your journey will be almost completed."

The sick man, now regaining consciousness, made a

desperate attempt to free himself from the awful position. Every stride brought him nearer to safe ground and away from the gaping pit. At last he reached the place where the two crystals stood. Then the soul whispered softly to its brother body, " Turn to the right and flee into the open jaw of Biggarroo, and you shall gain your freedom, and through eternity your body and mind shall feel neither sickness nor pain."

When he had completed his journey Biggarroo and Goonnear called softly in their musical voices to the sick man, " This way, my friend. To me you may come. We were once of the same totem as you. Our mothers are one. You are my brother, and I am your brother."

Then Biggarroo said, " To me you shall come, for the Great Father Spirit gave me the power to heal you, body, mind, and soul."

Biggarroo and Goonnear both proclaimed the same message. Biggarroo told the truth, but Goonnear lied. The sick man could not decide which one was the physician. He tried to recall warning words or past events that would help him to decide. In his half-conscious state he could hear faintly the two voices calling. He took three strides in the direction of the wicked Goonnear. Then his inner soul gave vision to the mental eye and perfect sight to the physical eye, so he could see things as they really were. He saw the deceitfulness in the wicked, cruel eyes of Goonnear. Straightway he turned and walked into the open jaws of Biggarroo, the good physician.

After he had walked sixty paces or more along the monster's throat, he stopped, and stood for a while, contemplating. He decided that he would choose a quiet spot where the grass grew like a green carpet and flowers bloomed upon a bush, and that there he would lie down and rest. He soon fell into a sound and healthful sleep. For one whole day he slept. On the second day he woke, and stood up on his feet. To his amazement he noticed that the bush had disappeared and had left behind it a sweet perfume. He walked along for about a hundred steps.

Then he saw a sight that filled him with joy. For upon the white pathway he noticed his mother's footprints. He was so overjoyed that he wept with gladness. He now knew that she lived within the Spirit Land, and that, in a few more days, he would behold her lovely face.

He pressed on eagerly until he came to about the middle of the snake. There he saw others of the human race. Some belonged to his tribe, and others to tribes that were strange to him in the outer world. But in this inner world they all spoke one language; each held intercourse as friend with friend, all being in sympathy. The thoughts of all were pure and free, but the people differed in their endowments. The more intelligent guided those of less understanding. All round in the interior of the snake there was abundant evidence to prove that the human race passes on from stage to stage until it is made perfect. Then all relatives, friends, and loved ones meet again and live within the Perfect Land. This thought urged the pilgrim onward. He became filled with joy and delight at the discoveries he made as he proceeded. These discoveries were so wonderful that he could find no fitting words by which to express them.

Returning to the place where he first fell asleep, he lay down quietly beneath the same bush, which appeared to have returned. He slept soundly and dreamed. He passed several hours trying to trace some meaning in his confused dream. But his mind was not equal to the task. He awoke and rose up slowly, and walked toward the open mouth of Biggarroo. He stepped to the summit of the cone and stood upright, with both hands clasped behind his back, with the dignity of some monarch beholding his kingdom. Suddenly there appeared a third eye upon his face. Its place was on the forehead, between the two other eyes. It was a wonderful eye, a magical eye, and it gave him wide vision and the power of looking through the veil of time. And this is what he saw. Impenetrable darkness reigned, but within him a light dimly glowed. A mighty tremor passed over the earth and space. The darkness rippled like water disturbed by a passing wind. He was amazed to see it roll away like a column toward the west. It passed over him as if urged by some greater force. Then a light appeared like the dawning of the morning. On the horizon of the eastern sky he saw a shapeless form, suspended between earth and space. He did not know how long he stood, but after a long interval he looked again at the hovering mass. He saw that it was assuming the form of a clothed woman. As it took definite shape the robes unfolded and fell apart from her body in four portions, opening from the head to the feet like the unfolding of a primrose bud, revealing the bright yellow flowers. She stood disrobed, with her golden hair streaming from the crown of her head to her ankles. With both hands she cast her hair from about her, and immediately the strands took the form of beams streaming forth like the rays of the rising sun.

The pilgrim gazed in silent ecstasy at her overpowering majesty and magnificence. The sight opened the gateway to his sense of mind and reason, and he spoke to the rays of the morn, and asked, " Whence come thy bright and golden beams, O Mother, Goddess of Love, Light, and Life? Is it thy purity that has maintained thy maidenly grace and youthful strength? For more than ten thousand years thou hast poured forth thyself as the enlightenment and the sustaining power of life! "

The pilgrim's soul desired to view the past once more, and his body, yielding to the soul's request, sank into a sub-conscious or visionary state. His single eye, the mirror of the soul, with keen vision traced the course of the sunbeams as they penetrated into the earth. First the frozen water, like a pavement of solid crystal covering portions of the earth, began to melt and to flow in liquid state. Then the earth staggered and rolled and trembled as if in dreadful agony. Rocks rose and formed mountains, hills, and valleys, and the silvery liquid rolled between as rivers, streams, and lakes. When this work was completed the Goddess of Light drew her mantle round her comely form, and retired into the darkness of everlasting night.

Then the pilgrim's soul led him again into the open jaws of Biggarroo. He walked on inside the snake until he came to the place where he had previously slept. This time he sank upon the grass beneath the same bush, not weary in body, but filled with divine wonderment. His soul was entranced with sacred meditation, for his eyes had seen the glory of the Mother Goddess, and he poured out his soul to her in prayer. " To thee I breathe my thanks and adoration. Thou gavest me wonderful and unmerited privileges. In thee I see my hope. I am corrupt within and without; my body is too frail to retain even a small spark of life and light. And yet thou hast placed me here on earth. When it pleases thee, take me hence to the unknown world. But while I remain in my corrupt body, and tread this earthly sphere with all its pain and woe, be pleased to extend to me thy everlasting defence whatever happens to me in this world or hereafter in the Spirit Land. I confide in thy omnipotent protection. But when this mortal form shall be no more my soul shall rise on wings to my everlasting home in thee, my Goddess of Light and of Life, and my Mother."

Then the pilgrim heard the melodious voice of Biggarroo, saying, " My child, it is the will of the Father Spirit that you, and all of the human race who resemble you, shall be like unto the Mother Goddess. The only way to attain to eternal youth is to dwell within me for a season, and time will impart to your body the elixir of life that comes from immortality. I am honoured by the Great Father Spirit to be the medium through which that life must pass."

The pilgrim slept soundly, and a century passed before he regained his self-consciousness. He stepped forth out of the snake, and once more he walked to the summit of the crystal cone. Then consciousness gradually passed from sense into vision. His single eye saw that a mist had risen from the ocean, rivers, lakes, and valleys, and had covered the earth like a shroud. Nothing was visible. Then the mist slowly melted away. He looked, and was amazed to see that the face of the barren earth had changed, and was covered with vegetation that was very beautiful to behold. The air was filled with sweet and reviving fragrance that was shed by flowers of every form and colour. Some of the trees rose to heights of many hundreds of feet, and their trunks at the ground were from thirty to forty feet thick. Vegetation reigned supreme. Generation after generation of forest life forms came, grew, decayed, and passed on, and were buried and changed into other forms of matter far below the surface of the earth.

He stood motionless, it seemed for only a day ; in reality centuries came and went, passing the boundary line of the evermore. The sun was concentrating her rays upon the water within the earth, and was bringing forth life in forms most strange to behold. Among these were Moolgewanke,[1] the *bunyip*, Harrimiah, the dark black goanna, Perindi, the striped yellow and brown goanna, Kendi, the frilled lizard, Uroo, the water-snake, as well as other mythical beings that are now known to us only in legends. Some of these were so large in size as to be beyond imagination, and some were very small. Some walked upon the earth, and others waddled like the goannas of to-day, while others hopped about like kangaroos, and some flew with great bat-like wings. Uroo, the great water-serpent, that is greater than all reptiles, returned to the water below the surface of the earth. He could not bear exposure to the light, because his body had no protection against the rays of the sun. He lives to-day in a subterranean creek a mile long.

Harrimiah, Perindi, Kendi, and others lived for many centuries, and then became extinct. The only evidence we have of their existence is found in bones or casts or impressions on stone.

The earth revolved, and time rolled on. The great monsters of the Reptile Age died out. Centuries again passed. Then came a pageant most wonderful to behold—

---

[1] A far-off booming sound which is frequently heard in Lake Alexandrina is ascribed to him, and the aboriginals think it causes rheumatism in those who hear it. He is represented as a curious being, half man, half fish, and as having instead of hair a matted crop of reeds.

the Bird Age, with the emu in the foremost rank, the insects following, and then the animals and fishes. Some of these were of great size and weight.

After the pilgrim had beheld this wonderful sight Big-garroo said to him, "Go now, my child; enter the Land of Perfection." So he walked into that land. Every morning and every evening the birds poured forth their love and gratitude in joyful song. The flowers unfolded their beauty at the rising of the sun, and when the sun sank in the west their sweet fragrance was diffused everywhere. For centuries he lived within the Land of Bliss. Then there came a time when a great and mighty storm arose in the south. It raised the water of the ocean with tremendous force, and drove it through the wall of the Land of Perfection. Then the great Father Spirit gave ear to the request of the Goddess of Light and Life, and transferred the Land of Perfection to the Sacred Land, now known as the Milky Way.

The Voice of the Great Spirit [1]

The Australian aboriginals have a deeper and more extensive sense of morality and religion than is generally known. From a very early age the children are instructed by the mothers and the old men of the tribe by means of stories and fables. This is one of the many stories that have been handed down from generation to generation.

In the beginning the Great Spirit used to speak directly every day to his people. The tribes could not see him, but they could hear his voice, and they used to assemble every morning to listen to him. Gradually, however, the tribes grew weary of listening, and they said, one to the other, "Oh, I am tired of this listening to a voice. I cannot see to whom it belongs. Let us go and enjoy ourselves by making our own corrobberies."

The Great Spirit was grieved when he heard this, so he

---

[1] It is interesting to learn something of the methods by which the various races of men have wrestled with the problem of good and evil. This is an aboriginal contribution to the subject.

sent his servant Nurunderi to call all the tribes together again. Nurunderi did so, saying, " The Great Spirit will not speak again to you, but he wishes to give you a sign." So all the tribes came to the meeting. When every one was seated on the ground Nurunderi asked them all to be very silent. Suddenly a terrific rending noise was heard. Nurunderi had so placed all the tribes that the meeting was being held round a large gum-tree. The tribes looked and saw this huge tree being slowly split open by some invisible force. They also saw an enormous tongue come down out of the sky and disappear into the middle of the gum-tree, after which the tree closed up again. Nurunderi said to the tribes, " You may go away now to your hunting and corrobberies."

The tribes went away to enjoy themselves. After a long time some began to grow weary of pleasure, and to long to hear again the voice of the Great Spirit; so they asked Nurunderi if he would call upon the Great Spirit to speak to them again. Nurunderi answered, " No. The Great Spirit will never speak to you again."

The tribes went to the sacred burial-grounds to ask the dead to help them, but of course the dead did not answer. Then they asked the great Nepelle, who lives in the Milky Way, if he would aid them, but still there was no answer. At last the tribes cried aloud. They began to fear that they would never again get in touch with the Great Spirit.

Finally the tribes appealed to Wyungare, the wise blackfellow who lives in the Milky Way. He told them to gather round about the big gum-tree again. When they were all assembled Wyungare asked, " Did you not see the tongue go into this tree? " The tribes answered, " Yes." " Well," said Wyungare, " take that as a sign that the tongue of the Great Spirit is in all things."

Thus it is to-day that the aboriginals know that the Great Spirit exists in all things, and speaks through every part of nature. The Tongue speaks in the voice of the wind; he rides on the storm; he speaks from out the thunder. The Tongue is everywhere and becomes manifest through the

183

bush, the birds, the flowers, the fish, the streams—in fact, everything that the aboriginal sees, hears, tastes, smells, and feels.

Witchcraft

Anyone whose reading on witchcraft, sorcery, magic, medicine, or rain-making has only been slight will find considerable difficulty in defining these terms. He will encounter, perhaps, still greater difficulty in classifying and describing the persons who practise the arts or perform the acts that are scientifically or popularly included under these terms. The reasons for this may become apparent when one remembers the large number of tribes that exist, or have existed, with different customs, languages, and environment. Further, it must be noted, and emphasized, that writers have too often assumed that rites, beliefs, and customs peculiar to one tribe conform in every respect with apparently similar rites, beliefs, and customs that exist in other tribes, whether far removed or in close proximity. Generalizing from particular instances is dangerous in many cases and in varied investigations ; in dealing with Australian aboriginals such logic is fatal to anthropological science. One should always understand that accurately recorded observations are true for the particular tribe or locality to which they refer, but that they cannot be assumed as universally or even generally true.

With this explanation, it may be said that a rain-maker may neither have, nor profess to have, any skill outside of his own profession of rain-making. A medicine-man is generally one who uses the pointing-stick or the pointing-bone, the *wirrie*, the crystal, the *thumie*, or the *ngathungi*. He professes to point the stick or the bone at a person and to cause it to enter the body ; and it is he who takes it or extracts it from the body, sometimes with the help of Puckowe,[1] a spirit who lives in the sky, and comes to his aid and operates on the patient when required. Some-

---

[1] Known as the Grandmother Spirit. She is supposed to inhabit the dark spot, the Coal-sack, in the Milky Way.

times he may compose a song to the spirit of the departed one, in order to hold communion with it regarding some coming event. When the medicine-man is in touch with the spirit he will say that the spirit, when granting a request, does not speak to him, but gives the answer indirectly by some sign, perhaps a sound, a rap on a tree, the rustling of a bough, the breaking of a bough on a tree, and sometimes, if he is beside a river, a splash of water. These sounds and signs the medicine-man is able to interpret.

It may be well, on the whole, to give some facts regarding the various acts done, and to use such terms as are generally employed by the aboriginals in the localities in which the particular arts are practised. In these records the operators are sometimes termed 'medicine-man,' 'doctor,' 'rain-maker,' '*munkumbole*,' 'magician,' 'medium,' apparently without accurate distinction. In this chapter the various terms are used without uniformity, very much in what might appear to be an indiscriminate fashion.

Rain-making. In every tribe there are usually one or more members who make a special study of the weather, and some become expert in interpreting signs and in forecasting happenings. Rain-makers belong to this class. They are men who profess to make rain through some incantation which causes a change in the weather by 're-leasing the elements.' Lightning, Thunder, and Rain are the name-totems of the tribe to which the rain-maker belongs.

Supposing a rain-maker wishes to impress his tribe with his ability to command the powers of the storm. He waits his opportunity. On some clear morning there may be no cloud in the sky, nor any sign of rain so far as the ordinary person can see. But the rain-maker notes indications that a thunder-storm is coming, and that it will arrive, say, within three hours. He begins his incantation, and his wife advises all present to warn their children that a storm is coming. The little children look about, but see no sign of it. After a while black clouds appear in the distance, followed by a flash of lightning. Then there is a peal of thunder. The children hasten to their wurleys, and almost immediately the storm is all round them. They are terrified. The rain-maker leaps out of his wurley, chanting his song of invocation to the spirits of the lightning, the thunder, the rain, and the wind, and repeating the words, " You have heard my call. Your response to it convinces the people that you are my friend and my servant and that you have come at my bidding." The children and youths and maidens are astounded at what they consider a wonderful performance.

An event like this becomes fixed in the minds of the young people, and they become easy victims to the deception of the professing prophet. Their belief grows with such convictions. Members of the tribe are therefore very careful not to offend the rain-maker; and they endeavour to gain his favour by ministering to his wants by gifts of food and of furs of animals for clothing. The gift that he professes to possess and to exercise belongs to his particular family and not to the tribe. While these persons may be weather-prophets, they may know nothing of the pointing-bone, nor have any skill in the use of it. They believe, however, in its deadly effects.

The Neilyeri. The employment of the *neilyeri* is a tribal means whereby one tribe takes revenge upon another for an injury. If, for instance, the Frilled Lizard totem tribe is desirous of doing an injury to the Carpet-snake totem tribe, one of its members would seek the aid of another person, say, a member of the Opossum totem tribe. The Frilled Lizard man would instruct the Opossum man to make the acquaintance of a Carpet-snake man. This he would do by asking a Tortoise totem tribe man to effect a meeting. After some palaver the Tortoise man would introduce the Opossum man to the Carpet-snake man. These two would sit by the fireside in the evening and discuss hunting and fishing, and the general topics of the day.

This would be repeated night after night for a week. Then one night the Opossum man would whisper into the ear of the Carpet-snake man a word of warning, saying that

186

the Frilled Lizard man was in possession of a great number of *neilyeries*, and was preparing them for use. Furthermore, he would say that he had heard that one of the *neilyeries* was to be used on a member of the Carpet-snake totem family, so he should be on his guard. As the Opossum and Carpet-snake men are sitting round the fireside exchanging thoughts and ideas about hunting and other important topics of the day the trained eye of the Carpet-snake man catches sight of something that strikes terror to his heart. There, about fifty yards away, sits the Frilled Lizard man with his eyes fixed upon him, and in his left hand he holds something which is only too well known to him—a pointing-bone. He is also making certain movements of his right hand.[1] The Carpet-snake man turns to his companion, and asks what the Frilled Lizard man is doing. The Opossum man says, " Do you see what he has in his hand? It is only too plain that it is a *neilyeri*. There is only one object that he sees at this moment; that is you."

The Carpet-snake man says in a whisper to the Opossum man, " Come, let us rise and retire to our wurleys." They both rise quickly and enter their abodes. The Carpet-snake man spends a restless night brooding over the deadly pointing-stick. He is the first to rise in the morning, and he sends for his companion of the previous night, and tells him that he has had a most dreadful night. He relates that in a vision or dream which came to him he was waylaid by some dreadful enemies. They were men, some having the appearance of the head of a dog, the body of a wombat, and the feet of an emu ; others had the head and neck of an emu, the legs of a kangaroo, and the body of a goanna ; still others had the head and body of an eagle-hawk and

---

[1] The method of using the pointing-bone may be described thus : The bone is held horizontally in the left hand, dorsum downward, the fingers folded over it firmly. The right hand is placed, fingers closed and downward, at the proximal end of the bone. This hand is then moved at first slowly along the bone, then increasingly in speed, while the fingers of it are kept closed. At the end of the bone, or a little beyond it, the fingers of this hand become firmly clasped. The motion still continues, and the hand becomes sharply thrown out at arm's length, with the fingers quickly extended. In all bone-pointing this is the practice.

MYTHS OF THE AUSTRALIAN ABORIGINALS

the legs of a native companion. All of these monsters were anxious to devour him, but he was favoured by Puckowe. She saw the danger which threatened him, and she came as a streak of smoke or white cloud, and enveloped him, so that his enemies were unable to see him; and thus by her timely protection he was saved, and was now able to relate the incident of the night.

The Opossum man says that this dream or vision means that there is an enemy who possesses many and varied qualities, so that the Carpet-snake man will be unable to escape him; there is only one tribe which is to be feared, and that is the Frilled Lizard tribe. He continues, " After what we saw the Frilled Lizard man doing last night I am convinced that he pointed the stick at you, and as you are not looking well I think you had better visit the medicine-man." So the Carpet-snake man decides to consult the doctor, but the cunning Lizard man has already seen the doctor, and has retained his services with bribes. The poor, worried, and despairing Carpet-snake man pleads with the medicine-man, saying, " Oh, is there no hope for me? Can you and will you stay the influence of the stick, or take it from my body? "

The medicine-man takes a bunch of feathers which he has brought with him, and shows them to his patient. He then goes to the door of the wurley, and sits quietly gazing at the sick man's body. Presently he closes his eyes as if to shut out an evil vision. Then he professes to speak with the departed spirit and the relatives of the patient. After the supposed conversation he gives the sick man two feathers, and instructs him to place these feathers before his eyes and then look through them at his body. The patient becomes startled, because he fancies that the body of the medicine-man appears to be transparent. The medicine-man inquires as to what he sees, and the patient answers, " It seems that your flesh has disappeared, and that I am able to see your spirit man."

Then the medicine-man removes the feathers from the patient's eyes and while doing so tells him to close his eyes.

THE POINTING-BONE

PUCKOWE, THE GRANDMOTHER SPIRIT, COMES TO THE RESCUE

This he does, and he keeps them shut until he is told to open them. The medicine-man then tells the patient that he, the medicine-man, has been endowed with the power of Puckowe, which gives life to the body or takes away life from it, but that there is a great deal of opposition coming from other spirits which are more numerous. The spirits of his great-great-grandfathers with their families, of his grandfathers with their families, and, lastly, of his father and mother and brother and sister, are awaiting him. He says, " They are here, just beside your bed, and I can see them. They are pleading with me in the spirit language to allow you to pass over to them, and it is for me to consent to their request or to deny it."

After this the medicine-man will place the two feathers before his eyes and look through them into the body of the patient, and with a few passes of the hand across the body will pull and tug, and produce a broken stick, which he had kept concealed, and will say, " I take a part of it ; your departed loved spirits have prevented me from taking the whole from your body, so nothing more can be done for you. They are determined that I shall not heal you."

The medicine-man sits silently watching the patient. He begins to cry softly, the tears flowing down his cheeks, and then he bids the patient good-bye. After his departure the relatives and friends congregate at the sick man's wurley, and the latter tells them that the medicine-man is unable to cure him, and that he must submit to the wishes of his loved ones, who are standing beside him ready to welcome him to the Spirit World. So he turns his face toward the west, that mysterious land, and allows his spirit to take its flight, and join that constantly happy company. After this the relatives and friends sit round and have great feasting. Thus the soul passes away through the power of suggestion.

The Wirrie and the Crystal. The *wirrie* is a charm-stick of wood or bone, and similar to the *neilyeri*, from which it differs only in the method of preparation. It is placed inside a dead human body, and is allowed to remain there until the corpse is decomposed.   It is then removed and wrapped in emu-feathers, and surrounded by kangaroo- or wallaby-skin.   Thus prepared, it is regarded as the most dangerous instrument of death.   It requires very careful handling, as a prick from the point of it is capable of causing blood-poisoning and death.   It may be, and usually is, thrust completely into the body of the victim while he is asleep.

Crystals composed of quartz are used in certain forms of ' medicine.'   The operator wears them in a bag fixed on to his upper arm with a bracelet.   Although he wears no clothing he is able to make it appear that he extracts a crystal from the body of the sick man.   He is further able to make one disappear as if it has gone into the body of the sick man.   The crystal is supposed to have certain powers of protecting the operator; it may injure or be of benefit to the person operated upon.

The Thumie.   The *thumie* is another death-dealing instrument.   It consists of a rope or string made from human hair [1] that has been taken from hundreds of people, living and dead.   It is believed that the minds of these people and their desires, loves, and hatreds are contained in the hair.

The hair is placed lengthwise in two strands, each about a quarter of an inch thick.   Each strand is twisted separately with the thumb and forefinger, and rubbed with red ochre mixed with the fat of the wombat, or opossum, or some other animal.   This retains the twist of the strand until such time as the performer places it upon his right leg.   He sits upon the ground with his legs so doubled at the knees that he is sitting almost or altogether upon his heels.   With his right hand he rubs the two strands while holding them in his left hand; in this manner he twists the strands until they form a single two-strand rope, about half an inch or less in thickness and from ten to twelve yards long.   The rope is then placed in a bag made of emu-skin turned outside in, in order that it will be lying on the feathers.   After the hair has been prepared it is allowed to

[1] In the *thumie* the downy hair of the body and the hair of the beard is not used. Only the fine hair of the head is taken.

rest for seven days, a period which is considered necessary to bring it into a fit condition to do its work effectively.

When one of the elders of a tribe is sick unto death the maker of this *thumie* asks a brother or a son of the sick one if he will take it to the sick man's bed and place it under his body, and let him lie upon it until he passes from this life into the Spirit Land. Thus his spirit will be absorbed by it. The brother or son conveys this wish to the dying man, and he gives his consent. He is watched closely. When he feels that he is departing from this world he bids farewell to his loved ones and relatives. Then the rope is wound about him, first at the hips, then round the trunk several times, and up under the arms, then loosely over the back of the neck and head. One end is placed in the dying man's hand, and the other is given to a person standing outside the wurley. Then all wait patiently until the spirit leaves the body. The rope is left for several weeks twined about the corpse, and by this time the body is putrefied or decomposed. Meantime the *thumie* has absorbed into itself the strength of the spirit of the departed. The *thumie* is considered to be sensitive to a wish or a desire on the part of the person who makes use of it, provided that it is cared for and kept warm and dry in the emu-skin bag.

The act of twining the rope round a dying person who submits to the process is symbolical. When many persons communicate to the hair rope a wish that some one shall give himself up as a victim to the ceremony that will cause death the sacrifice is willingly made without any effort to resist the demand. So it is thought that not only does the spirit assist in capturing a victim, but that in the pursuit it guides the operators through the forest of scrub, over mountain-tops, into fern-covered valleys, and across rivers, until they reach their destination. They say they walk on air, and that the spirits have made or caused the air for a foot above the earth to become solid and soft. The air is moving, and they are being carried along with it in a direct line toward their victim.

When the human hair rope is to be used the medicine-man will concentrate his mind upon it, and will speak to it as if he were addressing a human being, and will instruct it in what it is required to do. For example, a victim is chosen, say, Kartinyeri, from some tribe upon the Lower Murray. The *thumie* is taken to a sacred *boora*-ground [1] and stretched to its full length of about twelve yards. Twelve men stand away from it, each holding his spear and *waddy*, and chanting the song of hate and revenge. When the song is finished they will dance round the *thumie*, using words requesting it not to fail them in their mission. After singing and dancing thus for half a day they return to their wurleys and rest for the night, without a thought of the victim.

On the following morning about sunrise the medicine-man goes to the *boora*-ground, and makes a clear space, free from grass, sticks, and stones. He then makes a mound of the length of a man, and marks or draws as accurately as possible the figure of the victim, its feet toward the east and its head toward the west. He then returns to the camp and informs the other men that preparations have been made for another sacred dance. This is done in order that the hair may obtain even greater power as a spell. The twelve men go again to the *boora*-ground, and before performing the rites they paint their bodies with pipeclay and red ochre.

The women, young men, girls, and boys are forbidden to come near the *boora*-ground, or within sound of the chanting of the elders of the tribe who are assisting the performers. The elders sit in a circle about thirty feet in diameter, and the effigy of the victim is in the centre. A stake about five feet long is planted at or between the feet of the effigy. To this the *thumie* is tied. The rope is then laid along the body, and at the head it is tied to another stake which has been driven firmly into the earth. Then the rope is passed on to another stake, which is placed thirty feet due west beyond the head.

When everything is ready the elders, at a signal given by the medicine-man, chant in unison the death-song. " Let thy breath leave thy body. Thy day has already faded in

---

[1] The sacred ground for ceremonial rites.

the western sky." This is addressed to the effigy of the victim on the ground; but all the time they are singing they concentrate their minds upon Kartinyeri. They sing, "Die thou must, Kartinyeri," and they beat the ground with the palms of their right hands. The twelve chief performers stamp the ground with the right foot three times. The man who is standing at the head of the effigy stoops and takes hold of the *thumie* with his left hand, and walks in a crouching position toward the third, western, stake, rising gradually with the *thumie* in his hand, until he is upright when he reaches the stake. He now removes his left hand from the rope, closing his fingers as if gripping something, and then throws out the hand westward, at the same time opening his fingers as if to release something. For a few moments he stands thus facing the west, chanting three times, "Thou art going, and, with the sun, dipping into the western sky." Just as he turns to come back and take his place at the side of the eleventh man, about two or three yards from the foot of the effigy, the second man begins a similar series of actions, and after him the ten others repeat the procedure in turn. The elders meantime sit round in a circle and beat the ground with the palm of the right hand, chanting, "The sun is already nearing the end of her journey." This is repeated over and over again for two hours or more. Then after an interval of half an hour for rest the ceremony is resumed and continued until sunset.

Just as the sun is disappearing beneath the horizon the elders arise and stand, some on the right side of the effigy in a line toward the south, and the others on the left side, northward, all facing the east. The twelve men who have been performing with the *thumie* stand six in a line westward from the head of the effigy toward the sinking sun, and six in a line eastward, from the feet of the effigy, with faces toward the western sky.

While all are standing in these various positions each concentrates his mind upon Kartinyeri. The twelve men then leave the lines, and each takes a spear and stands with it in his hand with the point directed toward the effigy. Then they await an order from the medicine-man. After an incantation the medicine-man shouts, "Pierce the body!" and the twelve men thrust their spears into the mound. Then they all say, "*Shoo ho*, Kartinyeri!" and they blow out their breath toward the west. They feign sorrow, and cry with head bowed for a few minutes, and then they walk in single file toward the west, chanting, "Soon will the victim die," which is repeated all the way to the camp. They gradually turn in a curve and go to their respective wurleys. The medicine-man enters his wurley with the *thumie*, and coils the rope upon his bed, and then sits upon it. Every one is satisfied with the afternoon's proceedings.

On the evening of the seventh day the operators set out on the search for their victim. They travel during the night and rest in the daytime. It may be that in their line of travel they will pass the camping-ground of some tribe, and they will make a signal by striking the trunk of a standing or fallen dry gum-tree, or, if there should be no tree suitable, then by striking two sticks together, perhaps two *nulla-nullas*. When travelling along a river-bank, and approaching a camp, they will make a noise by throwing a stone into the water near to a wurley. When any of these sounds are heard in the evening, or during the night, or in the early hours of the morning, it is taken as a sign that a person or a party is travelling with a *thumie* and that the visitors have no fear, since they have indicated their presence and their wish to be allowed to pass by unmolested.

Sometimes a man who may be able to speak several languages stands erect in the blazing firelight in order that he may be seen. Then in a loud voice he will inquire who the travellers are, from whence they have journeyed, and to what destination their mission takes them. This inquiry may be made in the Kamilaroi tongue, and if no answer is received the questions will be repeated in the Wiradhuri tongue. Should either language be understood three knocks are given upon a gum-tree, or three stones are thrown into the river. It is a sign of acknowledgment as to the identity of the tribe, and nothing more requires to be said or asked regarding their mission, because it is the accepted sign given only by those travelling with a human hair rope. No one ever attempts to imitate this password or sign.

Sometimes a tribe will offer the travellers hospitality in the shape of food, perhaps fish, swan, kangaroo or opossum flesh, cooked or uncooked. This is taken to a spot about a hundred yards from the camp, and placed upon the ground; the travellers will sit down, and none will disturb them. After the meal is finished the fragments that remain are gathered up and committed to the fire, in order to avoid the possibility of anybody who is evilly disposed securing a piece for making *ngathungies*. This shows how careful the aborigines are in regard to their observances, even when, as in this case, the travellers are in possession of one of the most effective weapons of destruction, the *thumie*. When they prepare to leave the *nulla-nullas* are struck several times, or first one stone and then another is thrown into the river as a sign that all is well; then the party proceeds on its journey.

When they come within a night's march of their destination they set up a camp for two or three days. One, two, or three scouts, or more, are chosen to spy out the country; to obtain, without being seen, as much information as possible. On the third or fourth night the scouts leave their companions. They arrive, say, at the camp of the Black Swan totem tribe when the members are sitting round the open camp-fire. A scout creeps up beside some growing shrub, close enough to be within earshot of those sitting round the fire, and listens to the conversation, hoping to learn something of the whereabouts of Kartinyeri. If he should hear nothing of importance he creeps back to the bushes. Two other scouts are engaged in a like mission. Sometimes it is difficult to approach the camp, as the wurleys are on the bank of a river, with a very open or clear space at the back. In such a case a scout will wade into the river, either above or below the camp and about two hundred yards from the fire. He will then swim along the edge of the bank until he comes to within hearing distance, and then, among the reeds or rushes which grow along the bank, he will lie listening for some clue as to the whereabouts of Kartinyeri.

During the conversation of the tribe the name of Tilpulp is mentioned. This is the name of a member of the Lawarrie totem tribe. The scout is overjoyed at hearing this, as it means that now it will be possible to trace Kartinyeri by shadowing Tilpulp. So excited is he by the discovery that he ascends the bank, slips, and falls with a splash into the river. Every man of the Lawarrie tribe snatches up his *waddy*, his spear, and his shield. Some of them go upstream, and others go downstream. Each has his spear fitted into his *wommera*, ready for service to punish the intruder who dared to approach their home at night. But the scout has already disappeared. As soon as he knew he was discovered he took one deep breath, dived deeply, and swam under water until he neared the opposite bank. Then, after swimming about half a mile downstream, he landed in safety. When the pursuers failed to find him they returned to their camp, thinking perhaps they had heard only the splash of a water-rat or a Murray cod in pursuit of food.

The scout after reaching the bank is more careful than before. He hastens to his companions and tells them of his adventures of the evening, and also that he heard the name of Tilpulp mentioned, a name which belongs only to a man of the Lawarrie totem tribe.

All the men go out and try to find additional evidence. Each one wends his way stealthily through reeds and scrub and bush, scanning the ground carefully for footprints. One of the scouts finds a footprint of Tilpulp, and he follows it carefully until it leads him in the late afternoon to a great camping-ground. He hastens back to his hiding-place, and as he is the first to return he awaits patiently the arrival of the other scouts. The medicineman is the first to put in an appearance, and the scout tells him how he found the hunting-ground of the Lawarrie totem tribe by following the footprints of Tilpulp along the bank of the river. When all the others have returned from their search the first scout tells them of his success in locating the camping-ground of the Lawarrie totem. After this they partake of their evening meal.

Next day the medicine-man takes one of the party to accompany him to search for the wurley of Kartinyeri, and they take with them the human hair rope which will lead them there. When they arrive at the camping-ground they sit watching every movement of the individual men and women. They do this for several nights. When the medicine-man and his assistant are assured of the tribe's movements they select a very dark night, and enter the camp, brushing up against the Lawarrie totem men, who take no notice of them, thinking, perhaps, that they belong to their own tribe. After much searching the wurley is found, or perhaps, better still, Kartinyeri is found sitting in it, enjoying a meal. The medicine-man and his companion sit in a tree and watch every movement of Kartinyeri. This spying upon, or shadowing of, the victim continues, day and night, for a week. In order to keep an eye upon Kartinyeri during the day each one of the party does his turn in observing him. To do this they have to become acquainted with his daily going to and from the various hunting- and fishing-grounds. Some of the spies climb into trees which have thick foliage, or in which creepers are entwined. There they will spend whole nights watching the movements of the victim, and while they are thus hidden they will utter the death word, " *Shoo ho!* " toward Kartinyeri, silently and softly, so that he will not hear.

When they feel safe, and are confident that they will be able to work the *thumie*, and that it has become acquainted with Kartinyeri, they go about their work unmolested. On the evening before making the attack upon the victim they hold a consultation among themselves and the spirits embodied in the human hair, speaking to these as if they were gifted with human intelligence. The spirits in the hair rope give them an answer that Kartinyeri is already under the spell of the magic rope. After receiving this information the medicine-man goes to a shrub growing close to Kartin-yeri's wurley, and stays there till late in the evening. At about three or four o'clock in the morning all the others arrive separately, one after another, until the whole twelve are assembled. Then the medicine-man unrolls the hair rope, and places it upon a *nulla-nulla*, and the person holding the *nulla-nulla* winds the hair several times round it, and then creeps along toward the victim in the wurley, who, of course, is sound asleep. They wind the hair rope round his arms and neck in such a manner that they themselves shall not be exposed to the danger of allowing the sleeper to hold the rope with his hand.

The hair rope is placed once round the weapon of one of the operators, and then it is put once round the body, or arm, or neck of the victim. Those holding the rope are unanimous in their thought-suggestion. Kartinyeri arises from his bed as if awake, and comes toward the men who are sitting upon the ground. He walks forward of his own accord, and lays himself upon their knees, with his face turned toward the sky, as if about to rest upon his bed. He remains in this position, and the medicine-man comes forward, holding in his hand a flint knife made expressly for an occasion like this. He draws the skin of the victim from the hip toward the small rib. He makes a small hole in the body, and thrusts his little finger through it, and scoops out a small portion of the kidney-fat. Then the skin is allowed to return to its original position. The wound is pressed with smooth pieces of wood made for the purpose of keeping the edges together.

The victim is then removed from the men's knees and placed upon the ground, with his head lying toward the west, and his feet eastward. He lies so until Puckowe, the Grandmother Spirit, comes to the rescue, and puts life and sense into the apparently dead body. Then he rises to his feet, and faces east, turns to the north and yawns, turns again to the east and right round to the south and yawns. Finally he turns west, and, stretching his arms north and south, gives a long yawn. By this time he has regained

198

consciousness, and he goes into his wurley and lies down to sleep. Then Puckowe comes and heals the wound so that no one might be able to see the cut, and she takes from the man all consciousness of what has happened a few hours before.

Puckowe also goes to the place where the ceremony was performed and removes all signs of the enemy and blood, and makes the grass or broken twigs appear undisturbed. Then she returns to her home in the dark spot in the Milky Way. The medicine-man and the other men return to their homes, happy that they have secured their revenge and have taken a life for a life. When they return from their mission they go to the *boora*-ground and invite all the elders to come and see the fat taken from the kidney of Kartinyeri. When they are all seated one of the elders comes forward and unwraps a piece of bark of a gum-tree, taken from a tender bough, which has been treated by being dried in hot ashes and soaked in emu-fat to give it a polish. He gives this to the medicine-man with a request that it shall be the coffin of Kartinyeri.

In the meantime, the poor victim is uneasy. He knows that there is a pain somewhere in his body, but he is unable to say exactly where it is. He complains to his wife. Like a good and devoted wife she goes out among the shrubs and procures herbs which are used for medicine, and cooks these in the earth by steaming, and sets them before her husband, and pleads with him to eat, saying, " Eat and thou shalt be well, because I have sought the best food for thee." Owing to his bodily suffering the patient refuses to eat, but tries to recall something which has happened to him. Sometimes it seems that it happened a year ago, then it seems but a week ago, but his mind is unable to fix the exact time. He asks his wife to think for him. He says, " My wife, help-mate, and child-giver ! Can you call to mind any incident which may lead you to suspect that some one is pointing a bone at me, or whether some one may have a *ngathungi* ? " At this his wife becomes somewhat concerned. She hastens away to her elder brother, and asks him to come quickly, saying that Kartinyeri is talking strangely. He goes at once to visit his *ronggi*, Kartinyeri. He understands the message, and knows full well that his relative has been hypnotized by some of his enemies with the aid of a *thumie*, and that a portion of his kidney-fat has been extracted. He thereupon vows that some one or more of the offending party shall give life in return in exactly the same manner.

The medicine-man of the tribe is summoned to come and see who the people are, and where they are to be found, that did this injury which is causing the illness of their brother. The medicine-man is unsuccessful, so they send for a *munkumbole* who is living with another tribe a day's journey away. A smoke-signal is sent up, and a message is transmitted to the *munkumbole* to come at once because some one is dying, and his help is required to discover who committed the deed. The *munkumbole* comes with all haste, travelling all night and all the next day, and arrives at night at the wurley of the sick man. From his observations he is able to tell them that a Kamilaroi man did the act, that there were eleven men, and that they had the aid of a medicine-man. He tells them every detail of the days spent in making the acquaintance of the tribe and Kartinyeri, and also the doings on the night on which the operation was performed, and the distance from the wurley, and that he can point out the bushes in which the men hid themselves while they were spying. In order to satisfy them he tells them that he can see as in a vision all that has taken place. He tells them what their brother can see, but is not able to tell them. He removes the covering from the body of Kartinyeri, and shows them a scratch on his loin marking the place from which the kidney-fat had been removed. That night Kartinyeri dies, and his spirit returns to the west, to the home of all spirits.

The Lawarrie tribe now held a meeting, and decide to take the life of a Kamilaroi man. They go through a series of performances similar to that just described, and so the warfare goes on continually between the tribes.

Another form of revenge is to bruise the body on the

back in the kidney region, and also on the chest. The victim is first struck unconscious by a blow at the base of the skull with a *nulla-nulla*. Then the bruising is done by taking a weapon with a large head, a *waddy*, and by using the thin end of it as a handle. The body is struck gently, with just sufficient force to cause a little gathering of blood. Before the victim regains consciousness the performer, or enemy, has disappeared.

The Munkumbole. A *munkumbole* is regarded as a superior person. His profession is supposed to have an extensive, if not unlimited, range. He is well versed in all the arts of the medicine-man, and in the science of the weather and the conditions of climate. He knows, by his keenness of observation of animal, bird, reptile, and insect life, the effect of a temporary change, as well as of the changes of the seasons. He is an astronomer, geographer, and zoologist. He understands living beings and their anatomy, gives names to the various bones, muscles, ligaments, and other organs of the animals, birds, reptiles, fishes, and insects, and classifies them in their orders. He is a man who is naturally gifted as well as specially trained in arts that would be included in the scope of spiritualism, clairvoyance, or telepathy. He claims that he is able to cast his vision to distant places, and to observe what is happening there. He also possesses the power of looking backward and reviewing past events.

Although he excels the rain-maker and the medicine-man in their respective professions, he does not employ his knowledge in order to do anyone an injury. His one object is to do good to his fellow-men, either by giving advice or by relieving the sufferings of those pained in body or troubled in mind. He takes no part in tribal warfare. Even when his own tribe is at war he remains neutral. The only thing he would do would be to warn his tribe of an invading army, tell them its strength in numbers, estimate the time of attack, and advise the chief to be on his guard against the invasion. Sometimes the *munkumbole* sleeps with the chief on the night before the attack, and the chief gives to him his *wakkalde*.[1] The *munkumbole* takes this *wakkalde* and places it so that it becomes a pillow on which he rests his head.   He goes to sleep, and in a vision he sees the battle raging.   First he sees his tribe being driven back ; it rallies and withstands the oncoming enemy ; then the tables are turned and he sees the enemy being completely driven back.   After this he awakes.   Sitting by the fireside he sings a song to the spirit of battle, and pleads that his chief may be protected against the spear, the *waddy*, and the boomerang of the enemy.   He tells the chief that in his vision he saw that he, the chief, was the one who, because of his knowledge and agility as a warrior, had thrown the fatal spear.

Just before sunrise the *munkumbole* awakens a man whose duty it is to give the call to rise and eat.   This ' herald ' gives another call for the warriors to prepare the weapons of war, and he sees that all have their allotted number of spears ready to hand, and also that the attendants that carry the *waddies* and the boomerangs have a goodly supply of these weapons.   Everything is now in readiness, and every warrior sits with three or four sharp spears, about five feet long and a quarter of an inch thick, made out of a reed, with a wooden point.   The herald issues instructions that each warrior shall leave the camp, and go and sit away from the rest of the tribe, so that the women and children may be kept at a safe distance from the danger zone.   The instructions are given by the herald in the presence of the *munkumbole*, who retires, and takes no part in the fight.

The *munkumbole* has something higher to live for than to help his tribe to gain victory in battle, and that is to make each tribe live in harmony with its neighbours.   He is therefore present at the full moon assembly, which is a meeting preliminary to great gatherings ; and here it is that advice is given by the representative *munkumbole* of two or more tribes.

The Ngathungi.   The aboriginals believe that the fragments that are left over of the food that we touch when

---

[1] A shield.

eating retain our image, our thoughts, and our feelings. They also believe that a similar property exists in anything that belongs to us, such as the hair of the head and body, the nails of the fingers and toes, wax from the ear, and mucus from the nose and throat. This belief is very strong; hence, after meals, all remains of bone, flesh, feathers, and hair of animals, birds, and reptiles, and all fragments belonging to the human body, are carefully collected and buried.

These waste matters, if not destroyed, may be used for the purpose of inflicting some deadly injury in the following manner. Fragments of flesh and pieces of bone which remain over from some one's meal are bound to a stick, about four inches long and a quarter of an inch thick, which tapers gradually from one end to a sharp point. At the blunt end the flesh and bone are bound round with kangaroo sinews, and covered by the gum of the pine-tree. This instrument, which is known as a *ngathungi*, is then put away in a cool place. In most cases it is conveyed to some secluded spot and buried in the earth, from a foot to eighteen inches below the surface, although sometimes it is placed in the hollow of a rock or a tree until it is required for the purpose of bringing evil upon an enemy.

The *ngathungi* is regarded as a very deadly instrument. When any person has failed to accomplish his object by the use of the pointing-stick, the bone, or the crystal, he resorts to the *ngathungi*. It is possible for one to avoid injury from these others, but not so, to the same extent, when the *ngathungi* is employed.

The members of a tribe are taught to collect such articles as have been mentioned, and to barter them. For instance, a Dingo totem man has in his possession the brain of a black duck remaining over from a meal enjoyed by him and a Kangaroo-rat totem man. It happened that the Kangaroo-rat man was eating the back and neck and head of the black duck, and in a moment of forgetfulness hastened away to his camp for a stone knife or an axe, leaving the head behind. When he returned the head had disappeared. He inquired

203

of the Dingo totem man what had become of the black duck's head. The Dingo man said he did not know, as he had left a moment after the Kangaroo-rat man to see whether his camp was all right; perhaps when they were both absent, he said, a native wild cat or a crow had taken the head. The two then commence to rake up the refuse of their meal, and to commit it to the fire. The Kangaroo-rat man watches his opportunity, and by a little strategy procures a portion of the head or eye of a Murray cod left over from the Dingo man's dinner. The Dingo man is aware that the Kangaroo-rat man has this in his possession. Every family of a tribe has some one else's *ngathungi* in its keeping.

The person who operates with the *ngathungi* must be an expert. He must possess the power of concentration and of communicating without physical means or agency; he must also be a person with a good many years of training. In performing, the operator takes a *ngathungi* from a large collection which is kept in store.

Let us suppose that a man of the Pelican totem tribe feels that he has a grievance against Yong Keeng, a man of the Black Swan totem tribe, who some years previously had caused the death of a man of his tribe. He selects a *ngathungi* belonging to Yong Keeng and goes out of his wurley, looks round to see that no one is about, and returns to his fireside. He takes the *ngathungi* in his left hand, and utters a word or two very softly so that no one in the wurley is able to hear him. He says, " *Shooh ho !* Let the breath leave thy body, O boy ! " Then he begins to chant a song of hate, and after singing this for an hour or more he warms the gummed part of the stick, to which a portion of the brain of a black duck is attached.

With his eyes closed he concentrates his mind upon Yong Keeng until he is able to see a mental picture of him. Then, with all the hatred that he can command, he whispers, " Die ! " He then lies down on his bed as if intending to sleep, and remains in this position for an hour. Then he rises and sits up and takes the *ngathungi*, and concentrates his mind upon his victim until he obtains another mental vision. Then he whispers the death words, " Let the life-breath leave thy body, O boy! Die!" He goes through this performance about five times. Then he takes the *ngathungi* and places it in the opening left in the centre of the wurley which answers the purpose of a chimney.

He then lies on his back as if asleep, but his mind is concentrated upon his victim. He sees him plainly in his mind's eye, and says, " *Shoo ho !* I wish that the breath may leave thy body." He continues to do this all through the night, until the early hours of the morning.

Then he silently steals away from his camp, making his way toward his victim's wurley. Seating himself under a shrub about ten yards away, he begins to concentrate his thoughts upon Yong Keeng. He carries a bag which con-tains his *waddy*, his *kanake*,[1] and a bunch of emu-feathers which has been placed under the arms of the decomposed body of a human being. He takes the *ngathungi* in his right hand, and, extending the arm, he waves his hand forward and backward, whispering, " Go to sleep soundly, and feel nothing." The victim usually does so, but if he should not the performer will continue for about two hours, and then he stealthily creeps toward the door of the wurley. He peeps in to see whether there is any firelight, and finds there is none. He is on his hands and knees in a position for flight if Yong Keeng is not soundly asleep, and he watches intently and waits patiently. Perhaps the victim is feigning sleep, and waiting with a *kanake* to strike him should he come too near. But on this occasion the victim is very much asleep, as is discovered by his snoring or deep breathing, and, satisfied of this, the operator creeps forward and places the emu-feathers near the head, and gently rubs them about the face, so that the odour may cling to it. When Yong Keeng awakes in the morning he complains of an odious smell, which he ascribes to a *ngathungi*. He summons his relatives and tells them that he is unable to get rid of the smell in spite of washing with mud or pipeclay and water.

[1] A fighting club.

Something must be done. The relatives make inquiries as to the person or persons in possession of a *ngathungi* belonging to Yong Keeng. They go from camp to camp, until they come to the camp of the Pelican men, who do not directly admit that anyone is possessed of a *ngathungi*, but say that it would be a wise thing if a general inquiry were made, and that they would be willing to discuss the matter on condition that Yong Keeng's relatives would send out an invitation to all the surrounding tribes within a radius of one hundred miles to attend and bring their collections of *ngathungies* to a court that should be held at Wangarrawa at the time of the appearing of the next full moon. In due time all the tribes arrive and build their wurleys. On the day of the full moon the various chiefs come together and discuss the matter in a formal way. Each gives an undertaking that he will do his utmost to cause the members of his tribe to bring and show any *ngathungies* they may possess, so that they may barter one with another.

The night of the full moon is looked upon as an important one. All the members of the tribes gather together, with the *munkumbole* sitting in the centre. The *munkumbole* appears to be thinking deeply. By and by he begins to recite that on a certain night a Pelican totem man approached the wurley of a Black Swan totem man, seeking an opportunity to use the *ngathungi*. The *munkumbole* gives such a realistic description of the actions of the two men on that memorable night that the guilty man is forced to make a confession. Perhaps the uncle of the Black Swan man will challenge him, or perhaps the Black Swan tribe may decide to choose one of their expert fighters to deal with him. It is decided that the two men shall fight with the *kanake*. They go away from the camp, and the men of the tribes follow. The two men who are going to fight stand in the centre of an open space, and the men of the tribes stand about them in order to see that everything is carried out in the correct fashion. The opponents stand opposite each other. They raise their *kanakes* to about the level of the forehead in a horizontal position. The object of each is to strike the other upon the head and draw blood rather than make him unconscious. The first man to draw blood is accounted the victor. Meantime, the *munkumbole* attends to the man of the Black Swan totem tribe who has been charmed by the *ngathungi* of the Pelican totem tribe man, and by the aid of suggestion he makes him well again.

On the morning following the night of the full moon the oldest men of the different tribes will meet, bringing with them their collections of *ngathungies*. The audience sits in a large circle, and all the *ngathungies* are placed in an open space within the circle. A *munkumbole* comes forward and places each of these charmed sticks on the ground, so that every one may see if any of them should have attached to it anything belonging to him or anything that he may have touched or handled.

Supposing a Water-rat totem man should suspect or have a feeling that a *ngathungi* belonging to his elder or younger son is among the exhibits, he would ask the *munkumbole* to find out, and, if his suspicion should be justified, to procure it by barter in return for one belonging to a relative of the person who has possession of it. The first lot of charm-sticks to be examined belongs, we will say, to the Crow totem tribe. The *munkumbole* comes forward and sits within the circle beside the *ngathungies*. Taking each stick separately in his right hand, he speaks to it as if he were addressing a human being, and says, " Do you belong to the Water-rat tribe? " If a certain answer, which is known only to him, is not made he replaces the stick beside the others, and takes up another, and asks it if it belongs to the Water-rat tribe. He goes through the whole number, and if he should not receive any answer at all he is satisfied, and retires from the meeting.

Now a Black Swan totem man from the outside of the circle calls to the *munkumbole* that one of his tribe is sick and that it is suspected that there is in the collection a *ngathungi* belonging to this man. The *munkumbole* takes up a charmed stick and inquires. This time he receives an answer from the unknown. With the stick in his hand he turns to a Pelican man and asks whether the spirits have given a correct answer, to which the Pelican man replies, " Yes." Then the *munkumbole* will say, " Why did you do such an act ? " and he will reply, " I did it because one of the members of the tribe to which I belong is very sick, and thinks that the Swan totem man has his *ngathungi*. If the people of the tribe are willing to give it to me I will give them theirs."

Then an exchange is made of the *ngathungies*. Both men go to the river and dip the stick into the water, and allow it to remain floating for a while, say, about half an hour. A messenger is then dispatched to the Black Swan totem tribe to inform the sick man that his *ngathungi* has been got from the Pelican man, and has already been dipped in water to take away the spell which was imposed by the enemy. An encouraging message is also sent by the *munkumbole* to the sick man that he need no longer fear the deathful effect of the *ngathungi*, because Puckowe the spirit, who has the power to return the spirit of a departed one back into the body, will ever be ready to prevent his death until it is the will of the departed spirits that he shall join them. This message, naturally, has a magical effect upon the patient. He rises from his bed, and sits beside the fire, and asks to be served with food.

Now the *munkumbole* will spend a week selecting the *ngathungies* of individuals, and advising the parties to barter or exchange the one with the other. Each of the tribes is satisfied with the decision of the *munkumbole*, and they will collect their various belongings and silently steal away to their own country or their hunting-grounds.

CHAPTER IV : SOCIAL

Marriage Customs

WHEN a youth or maiden arrives at an age of between sixteen and eighteen years, which is considered the marriageable age, the uncle who is brother to the mother of the young person concerned will summon a meeting of the members of the family to discuss the all-important subject of matrimony at his home on a night specified. Before the meeting takes place the mother of the young man (or of the maiden) will seek a private interview with her brother, and she will express a wish that her child should be married to a member of some particular tribe, which she names. The brother will take a spear in his right hand as a sign to his sister that he will carry out her wish at the cost of his life. The mother departs to her home, awaiting the appointed night of the meeting.

The family gathering is representative, and each relative will speak of certain tribes or families with whom it might be desirable to form a marriage connexion. Usually the father and mother take no part in the exchange of views, but sit silently and listen. The important person in the assembly is the uncle. He sits patiently until every one of the family has had a say, then all eyes are turned to him, awaiting some sign of his approval or disapproval. He rises quietly, and takes his spear and *wommera*. He places the spear in position, and stands ready to throw it with lightning speed into the body of anyone who objects to his decision, which he proceeds to announce.

In the early hours of the morning the uncle, accompanied by the *brigge*,[1] sets out. At midday they arrive at the home of a strange tribe. The *brigge* explains their mission to the chief of the tribe, who asks them to rest a while and to be good enough to accept their hospitality. They sit down, and the *brigge* tells them any important or interesting news. By and by the two visitors continue their journey toward the tribe that the uncle selected as his choice.

[1] A messenger.

A day before their destination is reached the uncle and the *brigge* make a fire and place a green bough of the mallee or other tree on it, and a dark smoke ascends into the clear sky, followed by a white smoke column. The surrounding tribes understand from this that some one is in search of a wife or a husband. They wonder if he will call on them, so each family is on the look-out.

The uncle and the *brigge* arrive at their destination as nearly as possible at the time indicated by the smoke-signal on the previous day. Now this tribe feels greatly honoured by a visit of this nature. All the members of it are full of eagerness to gain the goodwill of the uncle and to help him in his search. One family brings along a swan baked in an earth oven with various herbs. Another brings fish rolled in clay, preferably pipeclay, placed in hot ashes. Others will bring a choice portion of the flesh of the kangaroo, wombat, or emu, and others bring mussels or cockles. Each is seeking to be favoured by being asked for a wife or a husband from his family.

Now the uncle spends a week with this tribe, visiting each individual family, studying the dispositions of the youths and maidens, and looking for one whom he would select. When he thinks he has found one suitable he approaches the uncle of the chosen one, giving him an invitation to visit him and to enjoy his hospitality, and to make the acquaintance of the members of his tribe. This invitation is accepted by the other uncle, who says he is gratified by the honour offered to him and to his tribe. So the first uncle returns home to tell his tribe of his successful mission, and advises them to be prepared for the visit of the second uncle, who will arrive a week later. The second uncle visits the first uncle, who introduces him to his brother-in-law and sister. He stays with them for a week, and then the two uncles fix the date and place of the marriage.

Here is another way in which the young people are joined together as man and wife. Away in the south-east of South Australia, on the Coorong, there is the Pumbala tribe, whose totem is the seagull. In the Lower Murray region there lives a tribe known as the Lathinyeri, whose totem is the black swan. There is a boy in this tribe who is just entering on the course of training to become a man, and is being educated in the law and traditions of his tribe, and at this particular time a girl is born in the tribe whose totem is the seagull. Some time after, at one of the great gatherings of the tribes, the tribe of the Seagull totem makes the acquaintance of the tribe of the Black Swan totem. The uncle of the girl allows his mind to pass in review the members of the tribes met together, and he carefully scans all the boys and youths whom he sees. Presently one boy stands out conspicuously among the others. It is the Black Swan totem boy. He calls his sister and her husband, and they discuss the matter together. He tells them of this boy, and expresses his intention that the girl should be pledged to become the wife of the Black Swan boy. The mother and the father of the infant girl are pleased with the selection. Then the uncle of the infant girl of the Seagull tribe sends a *brigge* to the Lathinyeri tribe to inform

FOREHEAD ORNAMENT
OF KANGAROO TEETH
AND GUM
British Museum

them that they are pleased to offer the infant girl, who is now twelve moons old, as a wife to the Black Swan boy. They ask if they will kindly accept the offer and send a reply. The father and mother of the boy receive the message, and the mother sends in haste for her elder brother, a Dingo totem tribe man. He comes to his sister, and she tells him of the offer. The brother is very pleased, and advises his sister to accept it.

When the girl is seven or eight years of age her mother will make it her business to relate stories of this wonderful young man. She will say that he is a great hunter, a fierce warrior, or will tell of incidents that will arouse interest and admiration, so that the girl, from her earliest youth, is looking forward to catching a glimpse of her hero. When she has undergone the training in the arts of overcoming fear and enduring pain without questioning she becomes more eager, and she approaches her father or mother with the question, "When shall I see this young man?" The mother sends for her elder brother, and he comes and whispers to her that at the next gathering for sport and story-telling, which will take place two moons hence, she will have the privilege of seeing him. By this time the two uncles have fixed a date and place for the marriage to take place.

Now the marriage does not necessarily take place at the hunting-ground of the tribe of the bridegroom or bride. Sometimes it is celebrated at the place of her grandmother on the mother's side, or at the place of some friendly tribe at a distance. The members of the two tribes meet at an appointed place, and they camp at a distance of about half a mile from one another. All aboriginal marriages are celebrated at midnight, usually when there is a full moon. Just before sunset the younger members of the families of the bridegroom and bride will bring bundles of sticks to the camp of the person who is appointed to announce the ceremony between these two parties. They make a huge fire, so that the surrounding camps can see where the man is stationed, and as midnight approaches his voice is heard chanting in the clear and still night, "The bridegroom comes to join the marriage-parties." Then the procession starts. Each member of the families that represent both tribes carries a fire-stick, and from each starting-point they move in a line to form the letter V, and as they join up they place their fire-sticks together. The respective uncles of the bride and bridegroom address them thus : "Children, the fire is symbolical of the severity of the law. Neither of you must abuse or make light of this privilege of becoming a husband or a wife, a father or a mother. It is the will of the Great Spirit that you shall honour and respect the bond of marriage. As fire consumes, so will the law of your fathers destroy all who dishonour the marriage-bond."

Another form of marriage is that of a widow remarrying. In the case of a husband's death the widow goes into mourning for twelve months. Every morning and evening she

A GRAVE WITH WIDOWS' MOURNING CAPS OF CLAY

By permission

DANCING INTO A FRIENDLY CAMP

The visitors are about to enter the camp, where their hosts await them.

From "The Arunta," by Sir Baldwin Spencer and F. J. Gillen, by permission of Messrs Macmillan & Co., Ltd.

224

wails in a loud tone, " Why did you leave me, O husband of mine?" On the first day of her wailing she beats her head with a *nulla-nulla*, and cuts her arm with a flint knife, and causes the blood to flow from her head and arms. Then she takes ashes from an old, disused fireplace, and with them she covers her head and smears her body. After a month of mourning in this fashion she takes pipeclay and makes a cap with it, which she places upon her head. She wears this for twelve months or more, removing it at night when she retires to bed. After completing the twelve months of mourning she lays aside the clay cap, and washes the pipeclay from her face and breast. She leaves her parents' home and seeks the protection and hospitality of her late husband's brothers. There may be four brothers in the family, and they all minister to her wants. Then she stays with her mother-in-law for three months. She says to her, " Mother of my husband and my mother, I want to be your daughter-in-law until I die, and meet my husband in the happy hunting-ground. To which of your sons shall I become a wife?" The mother-in-law will say, " My daughter, I would very much like that you should become the wife of the eldest of the four. But, my child, choose for yourself, and it shall please me and the whole tribe." The widow makes her choice. She tells her mother-in-law that she would like to marry the young man next to the eldest. At night, when every one is preparing to go to bed, the widow enters the home of this young man. He is lying in bed, and she goes and lies down crosswise at his feet. This she does night after night for about a fortnight. Her action signifies that she is willing to become his wife, and he accepts her as such. This procedure in the case of a widow is the only instance in which a woman is allowed any choice as to who is to be her husband.

When a wife dies the husband goes into mourning. He takes his children to his late wife's mother and sister, and leaves them for a while, say, for twelve months. Then he travels, and when he returns one of the wife's sisters volunteers to become his wife. So she takes the children and makes a bed for herself and them at the foot of the bed of her brother-in-law. This is a sign that she is desirous to be a mother to her sister's children, and if the man accepts her offer they become husband and wife.

The Spirit of Help among the Aboriginals [1]

The Chase. "Arise!" This is a call of daylight. Each young man goes forth. Some have a *wunde*,[2] and others have a *kaike*. The one with the *wunde* makes his way into the bush stealthily, in a crouching attitude. He passes from shrub to shrub, and watches keenly for any passing object. A *swish*! Then like a bolt shot from the sky the spear is sent on its errand, and finds its mark; the wallaby lies dying, with the warm blood trickling from a deadly wound. The hunter goes on so until he has secured three or four wallabies. He then returns to the camp. Others, who have been fishing, return with their catch of Murray cod, Murray bream, cat-fish, and turtles. Others, again, return laden with other sorts of game. Then the elder of the tribe comes, and the spoil is distributed to the various members of the tribe. After every one else is supplied the hunters receive their portions, which may consist of the head of a kangaroo, the head of a cod, or the head and neck of a swan, or suchlike. The hunters receive these trifles without a murmur, satisfied that they are fulfilling the will of the Great Spirit, the source of good deeds, by supplying food for those who are unable to obtain it for themselves.

---

[1] The aboriginals have traditional sayings and customs that have come down from generation to generation for thousands of years. Some of these stand out more prominently than others—*e.g.*, "Do unto others as you would that they should do unto you." The practice of this principle is carried out among the aboriginals. It is the foundation of their social and religious life. On this their educational system is built. There are various degrees in this education, as we have seen. First, the mind is trained to control pain through concentration and to master appetite, human desires, and fear. When the girls and boys have passed through these initial stages of education they are declared to be women and men, and they are then expected to take upon themselves the responsibilities of womanhood and manhood. They must think of their duty to their tribe, to other tribes, and to the whole of the race to which they belong. They fulfil this rule, not by preaching, nor by writing on rock or tree, but by deeds.

[2] A long, heavy black spear.

Duty to the Old. The wives of the young men take upon themselves the responsibility of making the old, the infirm, and the widows and orphans happy and comfortable. They supply them with yams and herbs.[1] The young men and their wives carry on this good work until they themselves become old and infirm; then those who, in the meantime, have been growing up assume the responsibility. This goes on for generation after generation, each individual living for the others, and the strong caring for the weak.

No tribe or individual will ever attempt to possess more than another. Perhaps the hunting-ground of one tribe may be a lagoon, and the food may thus consist chiefly of fish and wild fowl. A neighbouring tribe's ground may be the bush, and their food would consist of grubs, herbs, honey, and the flesh of animals. In such a case these two tribes would barter freely.

Trespassing. No person of one tribe would trespass upon the hunting-ground of another. To do so would mean death, since it is a capital offence to take food from another tribe's hunting-ground. There are occasions when one tribe will ask another, or be invited by another, to spend two or three months with them and partake of their hospitality, and when the tribe returns home it will invite the other to return the visit. Thus there always exists a spirit of friendship. There are, however, many instances where the chief of a tribe becomes dissatisfied with his hunting-ground, and becomes a danger to surrounding tribes. In such a case these tribes will combine to drive the offender out of the country, and the tribe of the defeated chief gradually becomes absorbed into other tribes, and ceases to exist as an individual tribe.

Ngia Ngiampe

Probably all races or nations practise certain ceremonies or rites that have a symbolic meaning and a strong influence

[1] *Food.*—All animal food is eaten in the early hours of the morning and late in the evening. Vegetables are eaten at intervals from an hour before midday to four o'clock in the afternoon.

on the creed, morality, or religion of the people. In their oral traditions or in their national records the origin of some such national or tribal ceremony is not infrequently ascribed to one individual. One needs only to mention Jews and Christians as illustrations. Even in modern times new laws are stated to have been promulgated by real or mythical authorities of long antecedent times in order to give them their necessary validity.

Among the Narrinyeri tribe of South Australia there is a custom called *ngia ngiampe*. According to this custom certain families are *ngia ngiampe* to certain other families. These families are forbidden in ordinary circumstances to have intercourse of any kind whatsoever with one another. But, although the families must not speak to each other, it is required of them to give help if either should be in distress or in want. One of the reasons given for not allowing them to speak to one another is the possibility that by some act or word one might hurt another. It is said that this prohibition was introduced by Nurunderi. There are certain ceremonies connected with it.

When a child is born a portion of its umbilical cord is taken, and is treated in a way that preserves it permanently. After this treatment it is placed within a roll of emu-feathers, and fibre from the bark of the mallee-tree is wound round it. It is now called a *kalduke*, and it is exchanged between the two families as a symbol that they are *ngia ngiampe* to each other. Only a certain woman of the tribe is privileged to be the giver of this piece of cord. She must be the daughter of a mother who also had been similarly chosen. These mothers must be in a direct line of noble womanhood, and must be of pure character. She gives the cord to a medicine-man of the tribe. He retains possession of it until he sees fit to present it to another tribe. If a break should occur in the line of descent of these women, then the woman who is the next of kin on the mother's side is appointed to this great and important office. This position is very greatly coveted among the women, and every girl, when she is educated to become a woman, strives to be accounted worthy to occupy it.

This cord has a double significance. On the one hand, it relates to that part of the woman wherein dwell all the feelings of piety, reverence, and sympathy—the elements

LARGE BASKET FOR CARRYING A CHILD
From Northern Queensland.
From *Among Cannibals*, by Carl Lumholtz (Murray).

of perfect womanhood. On the other hand, there is signified an inheritance of innocence and purity, which is capable of great development in the child. Beyond this, the cord is symbolical of a bond connecting the qualities of the mother and the child. And as mother and child are linked to each other before birth by this physical bond, so should the *kalduke* be emblematic of true love, true fellowship, true

217

pity; and as such it acts as a reverential bond. And it has come to be so regarded as a bond capable of binding any two tribes in good fellowship and brotherhood. Distance is no barrier to its efficacy. When it is conveyed to, and proffered to, and accepted by a tribe it is recognized and honoured, and the two tribes thereafter respect the responsibilities thus entailed. When a man is sent on a long mission he takes the *kalduke* with him as a symbol or token of friendship.

In respect to the method in which it is employed, suppose, for example, that the Ponde totem tribe and the Pomeri totem tribe are continually at war, the one with the other. Another tribe, the Tukkeri, steps in, not to take any part in the conflict, or with any wish to decide which tribe has right or wrong on its side, but because it is peaceful in its nature and is desirous of ending the dispute in a way that will be satisfactory and advantageous to both disputants. The Tukkeri totem tribe will perhaps say to the Ponde totem tribe, " Why do you continue fighting the Pomeri tribe? Do you not think it would be better to become friendly? " The Ponde tribe may reply, " We will not cease the conflict until our tribe shall conquer and entirely destroy the Pomeri tribe." Then a Tukkeri tribe man goes to the Pomeri totem tribe and pleads with them, but they too may be determined to continue the enmity. So the Tukkeri tribe man goes home and sends a message to the elders of two or more tribes who are of a peaceful nature. They hold a conference, and decide that some one shall go to either tribe, the Ponde or the Pomeri, in order to take steps to bring about peace. One of the elders of the Tukkeri tribe consents to go and stay with the Ponde tribe for some time. During his stay the wife of one of the Ponde totem tribe has a child. The Tukkeri man procures part of the cord, and, after being prepared in the usual fashion, it is sent through a *brigge* to the Pomeri totem tribe. If they accept the *kalduke* these two tribes that were previously at enmity now become staunch allies. They are now *ngia ngiampe* the one to the other.

218

Hunting

In the theory and practice of bushcraft and hunting the aboriginals are experts. No other of the primitive races excels them in this respect. As to power of observation, it may be claimed that they stand alone, having no equal. This is because they are trained from early childhood to make a careful and thorough study of forest, scrub, and plain, with their vegetation, as well as of river, lake, lagoon, and *billabong*. These are the haunts of animal, bird, reptile, insect, and fish life. The aboriginals have studied the effects of environment on animal life, and they know how the various forms of living organisms are adapted to and protected by the conditions in which they live.

In a hunting expedition an experienced hunter would not begin in a haphazard fashion, but would study the nature and habits of the animal he is hunting and seek it in its natural surroundings. If, for instance, he were hunting for a pheasant he would not search a plain country where there might be a few scattered shrubs, or choose a river-bank devoid of bushes. Nor would he venture to hunt teal, or black duck, or swan at a running stream near its source, where it tumbles down in a cascade or forces its way between steep, rocky margins ; or where the stream flows in the deep valley, where the huge gum-tree pushes itself up skyward and throws its branches across the stream, shutting out the sunlight ; or where the dense undergrowth of wild, clinging creepers and twiners hides the running stream from view. Nor would he think of watching and waiting for the approach of a thirsty kangaroo or emu at such places. These are not their haunts or their visiting spots ; but the little stream farther down the valley may be an ideal spot for Mr and Mrs Platypus to live and to rear a family. Again, the hunter would not seek the wombat in the upper reaches of rivers or in steep, rocky valleys or dense undergrowth ; nothing would entice the wombat to make a home there. Perhaps the lyre-bird would love to be in such an enchanting locality as this, but neither the eagle-hawk nor the swan would find it a fitting place to live in.

Suppose the hunter seeks the swan as food. He goes to the Murray River or some other large river alongside of which there may be low-lying land, over which the flood waters spread and form a lagoon. This is where he would expect to find the various kinds of waterfowl, black duck, teal, and swan. Some of these may be on the bank, basking in the sunshine, while others may be washing themselves by dipping into the water and ruffling their feathers and flapping their wings, and still others may be thrusting their heads under the water in search of weeds and gravel.

The hunter, hidden in the bush at about thirty to fifty yards' distance, allows his eye to take in every detail of ducks, swans, and other waterfowl. Presently he sees something that he is looking for. Away yonder his well-trained eye catches sight of a plover on duty as a sentinel. The plover is taking note of every moving object to see whether an enemy is lying in ambush awaiting an opportunity to pounce upon a bird. But the skill of the hunter enables him to outwit the plover. After planning the attack and being satisfied regarding the position of the sentinel, he begins with the alertness of a cat to glide from bush to bush. Presently he throws himself flat on the ground, and wriggles toward the water's edge, through rushes and water-shrubs. He halts and plucks some rushes and reeds and water-flags, and while lying flat he constructs a hat by tying the ends of the rushes and reeds. He places the hat upon his head and pulls it down over his eyes, and begins to wriggle along until he is clear of the rushes and the reeds.

The plover catches sight of the object, and gives a warning cry. All the birds—swans, ducks, and waterfowl—fly into the lagoon, and alight about fifty yards from the bank. They respond instinctively to the warning note of danger sounded by the plover. The birds then look around to see where the danger is. They see nothing. But the plover on duty, reasoning that the object now floating toward the ducks and swans is something not common or usual, and therefore an enemy, rises on the wing and flies toward the floating object, circles round it several times, still giving the warning cry of danger, but finally returns to the bank and settles down, satisfied that it is only a floating rush or weed.

The hunter is now peering through the rushes and waiting for an opportunity. He sees that the ducks are among the weeds. He eagerly but cautiously approaches nearer and nearer, until he is within arm's length of a duck. Then his arm goes out beneath the water and through the weeds, and with his hand he seizes the duck by a leg and suddenly pulls it beneath the surface. He then takes it by the neck, and, with a twist and a pull, he has broken its neck. The hunter then places the head of the duck under a rush belt which he is wearing round his body, and the bird is held there securely. He goes on capturing duck after duck in this manner. Then he swims over to the bank of the river opposite to where he entered the water, so as to give the birds the impression of a floating object. After relieving himself of his burden, which he does while lying upon his stomach, he returns to the hunt, and secures a few more ducks. He will then swim with these on the side of the lagoon from which he first entered the water and will dispose of them similarly. He will repeat this until he has captured all he requires. Then he will sit still until darkness sets in ; or he may in disguise creep under cover of the shrubs and make a bee-line for home. He will tell of his great capture, and will give details as to where he left the ducks, and some of the young men will go to the lagoon and fetch them. They make no attempt to cover their movements, in order to give the birds the impression that this journeying is unconnected with what has just happened to the flock, when they did not see the hunter. This makes matters easier for the hunter when next he goes on an expedition.

Other birds of the duck species, such as the teal, are captured in other ways. In midwinter the water is very cold, and the hunter does not feel inclined to risk his life, thinking that possibly the sudden cold may give him cramp, which may result in his being drowned. So he uses a method of capture that has been practised by his ancestors.

He takes with him his *waddy*, or probably two *waddies*, a boomerang, and a spear. He holds something else, namely, the flower-top of a reed. He may have three of these tied together. He steals silently and under cover to the river-bank, and begins waving the flower-topped reeds so that the ducks can see them. They become curious and swim toward him, and when they are within striking distance, say, about ten to fifteen yards away, he stands up suddenly. This surprises the ducks and they rise into the air in confusion. The hunter hurls first his spear and then his boomerang into their midst. When the birds rise in a flock it is quite possible that the hunter's spear will strike half a dozen of them, and the force with which they have risen carries the spear along with them, so that it becomes an obstacle to the other birds and they strike it. This accounts for perhaps another half-dozen. Then when the boomerang is thrown with force it cuts through the air, making a sound similar to the cry of a hawk. The birds hesitate, not knowing whether to continue their flight or to swoop down on the water. They usually decide to settle on the water, being more afraid of the supposed hawk than of the human hunter. The boomerang has come back to the thrower. He now takes it, and throws it again, but so that it skims close along the surface of the water, and if a duck's head happens to be in the way it is cut clean off the body. This may happen to three or four ducks at the one throw.

Another method of capturing ducks is first to watch closely their habits of flying from one lagoon to another, or from a river or lake to a lagoon. The hunters have a special net constructed from rushes which grow along the river-bank. It is made after the style of the European fishing-nets, and is from thirty to fifty yards long and from ten to twelve feet wide. This net is stretched from tree to tree across the line of flight of the ducks when they are passing from one body of water to another, and it is tied sufficiently firmly to bear its own weight. The hunters now await the ducks. They allow the first flight to pass unmolested, and presently the second follows in the same course as the first.

One man stands at each side of the net. A third man stands about forty yards away, in front of the net toward which the ducks are flying. As they pass him he imitates the whistle of the falcon, loud enough for the ducks to hear. Then suddenly he hurls his boomerang with great force, and the whirr of the weapon as it cuts the air is like the sound of a falcon on the wing. The birds are deceived. Thinking it is a falcon rising to attack them they swoop down in a body right into the middle of the net, striking it and carrying it along with them, and eventually becoming entangled in its mesh. The two men who are standing one at each side of the net now rush forward and draw the net so that all the birds that are in it are secured. At times from one to two hundred ducks are caught in this manner.

This method is the most effective and advantageous, insomuch as the hunters simply wait the approach of a flight of ducks, and the birds are caught in great numbers at once

NET FOR TRAPPING WALLABIES
From *Among Cannibals*, by Carl Lumholtz (Murray).

and near to the camping-ground. Sometimes as the birds fly past a stick like a spear is thrown into the midst of them. The ducks, flying at great speed, strike the stick; some fall to the ground with broken wings or broken necks, and some with their heads smashed.

The swan may be hunted and captured in several different ways. Firstly, perhaps the hunter goes to the same lagoon in which he captured the ducks. He creeps along its margin, in the same fashion as when hunting the ducks, until he arrives at a spot upon the edge of the reeds or rushes which are growing in the water to a distance of about five or ten yards from the bank. The hunter takes his place in a bunch of reeds, and he has with him a wing of a swan, covered with feathers. The swans are feeding in the middle of the lagoon, so the hunter begins to flap the wing in the water, imitating a swan in distress. The swans hear the noise of the water being struck; they see the wing of a bird belonging to their kind, and they swim to the supposed swan in distress. The hunter stops for a while and prepares his rod. The rod has a noose at the end, and the hunter prepares this as the swans approach to investigate. They do not suspect danger, but draw nearer and nearer, until they are within reach of the rod. Then the hunter places the noose over the head of one of them, and draws it toward him until he can grasp it with his hand. This he does so quickly that the other swans do not see what has taken place. The hunter then twists the victim's neck and throws it behind him quickly and deftly. He places the noose on the neck of another swan, and deals with it in the same manner. In this way an expert will capture half a dozen swans before their companions suspect danger and swim away.

Another method by which swans are captured is this. A hunter propels his canoe with a pole in and round the lagoon until he arrives at a spot where there is a passage in the reeds or bulrushes through which the swans are accustomed to travel from one clear spot to another. The hunter makes that passage of reeds or bulrushes so narrow and low that it is just large enough to allow one swan to pass at a time. Two to four passages may be made in this fashion, all side by side. A noose is set in each passage, so that when a swan stretches its head and neck forward it is caught in it. When the bird finds that it is hindered from further progress it begins to struggle, with the result that the noose tightens on account of its being tied firmly to two poles which have been fixed in the bed of the lagoon. When the hunter returns on the following morning to examine his traps he releases the dead birds and returns home, perhaps taking the snare with him, as the birds are only trapped as they are required for food.

In hunting the kangaroo a great deal of skill and patience is needed, because there is something that almost amounts to human reasoning in some of these animals. The kangaroo always takes shelter at midday in the scrub, which may be in low mallee- or tea-tree country. It will dig an oblong hole at the root of a shrub or bush, just large enough to take in its body and legs. The forelegs and head rest on the surface of the ground outside the hole, while the body is hidden from view. In this manner kangaroos rest at midday, and it is very difficult to come near to them. Usually one or two of them act as sentinels and give warning of the approach of an enemy. It is possible that the method of resting with the head against the ground may assist the animal to hear sounds.

Kangaroos are like human beings in that they choose to live in one locality, and to frequent regularly one particular feeding-ground. A hunter never searches for kangaroos when they are resting, but waits until just before they set out for their feeding-grounds. He is already equipped with a spear and a *waddy*. Before the expected arrival of the kangaroos the hunter has constructed a shield cunningly made of the boughs of shrubs that are growing round about the feeding-ground and sufficiently large to conceal him. When the kangaroos are feeding he gradually draws nearer and nearer to them. At first they will stop feeding and look round as if expecting an enemy. They seem instinctively to sense an approaching danger. They look around, scanning every tuft of grass, shrub, or tree, and then they resume feeding. They have failed to notice that behind one of the shrubs that appears to be growing in the feeding-ground an aboriginal is gradually drawing closer to them. In the right hand of the hunter is a spear made of tea-tree, with a keenly tempered point. When within striking distance he thrusts his spear into a vital spot of a kangaroo. He then moves to a second victim, which he treats after a similar fashion. An expert hunter will always spear a kangaroo when it is stooping to feed. By this method there is less danger of one kangaroo alarming others by its struggles.

There is another method of hunting the kangaroo in which the *waddy* is used. The use of this particular weapon requires a strong and skilful hunter. All members of the tribe volunteer to take part in the hunt. Some are distributed in the bush to disturb the kangaroos, which rush out with great speed. Others are posted at intervals, and when the kangaroos come in sight they make a great noise by shouting, which excites the animals and causes them to rush straight ahead. The picked men with *waddies*, numbering about two dozen or more, are placed in a line, along which the kangaroos are driven. Presently a hunter hurls his weapon at the head of a kangaroo, and the animal falls to the ground with its skull smashed. The others continue to race along for safety, and another *waddy* is thrown. The hunters are always specially selected for their skill in throwing this weapon, and sometimes each of them obtains a kangaroo.

Should the weather be unfavourable for hunting with the spear or *waddy* a party of young men is sent out to a spot where kangaroos are numerous. They dig a series of large pits about five feet deep and twelve feet wide, which they cunningly cover with small boughs and sand. These pits are made right in the beaten track of the kangaroos. The hunt takes place when two or three tribes meet to discuss tribal matters, and the members of each tribe are represented in the hunting-party. At intervals of about fifty yards men are stationed on both sides of the kangaroo-track. Others go into the bush to raise the kangaroos from their lairs or resting-grounds. When the animals are disturbed they rush along this laneway, seeing no danger. Suddenly some of them fall into a pit. The others continue their course, and some of them fall into the second pit. If half a dozen pits have been made each pit will account for four or five kangaroos, which is a good day's sport.

Hunting the opossum is not a very difficult matter, since this animal is very easily caught. A few scratches on a gum-tree will show that he is resting within the hollow trunk of the tree or among the thick boughs. A few hairs among the rocks leading to a hole, if the hole has a smooth surface round its entrance, will indicate that Mr and Mrs Opossum are having their daily nap.

The wombat is another animal that falls an easy prey to the hunter, but it is sometimes difficult to handle after it has been captured. Although wombats live in holes like rabbits, they come out late in the afternoon. If the hunter sees a wombat he watches it from a bush near by. When he thinks that he will be able to reach its hole without being seen he cautiously approaches this, and blocks it inside, about two or three feet from the entrance. Then he steals back to his ambush, and, taking his *nulla-nulla* in his hand, boldly walks toward the prey. Presently the wombat sees the hunter, and makes haste to get into its home. When it has entered the hole it finds that it is imprisoned at a distance of a few feet within the entrance. The hunter takes the wombat by the hind-legs, and then there begins the tug of war. The wombat is very obstinate, and sometimes is extremely difficult to handle.

Hunting the emu is not a difficult matter. It may be hunted in the same manner as the kangaroo, with bough shields or by digging a hole or holes which are concealed by boughs and bushes. A hunter who is acquainted with its ways usually waits alongside its path, which leads to the river-side or to a water-hole. He conceals himself inside a thick bush, just within arm's length of the emu's path. When late afternoon approaches the emu wends its way to the river-side, unconscious of the danger awaiting it. As it comes close to the shrub in which the hunter is concealed the hunter thrusts out a hand and grasps the emu by a leg. Rising from the ground and still clinging to the leg of the emu, he strikes the bird on the head with his *nulla-nulla*. After it is dead it is carried away to the camping-ground, and is cut up in pieces and distributed to the various members of the tribe, or it may be cooked whole.

The emu is cooked in the following fashion. A hole is

made in the ground a little larger than the emu, and in this a fire is made. The earth in the hole becomes hot, and the bottom is covered with live coals; then grass and boughs of shrubs are placed in the hole, and the emu is laid on the grass and the hot coals. It is then covered with more boughs and grass and earth, and a fire is made on the top. The head with part of the neck is left exposed. The emu is let alone until steam issues from the mouth of the oven. This is a sign that it is cooked. After this it is taken out of the hole and allowed to cool for half a day, or perhaps for a day, before being eaten.

Fishing

Just as the aboriginals have made an exact and detailed study of animal, bird, and reptile life, so with a similar proficiency and thoroughness they have given their attention to fish life. The possession of a knowledge of animal, bird, and fish life makes the hunter more skilful in capturing these animals. This accounts for the fact that people never hear of aboriginals dying from lack of nourishment. The aboriginal is well informed as to where water is to be found and how to procure it, and this applies also to food. These are the two things that constitute the means of subsistence for an aboriginal. Every boy and girl, especially if living close to water, is taught to study the life and habits of fishes, and to recognize and watch them in the shallow water among the weeds and the rocks and hollow logs that lie beneath the surface of the waters of rivers, lakes, and *billabongs*.

Much interest attaches to the fish found in the great river Murray and its tributaries the Darling, the Murrumbidgee, the Wagga Wagga, and other streams. These waters abound with that wonderful fish the Murray cod, and with lesser fish such as the Murray perch and bream, the silver bream, which is very bony, the cat-fish, and mudfish. To the Australian aboriginal the Murray cod is *the* fish. There is none to compare with it in freshwater lake or river or in salt-water lake or sea. According to a legend, there was a great earth shock or tremor at the source of the Murray, which continued for some days. Then suddenly the earth was rent right along where the Murray now flows, but at first there was only a small stream of water trickling and winding its way to the Southern Ocean. Presently there was another earth tremor, more severe than the first, and there burst forth from the depth of the earth a huge fish, the Murray cod. As it came out of the earth it was followed by a flow of water. The cod, struggling along this narrow stream, digging with its head and swinging its powerful tail, acted like a great steam shovel, making the river deep, and forming all the bends in it as far as what is known as Lake Alexandrina. Then Nepelle, the Great Prophet, caught it and cut it in pieces, and, throwing the fragments into the river, named them the *ponde* (Murray cod), the *pomeri* (mud-fish), the *tarki* (perch), the *tukkeri* (a flat silvery fish), the *kundgulde* (butter-fish), the *tinuwarre* (bream), the *mallowe* (Murray mouth salmon). Fresh-water fish are more easily caught than salt-water fish. All the fish mentioned above live in the lagoons and *billabongs*, as well as in the Murray stream. In the low-lying country, alongside of the river, trenches are dug two or three hundred yards long and from four to five feet deep. When the Murray becomes flooded it overflows its banks to the extent of a mile or more on each side, and frequently the Murray cod, the bream, the butter-fish, and other fish are living in this water. When the waters become low through evaporation and soakage the fish are easily caught. This is the time when the women, girls, and boys enjoy themselves. They wade into the shallow water and scoop the fish into baskets made especially for this purpose. These baskets are shaped somewhat after the pattern of a fisherman's landing-net, except that there is no handle. Some of the boys take their little spears and try their skill in spear-fishing.

When the water becomes low, and is only about a foot deep, many of the fish die. This is often due to rapid changes in the temperature of the water. The falling of the water in the Murray River drains the lagoons and *billa-bongs* very considerably at times, and sometimes to such an extent that they become quite dry, and the fishes and turtles and yabbies [1] seek the main stream of the Murray. When this happens another mode of fishing is adopted. The fisherman floats down the stream in a canoe, sometimes tying the canoe to a gum-tree, and waits patiently until a fish swims by. He scans the still waters intently. Presently he discerns a ripple, and with the speed of lightning his spear is sent into the middle of the ripple. The fish, struck by the spear, struggles to free itself, becomes exhausted, and then rises to the surface, and is captured and placed in the canoe.

Fish-spearing is a most interesting and exciting occupation, and one that requires a great deal of skill. The fisherman gets into his canoe, taking with him a spear about nine feet long. One end of it is a plain tapering point, and on the other end are two prongs, made of hard wood, which have very sharp points. The two prongs are tied to the spear with string made of rush or the fibre of the mallee-tree. The prong end of the spear is suddenly thrust into the water, which must have a depth of at least four to five feet. When this thrust is made it carries a quantity of air right to the end of its travel, and the air, being compressed, but lighter than the water, rises, and comes to the surface with a report that can be heard fifty or sixty yards away. The fish is startled, and in its movements it causes the reeds to quiver. The fisherman knows that it is a *tinuwarre*, and, knowing the depth of the water and the size of the fish, he takes up his spear. All this is done in a moment. Ten yards away the fish is racing for life, and allowance has to be made for the speed at which it is travelling and the depth at which it is swimming, and the spear has to be thrown unerringly to strike the fish. An expert will probably strike six times and miss twice. This method of fishing is used mostly near the shores of Lake Alexandrina and Lake Albert, and on the Lower Murray in South Australia.

[1] A small crayfish found in water-holes.

SPEARING FISH FROM A BARK CANOE

By permission

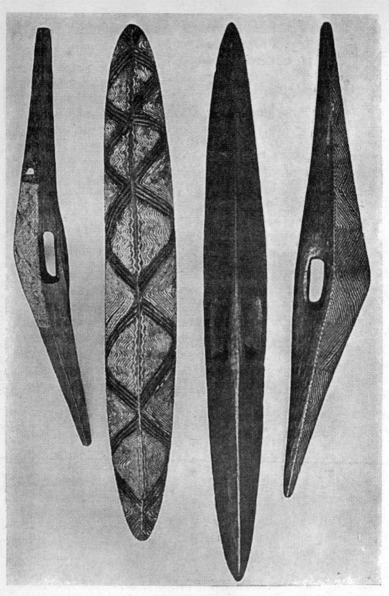

PARRYING SHIELDS

British Museum

236

FISHING

Here there are shallow waters having a depth of from four to five feet, extending from the banks of the lake for about two or three hundred yards, and in these shallow waters there is a growth of water-weeds of a ribbon shape. They grow from the water-bed right to the top, with a foot or more of their length upon the surface of the water. Sometimes these weeds are very dense in growth, and make it difficult for a canoe to pass through them. There are other water-weeds as well—namely, bulrushes and reeds. These growths form feeding-grounds, resting-places, and spawning-grounds for the fish.

Oftentimes one tribe will challenge another tribe to a trial of skill. The Piltinyeri tribe, whose hunting-ground is on the southern shore of Lake Alexandrina, will challenge the Coorong tribe of the western shores of Lake Albert. The issuing of the challenge is made known to all the adjoining tribes, and people will come from a distance of even two hundred miles. The place chosen for the competition is the southern shore of Lake Alexandrina. After the challenge is issued, with the information of the locality chosen and the time at which the meeting will take place, the two tribes are out every day on their respective hunting-grounds, training and making spears for the event. A week before the date of the meeting people commence to arrive from all quarters, and the evening before the day on which the two tribes introduce their picked men the men of the Raminyeri tribe give a corrobbery, and imitate the competitors in their canoes on the water, spearing fish. Perhaps they go so far as to personify the Piltinyeri man making an attempt to spear a fish, and missing his object, which causes the others to laugh and to tell him that he would be better occupied at home going into the bush and assisting the old women in digging roots and gathering herbs. The Piltinyeri are sitting quietly, never expressing their feelings, but the Coorongs, on the other hand, are enjoying the joke. They laugh and shout, " *Kai hai!* " which is equivalent to the European " Hurrah ! " or " Encore ! "

Before sunrise both parties are astir, overhauling their spears and making sure that the canoes are in order, examining them to see that they have not been tampered with during the night. By this time all the camp is awake. The tribes that have come to witness the event encourage each competitor, and speak words of cheer and hope to embolden them for the trial. About nine o'clock each of the selected men of the Piltinyeri and the Coorong takes his place in the prow of his canoe. A man belonging to the tribe will push the canoe from the shore, and then he will get in at the stern and use a pole to propel it through the weeds. The canoes make a straight course for the fishing-ground. A referee in another canoe calls upon the competitors to halt in order to await the arrival of the spectators, who come in their own canoes. Some canoes carry three or four spectators. The number of canoes may be from three to five hundred, and they form a large circle round the area in which the competition will take place. This circle may be three hundred yards in diameter. The water is of a chalky or milky colour, and the fisherman is not able to see an object if it is more than four inches below the surface. Among the weeds the fish have the appearance of resting. They mostly swim or rest midway between the surface and the bottom, where the depth of water is from three to four feet.

Perhaps the Piltinyeri, being the challengers, will enter from the eastern side. A canoe darts forward with a single occupant in it, whose duty it is to arouse the fish from their lair. He is equipped with a spear, which he thrusts into the water, and the startled fish swim away. He shouts aloud so that all onlookers shall hear him, and he tells them that it is a *tinuwarre*. As the fish is passing rapidly through the water the disturbance of the weeds indicates what kind of fish it is. The *tinuwarre* has a small head, and so lightly touches the weeds that no one but a skilled observer is able to notice the weeds moving. Suddenly the *tinuwarre* stops, and the Piltinyeri man takes up a *kaike*, places it upon a *taralye*,[1] stands at the prow of the canoe, and raises the

[1] A throwing-stick.

spear in a position to throw. Again the man
appointed to rouse the fish from their lair thrusts
his spear into the water to set the *tinuwarre* moving.
Quick as lightning the *kaike* is sent from the *taralye*,
straight into the fin or through the body of the fish.
The referee goes forward. He picks up the spear
and exhibits the fish to view. Then, as with one
voice, a shout goes up from the onlookers, "*Kai
hai! Kai hai!*" The Piltinyeri man retires and
takes his place in the circle of onlookers. Then
the Coorong man enters, to take his turn. The
referee speaks, and the man whose duty it is strikes
the water and starts another fish, a *pomeri*. The
Coorong man rises in the prow of his canoe, and
presently another fish falls a prey to the hunter.
The referee goes forward, takes up the spear, and
holds up the fish for all to see. Again the cry is
raised, "*Kai hai! Kai hai!*" All the women and
children who have congregated on the banks of
the lake respond, "*Kai hai!*" and the representatives of the tribes take their place alternately in
the arena until midday. Then they go ashore, and
partake of the catch for their dinner. It may be
that a hundred fish have been caught. These are
given to the elders of each tribe.

After having rested, and having listened to a
person whose duty it is to entertain them with a
legendary story to pass away the time, the referee
tells them it is time to resume. The competitors
enter their canoes, and go through a similar performance to the previous one. Sometimes the
tinuwarre are seen swimming through the weeds,
and the Coorong man is in the arena. He takes
up his first spear and throws it with unerring aim,
striking the fish, which is swimming about fifteen
yards away. Then, with all speed, he takes up
the second spear, and strikes another fish through
the body before it has gone twenty-five yards.

SPEAR WITH PRONGS USED IN FISHING
British Museum

This performance causes a great deal of shouting and *Kai hai*-ing on both sides. Even the opposing side gives the Coorong man a hearty cheer. This competitor is accounted a hero for such a wonderful display of skill in spearing two *tinuwarre* so quickly within such a short interval. It is possible that the time between the spearing of the first fish and the second would be only two seconds.

When the competition is over all the canoes set out for the camping-ground. Upon reaching the shore the competitors go quietly to their wurleys, and sit, without uttering a word to their wives or children. When bedtime comes they retire with but one thought—fish-spearing. In their sleep they dream they are still in the arena with the *tinuwarre*, the *pomeri*, and fish-spears.

Early in the morning all are cooking fish at their respective fires for breakfast. Again the fish-hunters get into their canoes, but this time each is alone, and is armed with a spear that is made of young pine, well dried and greased, having two prongs made from the she-oak tree. They proceed to near the bank of the lake, where the reeds and the bulrushes and several other species of rushes are growing. Among this growth fish are also found, not in the midst of the growth, but along the edge of it. The competitors guide their canoes, and the noise of the canoes passing through the water startles the fish, and they dart through the reeds or bulrushes out into the open water. Fish are distinguished by the indications which they give in swimming. A *tinuwarre*, swimming through the reeds, divides them neatly, causing a quivering motion. A *ponde*, with its large head, carries the weeds toward its line of travel, as does also a *pomeri*. When the hunter sees the movement of the reeds caused by the flight of the fish he thrusts his prong-spear down to strike the fish in its line of travel, with the result that the fish is caught, with the prongs firmly embedded in its flesh. The competitor raises his spear with the fish for the referee and the onlookers to see, and in order to have their approval. Then one of the Piltinyeri competitors, eager to secure an advantage and to show his skill, keenly watches for an opportunity. Presently two *pomeri*, startled by the splashing of the paddling-pole, rush from among the reeds to an open space of water for safety. The hunter, with the agility of his race and the skill of a fish-spearing expert, thrusts his spear with lightning speed into the first fish, and in less than two seconds takes up another spear and drives it into the second one. This is done so quickly that the eyes of the referee and spectators are unable to follow the movements of the Piltinyeri man, and they are therefore unaware that he has speared two fish until he lifts both spears and shows them, with a fish on each. Instantly and simultaneously a shout goes up from all sides. Then, without any outward show of elation, the Piltinyeri competitor sits in his canoe, and allows the others to tow him to the camping-ground, where he is met and received as a hero, satisfied that he is as good as the Coorong man. Every individual male among the tribes congregated there comes along to congratulate him for having accomplished what is considered a wonderful achievement. Even the Coorong tribe will come and express their pleasure at having been eyewitnesses of his ability as a fish-spearing expert.

One thing is very noticeable. No competitor who has taken part in the proceedings is allowed to eat of fish that he himself or any other competitor has speared. There is always an elder who was an expert in his younger days, and he provides the fish for them, and his wife does the cooking. The competitors are not allowed to eat their food while it is hot. It is taken aside and placed upon the tree boughs to cool. Sometimes the food is cooked a day before, and is wrapped in herbs, which are also eaten with the fish.

Another custom is that the competitors are not allowed to camp near their wives. They occupy a camping-ground that is set apart for them, and no female member of any tribe is allowed to come within speaking distance of this ground. The women are not even allowed to go near the path by which the competitors go to their canoes, nor are they permitted to touch their canoes or spears.

A gathering of this nature takes place usually during the summer months—that is, from November to April; but if the weather is favourable it would commence in September.

This manner of fishing requires a great deal of knowledge, founded on observation and practice.

Sport

Wrestling and foot-racing between two or more persons were common sports to be witnessed every day among the aboriginals, especially among the boys and young men. Another form of sport was the throwing of the spear and boomerang. In wrestling the object was not to clinch or grip an opponent in such a way as to overpower him by main strength or to make him helpless to move. What was aimed at was skill and agility in grappling with a rival, and throwing him to the ground clear away, without giving him an opportunity of holding on to his opponent.

Let us suppose there is to be a contest. Three persons are chosen from the Emu totem tribe and three others from the Pelican totem tribe. The ground is selected before the competitors arrive. It must be a soft, sandy spot, free from shrubs and stones. The members of the respective tribes congregate to look on, and to encourage either side. Now the boys or young men who are to wrestle arrive. They may or may not be smeared with oil and red ochre. Presently a man steps forward. He turns to the contestants, and addresses them. "Now, boys, you are called on this day to uphold the honour of your tribe. One of you may win and take this coveted prize." And he holds before them a newly made boomerang and a *waddy*. These two weapons are stuck into the ground endwise. The referee then calls for the boys who are to defend the weapons. Perhaps the Pelican totem tribe offers to do this. The onlookers shout, "*Kai hai!*" Now one of the Pelican boys stands in front of the boomerang and *waddy*, and faces the Emu boys, who stand from ten to twenty yards away. After a while the referee calls to the Emu boys, "Take the weapon

236

from the Pelican boy!" One of the Emu boys walks forward to take the weapon, and when he has gone half-way he is met by the Pelican boy, who grapples with him to prevent him from coming any farther. Supposing the Emu boy throws the Pelican boy to the ground, he rushes forward, and is met by a second Pelican boy. He serves the second boy in the same way, by throwing him upon his back. By this time he has almost reached the coveted prize; but he has to encounter a third Pelican boy. And now the struggle begins. The Pelican boy strains every muscle of his body to defend the prize and maintain the honour of his tribe. Both boys fall to the ground, but they are up again at once. The Emu boy gets nearer and nearer to the prize. He reaches out one hand to take hold of the *waddy*, but fails. At last he gives up further attempts to capture the prize, and he returns to his fellows with a feeling of defeat.

The second Emu boy now makes the attempt, but he has not the strength or skill to succeed, because he is the youngest of the three. The third Emu boy now advances. Instead of walking he runs, and perhaps knocks the first Pelican boy down, and meets the second boy, and throws him also to the ground. He then grapples with the third Pelican boy, and throws him to the ground. Then he takes the *waddy*, and returns with it to his two companions, amid the cheers of the onlookers. He feels a very proud boy.

Now the competitors are given a rest for perhaps an hour or more. The referee takes the boomerang, and places it on the Emu boys' side. He faces the Pelican boys, and says in a loud tone, so all those present may hear, "Take the weapon from the Emu boys!" A Pelican boy goes forward, and is met half-way by an Emu boy. They begin wrestling. Perhaps the Emu boy manages to throw his opponent over his shoulder, and to carry him to his company. A second Pelican boy also fails, and it then comes to be the task of the third Pelican boy to wrest the prize from the Emus, but he also fails. Then the friends of the

Emu tribe become excited, because the Emu boys have won the two prizes, the boomerang and *waddy*. The Pelican boys take their defeat in good part, and wave their hands to the Emu boys as a sign of friendship and the expression of a desire to meet them in the future in a similar contest.

The sport of running races is somewhat similar to the European running. There is no method of training for the competition.

Another subject of contest is spear-throwing. First, a selection is made of boys or young men. This time a Dingo boy and a Wombat boy meet in a contest to test their strength and their skill in long-distance throwing of their spears. The spears are made of reeds that grow on the banks of the river Murray, or Lake Alexandrina, or Lake Albert. The spear is about six feet long.

The Dingo boy outclasses the Wombat boy in distance-throwing. Now the Wombat boy challenges the Dingo boy at target-throwing. In this the Wombat boy excels, and wins the prize. This may be a newly made shield.

SHIELD FROM CENTRAL
QUEENSLAND

From *Among Cannibals*, by Carl
Lumholtz (Murray).

Another kind of game is played, and it is of such a nature that anyone who was not acquainted with it would think that the players showed a spirit of hatred toward one another. But it is only a friendly game in which they indulge. Let us imagine a large camping-ground, where representatives of half a dozen tribes have assembled. They are just sitting round in groups, enjoying their breakfast. Presently, without warning, a person appears on a hill-top not more than three hundred yards away. He shouts so loudly that all the tribes hear every word he utters, and all eyes are turned toward him. Then he cries, "An emu is climbing to the top of the hill." Now the hill that he is climbing is regarded as the property of the Karatinyeri tribe, one of the tribes present at the gathering, and the Emu man is trying to arouse their ire by climbing upon their property without permission. Once more he cries forth his challenge, and at the same time he flaunts in the air a bunch of emu-feathers, which he waves above his head. He dances round, and, in imitation of an emu in flight, dodges the imaginary spears, jumps into the air, and once more shouts his challenge. This is too much for the Karatinyeri men. They cannot remain quiet any longer. They rise to their feet, and give chase. The man who gave the challenge reaches his tribe just as the Karatinyeri are about to seize him. Every man in the great gathering rises to his feet to witness the coming struggle. The Karatinyeri are determined to capture the bunch of emu-feathers. The men of the Emu tribe, from which the man has come who challenged the Karatinyeri, form a ring by joining hands round him. He stands in the centre, holding the feathers. Now the Karatinyeri may have to pass a hundred or two hundred men before they get to him. The Karatinyeri press their way in, and the Emu men do their best to prevent them from reaching the man with the emu-feathers. But presently the Karatinyeri break through the circle and reach the man. Then they wrestle with him, and take the feathers. It may take them a whole day to accomplish this. On account of their success in the contest the Karatinyeri are looked upon as the heroes of the whole camp.

There is another game, in which thirty or more boys stand in a row extending for seventy or eighty yards, and two boys at the ends stand in a line parallel to this, each at a distance of forty yards from it. They have a weapon made of two crossed sticks, each nine inches long, three inches wide, and half an inch thick. One boy takes this weapon and discharges it in the direction of his companion who stands at the other end of the line. It trundles or spins along the ground, like a hoop or wheel. The other boys who stand in a row have spears or boomerangs, or any weapons they may fancy. With these weapons they try to stop the motion of the sticks. The crossed sticks are supposed to be a wallaby or a kangaroo, and this sport is designed to teach the boys to become skilled hunters of game that is in the act of running. Sport is more keenly exciting when the animal is running, or when the bird is on the wing, than when it is at rest on the ground.

There is a ball-game, called *pulyugge*, that is very popular. This is played by picked men, young or old, even up to fifty years of age. Six men, say, represent the Water-rat tribe, and six others the Eagle-hawk tribe. The Eagle-hawk men will oppose the Water-rat men just as players would at football. Presently a Water-rat man throws the ball to one of his companions. Then an Eagle-hawk man will try to catch it. If he succeeds, he throws it back to his companion, who perhaps catches it again. They try to keep the ball between them, catching it and throwing it, and dodging the Water-rat men. This play is kept up indefinitely until one party tires; or perhaps they will keep going until sunset, when both sides agree to abandon the game until the following morning. Then they resume their play and continue until some one of another tribe, perhaps the Ibis tribe, steps in as referee and declares the game drawn.

Boomerang-throwing is another great sport. This is a game in which men of fifty years of age will take part, as well as young men and boys. The Turtle tribe may send a challenge to all the surrounding tribes within a range of three or four hundred miles. On a calm, clear day a smoke-signal is sent up, and a message is sent that the Turtle tribe has made a number of boomerangs that cannot be equalled for quality. All the tribes are challenged to come and test them. They are invited to a certain place, on the shores of Lake Albert, where there are plains free from trees or shrubs. Now, for a busy fortnight, each tribe is engaged in making and testing their boomerangs. Then they come out on the ground, fully equipped, their bodies painted after various fashions, and their boomerangs carved in a variety of designs representing their tribe. A Turtle tribe man is the first to perform with his boomerang. Perhaps it is made to circle round him three times before hovering about his head and descending to the earth within two or three yards of where he stands. A Goanna tribe man will next accept the challenge and enter the ring. He throws his boomerang, and it goes in a straight course from him for about seventy yards, and then gradually works itself round and passes across the line at about forty yards, travelling in a spiral toward the performer. Next time it passes the line it comes within twenty yards; then it comes nearer, until it hovers about the Goanna man, and spins until its energy is exhausted. It touches the earth, and falls inside a circle about two feet from where the thrower stands.

CHAPTER V: PERSONAL MYTHS

Kirkin and Wyju

IN the vicinity of Coolgardie, on the east side, is a rocky hill standing in a tract of country a hundred miles in extent. In this land, which was named Maljarna, there was a distinguished personage named Kirkin. He lived by himself, and would not associate with any other beings.

Now there was a reason why Kirkin lived alone. Nature, in its mysterious workshop, had endowed him with long, beautiful golden hair, which had become the admiration of the whole animal, bird, reptile, and lizard tribes. Kangaroo, wallaby, emu, goanna, and carpet-snake people would travel at great risk to their lives and from great distances north, south, east, and west, and endure much hardship, in order to behold Kirkin. He was spoken of in every tongue as " the man with the golden hair." Many sought his favour, and a greater number offered their daughters to him if he would only condescend to marry them. But with his beautiful appearance and golden hair he was very conceited, and even the girls shrank from him and despised him. They would say, " O Father, why should you offer me to this vain person? Dost thou not see that he is altogether wrapped up in himself and sees nothing apart from him, but thinks only of his golden hair? "

No girl of marriageable age, nor any girl old or young, ever spoke one kind word of Kirkin. Because he tried to make himself believe that he was more beautiful than the maidens he was therefore hated and shunned by all women. No female of the animal, bird, reptile, or lizard tribe would go to see him. His admirers of every tribe were confined to the males.

Every morning at sunrise Kirkin would mount a high boulder and comb his hair. Then with both hands he would bring the golden shower from the back of his head to hang in front, and through the curtain of hair he would watch the people—I mean the bird, animal, and reptile folks—and become mightily pleased with himself because of

242

the admiration of the crowd. This continued for a great many years.

One day it occurred to him that he would like to have a companion, that it would be good to take to himself some one as wife and partner. So one morning as the animals, birds, reptiles, and lizards stood admiring him he said to them, " O my friends, some of you have come from a country beyond the rising sun, and some of you have come from the birthplace of the hot north wind, and some from the place of the cool, refreshing sea-breeze, and some from the mysterious west. All these climes have their beautiful maidens. I have now arrived at a time when I feel the need of a wife. Will some one give me his daughter? " Every one answered, " I will."

There was another being, named Wyju, travelling about the country, who, though he was a very humble man, did many wonderful acts. On one occasion a huge carpet-snake swallowed a child. The poor mother was prostrated with sorrow ; the father was at a loss how to recover the child. Wyju happened to be passing as the distressed parents were being comforted by a large number of sympathizers. Curious to know what had happened, he mixed with the crowd and inquired. One said to him, " Are you a stranger ? Have you not heard what has happened ? A child was swallowed by the Great God Snake in yonder valley. We dare not slay the snake, for we depend upon the snakes for all our water-supply, the springs on the hill-side and in the valley. If only we could make the snake straighten itself we might slay it, and then the water will flow in streams above the earth or in rivers underground ; but if it remains coiled in that position, and be slain so, then the streams above and beneath the earth will cease to flow." " Come," said Wyju, " show me where the Great God Snake lies, and I will slay him and rescue the child." So they showed him where the snake was coiled up asleep on a flat rock ledge.

Wyju took a mallee-root [1] containing water, climbed a

---

[1] A mallee-root running laterally, usually about a foot deep, under the surface of the ground for a distance of ten or twelve feet will yield a pint or two of water.

tree beside the snake, and sat upon a branch overhanging the reptile. Holding one end of the mallee-root in a direct line, with the other end of the root toward the sleeping snake's head, he allowed the water that was contained within the root to trickle, drop by drop, upon the head of the snake and to fall between its eyes. Presently the snake raised its head as if reaching up to where the water-drops came from. Up and up it stretched, unwinding itself coil after coil, till it stood upon the end of its tail, its nose touching the tip of the mallee-root. Springing from his perch, Wyju threw both arms round the neck of the snake, and, holding firmly in his right hand a sharp flint knife, he slid down the snake's back, cutting its belly with the knife as he descended. Thus did Wyju recover the child and restore it to the happy mother and father.

The fame of Wyju was carried abroad by message-stick and smoke-signal, and his praise was proclaimed in every song. The story of his wonderful deed reached even the conceited Kirkin, who became very jealous, and decided that if Wyju should come within the bounds of his hunting-ground he would endeavour to slay him.

In appearance Wyju was just a simple, ordinary-looking man, with certain marks upon his body to show where he belonged to, perhaps with a feather or two stuck in the hair of his head after the usual fashion, and some smears of pipeclay upon his body and face. He could not boast of such good looks as Kirkin nor of such a decoration as Kirkin's beautiful golden hair. And yet Wyju won the admiration of all the fair maidens of Ge Rill Ghillie and Wonboona. He possessed qualities that never die. He was good, kind, sympathetic, and thought little of himself, but much of serving others. Endeavouring to relieve the suffering of the afflicted, he spoke words of comfort to those who mourned, was a friend to the widows and the fatherless, and a support to the aged. Wherever Wyju went he found a place in everybody's heart.

At the time when Kirkin began to think seriously of taking a wife he heard that Wyju's name was upon the lips

KIRKIN COMBING HIS GOLDEN HAIR AT SUNRISE

"CHEEROONEAR BEGAN TO BREATHE VERY HEAVILY
AS HE CLIMBED THE HILL"

of all the fathers and mothers of eligible daughters, and that every maiden was willing and anxious to become his bride. Wyju lived about half a day's journey from the home of Kirkin. One morning, as the people were admiring the golden-haired Kirkin, some one remarked that with his beauty and vanity Kirkin was despised by all females, while Wyju was loved and sought after by every maiden. As soon as the people had gone their way Kirkin came down from his exalted position and inquired of the crow the whereabouts of Wyju. The crow said he was half a day's journey toward the rising sun. Kirkin set out in search of Wyju, and found him lying under the cool shade of a tree.

Kirkin said to Wyju, " Why have you not paid me a visit? Surely you have heard of my fame ! " Wyju said in reply, " Yes, my noble Kirkin, your fame has reached the uttermost parts of the country, even that magic Land of Sunrise where the golden sunlight dances upon the surface of the rippling water of the great ocean, and where the dewdrops sparkle on the leaves of the gum-trees, and where the sun shines upon the waving boughs, sending forth a thousand gleams, even unto the golden daylight. Thus far thy fame has reached."

" Then," said Kirkin, " why did you not come with those who worship me? And why have you not honoured me by coming to pay your respects to me? You are the only man who is so indifferent. Is it because you are conscious of the favour of the fair sex that you have forgotten that I reign supreme in the land of Ge Rill Ghillie and Wonboona? Should I so desire I could, for your impudence, command my admirers to take your body and commit it to the ant-bed. But I will forgive you for this, your first offence. Come to-morrow and pay homage to me and I will consent that you shall continue your journey in peace."

" Nay," said Wyju, " I pay homage to no mortal being. Only to one Supreme Spirit unseen by mortal vision do I submit, and to him I bow in reverence and admiration You know well that within the country of Ge Rill Ghillie and Wonboona my fame is upon the lips of great and small, of

male and female, of young and old.   Furthermore, the fair
sex wield a power for evil as well as for good, and should
they hear it whispered that the Golden-haired designed to
take my life they would rise in indignation and cry, ' Away
with Kirkin, the vain, conceited, selfish one.' "

So Kirkin thought deeply, and planned some other means
of getting rid of his rival.

" O Wyju," said he, " you have touched a kindly spot in
my heart.   Will you come and stay a while and be my guest
until you decide to go and continue your glorious work ? "
Kirkin said this more in flattery or sarcasm, but yet in tone
and manner disguised as a compliment, and Wyju, like a
good man, would not allow himself to entertain a suspicious
or evil thought at this sudden change of attitude of the
vain and conceited Kirkin.   He willingly accepted the
invitation.

This was how Wyju was the first to find an entrance to
the secret and forbidden Maljarna, the rocky home of the
golden-haired Kirkin of Wonboona.   During the evening
meal, as they sat round the fire, Kirkin, having almost completed his plan, began to tell of localities within the bounds
of his hunting-ground where numerous kangaroo, emu,
wallaby, opossum, and the walliow [1] could be easily found
and captured.   He began to wax eloquent, because the
hunting of the walliow would complete his evil design to
injure the unsuspecting Wyju.   "To procure this most
coveted prey no spear, boomerang, or *nulla-nulla* is required," he said.   " You simply walk cautiously without
a weapon into the nesting-ground, and when you see the
grass moving you know that beneath it lies the walliow, and
with a mighty leap into the air straight above the prey you
come down and let your feet land right upon it."

Wyju listened attentively to all that Kirkin had to say,
and then, feeling tired, he asked to be excused, and lay
down and fell asleep.   Kirkin went out into the moonlight
night, and with hurried strides walked rapidly to the
walliow ground, and in a walliow's nest he placed sharp,

[1] An animal of the kangaroo-rat tribe.

pointed sticks, each with one end stuck in the earth, and between these a dead walliow, with a string, very cleverly concealed from sight, leading to a shrub not more than twenty paces away. Returning home within two hours of sunrise, he found Wyju still asleep. Wyju was dreaming of the happy hunting-grounds. He dreamed of walliows. They were all about, peeping out of every bush and shrub. Some stood upon stumps doing acrobatic feats ; some were chasing one another all round and along a leaning log ; some ran upon his body, and one, more bold and venture-some, sat upon his head for a while, and then for a moment in his hands. Wyju quickly closed his hand—the walliow was not there, but sat peeping from within a shrub. Then Wyju, straining every muscle in his body, chased and chased the walliow, and caught it and held it fast, then struck it hard upon the head and killed it instantly. He put the fat walliow on the fire to roast slowly. Then he took it up and placed it upon the bough of a bush near by to cool gradually. When Wyju felt it and found that it was cold and ready to be eaten he tore off a hind-leg, and was just about to take one mouthful when Kirkin touched him gently and whispered softly to him, " It is time that you should rise and break your fast, for we go a-hunting. The sun is just risen. Will you please awaken ? "

Never before during his travels had Wyju wakened from such a realistic dream, and he could not help telling Kirkin of his experience, and saying that he hoped the day's hunting would give occasion for as much excitement.

After they had broken their fast Kirkin bade Wyju follow him. They went on until they reached the spot where Kirkin had set the trap. Kirkin pointed out a shrub where they should wait and watch for their opportunity. After a while Wyju crept cautiously forward, until within six feet of the trap. Then Kirkin pulled the hidden cord, which caused the grass in the squatting spot to shake as if moved by a walliow. Wyju jumped with all his might, and came down with both his feet upon the sharp spikes, which pierced them deeply.

Poor Wyju, rolling and groaning in an agony of pain, said, " O Kirkin, save my feet from the cruel spikes." But Kirkin said jeeringly, " I have planned this to entrap you, and you shall not escape my vengeance. Now I shall take a *wommera* and strike the spikes further into your feet." Wyju fainted, and remained unconscious for a long time. When he came to himself Kirkin said to him, " O my friend, when you walk upon your feet please don't forget to look me up. The sign by which you will find me is a white smoke column that rises on a still, clear day. You will know that it is the signal of your friend, who will be glad to renew acquaintance; so now, my good Wyju, my esteemed and honoured friend, good-bye."

Kirkin walked off, leaving Wyju to suffer until kind death should come and place him in the Spirit Land among the many stars that shine overhead. But some one greater had willed that Wyju should not die, but live until the day when Kirkin should receive punishment at his hands.

From new moon until next new moon did Wyju, over-come with pain and suffering, weep and cry unto the All Father Spirit: " Come, O my Father, the Father of All. Thou who dost grant favours to evil men as well as to good, and bestow the sunshine and the cool, refreshing rain, send unto me thy servants, the Winjarning brothers. Let the sacred brothers come and give me relief, and strengthen me to endure this pain." During the period of his suffering Wyju bled and rolled about until he made a great valley, and stained the earth all round it with his blood. Ever since that memorable event the aboriginals go to that valley and collect red ochre, which they use to smear the bodies of youthful candidates for initiation.

The Winjarning brothers heard Wyju's cry of the pain that he was enduring just at the appearance of another new moon. They came and extracted the spikes from his feet and bound up his wounds, and with the magical power of the All Father who rules over the destiny of men they gave health and strength to Wyju, so that he was able to go forth to destroy the wicked and conceited Kirkin, the Golden-haired. Wyju went in haste far away into the northern land, and saw a white smoke column rising straight into the clear blue sky. He ran forward until he came within a mile of it. Then he sat down beneath the shade of a tree. After resting for an hour he walked toward the smoke in a spiral course, nearer and nearer, until he came in sight of Kirkin, who was walking round and round the fire. Wyju watched him for some time, thinking how to attack him. Then he thought that it would be best to wait until the early hours of the rising sun, when Kirkin would be so absorbed in the care of his hair, fondling and combing his golden locks with his fingers, and thus being at a disadvantage.

At sunrise on the following morning Wyju approached the home of Kirkin with a warrior's boomerang in his hand, dodging from bush to bush until he was within ten paces of Kirkin, who was facing toward the east. Wyju came up from behind just as Kirkin threw the golden hair over his face. He raised his weapon, and with a mighty stroke severed the head with its golden hair from the trunk. He then committed Kirkin's body to the fire.

The spirit of Kirkin rose out of the flame and entered the body of a little hawk-like bird which one now sees resting motionless in the air, but fluttering its wings. The eye of the bird is always turned earthward in search of beetles, roaches, and other insects. One often sees this bird where a fire is raging or where there has been a fire. This was the fate of the vain and conceited Kirkin. Like all his predecessors, from being a very great personage he was changed into the form of a small and insignificant bird.

The Love-story of the Two Sisters

There were two sisters living at Pulluwewal, an isthmus between Lake Alexandrina and Lake Albert, on the Lower Murray River. They had been well instructed in all the tribal customs, and also in all details of bushcraft. It is the custom of the aboriginals to name their young people after some particular characteristic or peculiarity that they may show. These two girls had not been given individual names

249

because they were so alike and so attached to each other that, although there was a slight difference in their ages, they were almost indistinguishable from one another. So the elders called them Mar-Rallang, meaning 'two in one.'

Now there was a fine young man called Wyungare. He was a gift from the great leader Nurunderi. Years before, about the time the two sisters were born, a widow was mourning the loss of her husband. She had plastered her hair with white clay, and had cut great gashes in her body to express her intense grief. In her distress she cried to the Great Spirit, Nurunderi, "Why did you take my husband? Why have I not a son?"

Nurunderi heard her, and placed a young baby boy in the bush near by. When the baby cried the widow went and found him. She was delighted. She took the boy and reared him, and her brother helped her to educate him. They called the boy Wyungare, which means 'he who returns to the stars,' and, because the boy sooner or later must return and become a deity, great care was taken with his instruction in bushcraft and the habits of the birds and animals.

The uncle also sent a messenger round to all the families of the tribe, saying, "No girls are to be given to Wyungare in marriage. I have set aside a narrow strip of hunting-ground by the lake for him to live upon, and nobody else must trespass upon that ground." The families of the tribe answered, "True; let it be as you say."

The spring-time of the year is a great time in the training of the young people of the tribe. They are taught to become quick and observant in detecting the different love-notes of the wooing birds, and the mating impulses of the animals. One spring-time, when all nature round the lake had become alive again, the two sisters caught the spirit of the season, and felt a great urge to meet the young man Wyungare. So, early one morning, the elder sister hid herself in the bush near the camp of Wyungare and imitated the cry of an emu. Instantly Wyungare sprang up to hunt the supposed emu, but when the girl saw him she revealed herself, and asked him to help her to find her lost sister. This was only a trick in order to make the acquaintance of Wyungare and to tempt him to love. Later on the younger sister played a similar trick by giving the love-note of the swan. The result of this was that both the sisters married Wyungare.

When the uncle heard that Wyungare was married he was very wrathful, and he went off to Nepelle, the great man of the heavens, to ask him what he should do. Nepelle answered, " You will have to separate them." The uncle then took some ashes, and wrapped them in paper bark, and placed them near the camp of Wyungare, thinking that a fire would separate him from the two girls. During the night the ashes burst into flame, and set fire to the bush. Gradually a huge bush-fire encircled the camp. Wyungare was awakened by the smoke and flames, but in the danger and excitement of the burning flames and the blinding smoke he did not lose his presence of mind. He seized both of his wives, and, with one under each arm, set out for the lake. He dived again and again under the water to escape hurt from the flames. But the fire came close up, and began to burn all the dry reeds round the lake. Wyungare took his spear, to which was attached a coil of rope made of rushes. Then, calling to Nepelle, the great God of the Stars, he uttered a prayer, " O Father of Mankind, hear me, not for my sake, but for the sake of these my wives. Take hold of this spear until they have climbed into safety ; then in your pleasure do unto me what to you seems best." Then he threw the spear with great force right into the heavens.

Nepelle heard the cry, and he held the spear as the wives of Wyungare climbed into heaven. Then Nepelle called to Wyungare, " Come, my son, take thy place in heaven and reveal thy mission by shining forth and showing the children of earth that thou didst think more of the safety of thy wives than of thine own life."

The aboriginals still point to the three stars in the eastern sky that represent Wyungare and his two wives.

251

Cheeroonear

Cheeroonear, his wife, and the dogs lived in the midst of a dense forest. No human being ever met these peculiar beings, or even caught a glimpse of them. They were very cunning in carrying out their raids upon men, women, and children. The only signs of their existence were foot-prints leading to and from a camp from which a person was missing, or the sound of their harsh voices when one of them spoke to another. The barking of their dogs was much louder and deeper than the barking of ordinary dogs or dingoes. Cheeroonear and his wife and dogs would have remained merely as names in a spirit story of the dense forest had not changes come about in the following fashion.

It was midsummer on the Plain of Nullarbor. A severe heat-wave came and lasted for three days. Animals, reptiles, lizards, insects, and other creatures sought refuge in caves, of which there were a great many at the time of this story. Men, women, and children took shelter under the shade of trees in the valleys and on the hillsides, or under ledges of rock. The animals, birds, reptiles, lizards, and insects mutually agreed that they should herd in common, side by side, without fear of injury. Never before in the history of living beings had there been a sight so wonderful as this peaceful gathering of animals. Common danger, difficulty, and sorrow begat sympathy and made for friend-ship.

For two days men, women, and children sat quietly be-neath the trees, and were visited by snakes, lizards, and birds. Those who sat on the hill-tops and hillsides could view the large plain that stretched away toward the sunrise as far as the eye could see. Their attention was attracted by something peculiar-looking that made them curious. After watching for an hour they saw that it was an object resembling a human being. They began to say among them-selves that it could be no ordinary man who was walking across the plain on such a hot day. It might be one of the Winjarning brothers, the medicine-men. With this sur-mise they felt satisfied, and did not take any more notice.

CHEEROONEAR

To sit gazing at a medicine-man as he approached would have shown a lack of courtesy and good manners.

After sitting in concealment for an hour a man on the look-out gazed across the plain to see where the person was, so that they might be prepared to receive him in a manner befitting his rank. But what he saw caused him to tremble, and he was unable to speak for a time. After a while he asked the others to come and look at the strange sight. There, walking before them, was a being with ears and face like a dog, but without a chin. From the lower jaw there hung a flesh-like bag, shaped like the pouch of a pelican, and leading into the stomach. The ribs did not join in the centre to form a chest with one cavity, but were arranged so as to make two compartments. The compartment on the left side contained the lungs, and the one on the right side held the heart and its vessels, leaving the throat like a wide sack between the two, so that when it held water or food it looked like a tube. This was the dreaded gigantic Cheeroonear, of whom they had heard much, but whom they had never seen. He stood eight feet high. His arms reached below his knees to his ankles. When he stretched or opened his fingers he could touch the ground. He could pick up objects from the ground without stooping. The trained eye of the bushman or the hunter could take in these details at a glance. The men, women, and children hid themselves in fear lest they might be seen by this horrid monster.

Cheeroonear walked straight up the hillside without hesitation, as if he knew the locality well. When he arrived at the summit he went to a rock hole that contained a large supply of cool, refreshing water. After his long journey across the treeless and dusty plain, under the fierce glare of the scorching sun, he felt very thirsty. He removed the rock that formed the covering lid of the hole, and he stooped down and began to drink. As he took mouthful after mouthful the sound of his gulping could be heard about a hundred yards away.

After drinking he rose, stood upright, and looked about.

253

He was conscious that there were human beings near by. He sniffed like a dog scenting, first toward the north, then to the south, then to the east, and lastly to the west. He stooped to drink once more, and again stood up. His stomach looked like a huge ball, the pouch presented a very much inflated appearance, and the water almost came out of his mouth. He strode toward the west, where his home was. After he had gone about fifty paces he began to vomit water and human flesh, the remains of a meal that he had eaten. Among this were the heads and feet of infants that had been swallowed whole. After being sick he felt very weak, and staggered toward a tree that, only a few moments before, had been deserted by frightened men, women, and children.

When he had rested for a while he once more rose to his feet and looked about him in a suspicious manner. He felt that human beings were watching him from behind rocks and trees. He then saw that men and women were peeping at him, and he became exceedingly angry. When he first came into being he had vowed boastingly that he would never be seen by mortals, and that he would always prey upon them without their knowing who their enemy was. His most important reason for this was that it had been decreed that if he were to be seen by a human being he would surely meet his fate and be slain, and so destroyed for ever. This was not a very pleasant thought for Cheeroo-near, for he loved to live and to eat. Angrily he turned toward the peeping crowd, and said, " I shall come in the morning and command my dogs to slay all the men, women, youths, and maidens, but the children I shall save until I am hungry. My wife can prepare an infant for me when I wish to eat." Then, full of rage and fear, he hastened off to his home in the forest.

As soon as he had descended the rocky hill the people gathered round the spot where he had been vomiting, and to their horror they saw skulls and feet and hands of babies. Before them was the solution of the disappearance of their people. They saw also the footprints made by their visitor

254

a few moments before, and recognized them as being the same as those that were often seen coming to and going from the camps of people who were afterward found to be missing. Then they remembered Cheeroonear's parting words, " I shall come in the morning."

In consternation they sat down beneath the shade of the trees and began to discuss what would be best for them to do, and whether it would be advisable that they should flee to another country. But some one asked, " If we do this what shall we do with the aged, the blind, the sick, and the lame? We cannot leave them to the mercy of this wicked monster. Let us build a fortress in case of an attack by Cheeroonear and his dogs." But the elders persuaded the people to send two of their number who would go and find the Winjarning brothers. They would probably receive information of the whereabouts of Winjarning the elder from his brother. The brother had been heard of only four days before, when he rescued from drowning some youths who had been carried out to sea. Two youthful volunteers set out, going southward toward the coast.

Now at this time the Winjarning brothers were enjoying a rest on the seashore. They had caught some fish, and had just cooked it and put it aside to cool, when they looked up and saw the two messengers of the tribes approaching. As soon as they saw them the brothers rose to their feet to receive their visitors kindly. They asked them to be seated and to partake of some of the cooked fish that had been allowed to cool. But the youths, remembering the seriousness of their errand, refused to take food until they had delivered their message. They cried, " O protectors of the aged and the sick and the blind, forgive us if we refuse to eat, although we have eaten nothing for three days. We are in great distress. When after midday the sun had travelled a little to the west, and the trees and all objects cast their shadows toward the east, there appeared to our tribes a very strange being. He is one whom we have reason to fear, for we have seen with our own eyes that to satisfy his hunger he eats human flesh, especially the bodies of infants. For the sake of the aged, the sick, the women who give us our manhood, our tribes, and our people, will you protect us? We must return at once." The Winjarnings replied, " We shall come to your people at midnight, and we will deliver them from this evil monster. Be pleased to eat and be strengthened ; then you both will have fulfilled your duty satisfactorily."

The Winjarnings said this to encourage the youths, and also to convince them that it would be a wise course for them to follow. When the youths heard it they both sat down and enjoyed a good meal. Strengthened by the food, they made haste to return to their homes and their tribe with the good news that the Winjarnings, the protectors, were coming at midnight. The men, women, and children greatly rejoiced, and none laid himself down to sleep until the arrival of the Winjarnings.

At midnight, when the brothers arrived, an elder told them what Cheeroonear had said. The Winjarnings listened attentively. They were greatly moved with compassion, and wept to think that innocent babes had been killed and eaten by this cruel monster. They said to the elder, " Choose from among your people two hundred young men. Let them take their flint axes and go into yonder valley and each cut twenty bundles of brush scrub. Let as many as are willing carry the bundles to the summit of this hill, and let them make a race a hundred yards long and ten yards wide at the entrance, and let the outlet be sufficient for only one dog to pass through." Now while this race was being constructed it happened to be full moon, so all the men, women, and children took part in helping to make this trap that was to be used in dealing with Cheeroonear and his dogs.

Just as the dawn showed up in the eastern sky the men and women heard Cheeroonear calling to his dogs, and bidding them follow his footprints back to the hill and kill all the men and women, but to guard the children until he should arrive. They heard him shout, " Go, my faithful dogs ; do your duty. Do not fail me now. Man has seen me, but you, my good dogs, have never seen me. When the men and women see you may it be their last moment in this life! Kill them." Then Winjarning the elder gave instructions that all the warriors of the tribe should arm themselves with spears and boomerangs in case of emergency. He himself stood at the north end of the race with his brother; and each held two warrior-boomerangs. The aged, the sick, the blind, and the mothers with their babes sat along the outside of the race in a safe position, and some of the young men and maidens were told that they were to be ready to climb into the trees the moment that Cheeroonear approached. The Winjarning brothers and the warriors stood waiting the coming of the dogs. They could be heard barking and yelping as they came running at full speed.

Now there were six dogs in the pack. The fleetest of them was two hundred yards ahead of the second. When he came to the narrowest part at the end of the race Winjarning the elder struck him upon the neck and severed his head from his body. The head fell at his feet. A warrior standing beside Winjarning thrust the body to one side, and another warrior with a sharp knife cut off the tail and gave it to another man. Then the second dog came along, about a hundred yards ahead of the third. He followed the scent and track of the first dog, and he met the same fate, and in a similar fashion, at the hand of the younger of the brothers. In the same way each of the four dogs that followed was treated as he came along the race. When the last dog was slain there were six men each holding a dog's tail. These men were selected to play a certain part as soon as Cheeroonear should put in an appearance. They were told to conceal themselves under the trees, and to wag the tails as if the dogs were hunting the youths and maidens.

Cheeroonear waited some time for the return of the fleetest dog; it would be a sign that the dogs had fulfilled their master's command. As they did not return Cheeroonear decided to go and see how matters were progressing. He told his wife of his intention, and said that if he were

257

away longer than seemed necessary she should come to the hill-top. As Cheeroonear ran toward the top of the hill Winjarning and his brother prayed to the Great Father Spirit to tell the God of Dewdrops to send along a great fog so that Cheeroonear should not be able to distinguish objects clearly. Just as Cheeroonear came out of the dense forest which sheltered his home from prying eyes, in obedience to the command of the God of the Dewdrops a fog suddenly spread over the surrounding country.

As Cheeroonear began to ascend the hill the God of the Dewdrops said to the fog, " O fog, remember that I have given thee to the service of Winjarning." Cheeroonear began to breathe very heavily as he climbed the hill. Winjarning and the people could hear his laboured breathing as he came nearer and nearer. As arranged, the youths and maidens climbed into the trees that were near the race, and began to sob and cry as if in distress or in fear. Cheeroonear stood for a moment at the entrance to the race, looking about him. He could hear shrieks and cries. He saw the youths and maidens clinging to the trees and looking down toward the ground. He followed their gaze, and saw the dogs' tails wagging. " Oh," said he, " I see the dogs are at their work killing the people ; I must hasten forward to assist them." He hurried along the race until he came to the narrowest part. Here Winjarning and his brother were waiting in ambush. They both rose, and with the skill of born hunters they hit Cheeroonear on the head with their warrior-boomerangs. Another blow on the knees brought him instantly to the ground. Then the people came out and beat his body until there was no life in it.

The wife of Cheeroonear, after waiting some time, thought it would be well to go and look for her husband. She climbed the hill and came to the race. She fancied she could hear the dogs barking, and on looking round she could see the dogs' tails wagging. She rushed up the race, and was slain by Winjarning. Then some of the warriors took her body and cut it in halves with flint knives, and from within it there came forth a full-grown boy of twelve years. As soon as he was freed the boy ran away. He became a devil, and was able to transform himself into a bird, a reptile, or a lizard. At the present time he has the form of an evil man, but he is as evanescent as he was when he escaped at the death of his mother. The only evidence left of the existence of Cheeroonear and his dogs is the footprints to be seen to-day on the rocks in the land of Ge Rill Ghillie.

The Keen Keeng

Between Ge Rill Ghillie and Western Australia there lived in a cave a great number of strange beings. They were more human-like than Thardid Jimbo and Cheeroonear, or even the proud, conceited Kirkin. They did not look so fierce or cruel as did Thardid Jimbo and Cheeroonear; they were more pleasant in their appearance and manner. They differed also in some other respects. Firstly, the hand of the Keen Keeng consisted of the thumb and the last two fingers. Secondly, the Keen Keeng were great deceivers. Thirdly, they possessed a wonderful gift: they were able at a moment's notice to raise their arms above their heads and to transform them into large and powerful wings, one stroke of which would carry them a distance of five miles while one could count ten.

The Keen Keeng were related to a giant family. This family was noted for its cruelty. They neither feared a god nor respected man, but believed themselves to be gods. The Keen Keeng, however, believed in a god, a Fire and Flame God, whom they worshipped and to whom they offered gifts in sacrifice. The God of Fire and Flame continually burned in the centre of the cave in which they lived. When the Fire and Flame God was pleased with their doings he would disappear into the bowels of the earth, but if he were displeased the fire would rise like a great wave of the sea, and the flame would leap up against the ceiling of the cave. Then the only way to appease the god's anger was to offer a living human being as a sacrifice.

At this ceremony, to which all the Keen Keeng were invited, the men sat round the mouth of the fire-pit, singing and beating drums, and the women danced to the music. A priest, assisted by his wife, offered up the sacrifice.

Now there was one particular Keen Keeng appointed as scout or spy. His duty was to travel all round the country in order to collect information, and to secure human beings to be sacrificed as a means of appeasing the angry god. The Keen Keeng were well informed regarding the outside world. They knew all about the happenings to and all the doings of Thardid Jimbo, Kirkin, Cheeroonear, Newal, and other strange beings.

One day in midsummer the Keen Keeng scout on his usual round thought that he would rest himself under the shade of a huge tree. After hovering round he selected a clear spot, and sat down on the ground and folded his wings by his side so that they became arms. After resting for an hour or more he decided to walk about and admire the beautiful flowers that covered the ground. Going farther on, he came to a dry and parched country, where mallee grew in scattered clumps. He came to a spot where two men sat sipping from a wooden bowl the water which they had procured from mallee-roots.

These two men were known to the whole of Western Australia as the Winjarnings, brother medicine-men. They were respected and worshipped by all who came under their influence. Their object in life was to protect the human race from the cruelties of Thardid Jimbo, Cheeroonear, Kirkin, and other wicked beings. Without hesitating the Keen Keeng walked toward Winjarning and his younger brother, and stood within five yards of them. The Keen Keeng was a perfect specimen of manhood, eight feet high, with a pleasant and kindly appearance. He was surprised when one of the Winjarnings addressed him in the Keen Keeng tongue, and said, " Will you sit yourself down? " indicating with his hand a spot about ten yards away. The Keen Keeng sat down. Winjarning, his brother, and the Keen Keeng sat for half an hour in silence.

THE KEEN KEENG

During this time the Keen Keeng was thinking very hard and controlling his emotion. " I should like very much," thought he, " to take these two men to our home. I know it would give my friends a great deal of pleasure to have such intelligent beings living in captivity. There is also a possibility that, by having them as captives, we might be able to discover wherein lies the secret of their knowledge and their power to combat our evil designs." The Winjarnings knew what the Keen Keeng was thinking. Suddenly the Keen Keeng rose to his feet. So did Winjarning and his brother. They stood thus for a moment. Then the silence was broken by the Keen Keeng, who said, " I was wondering whether you two would care to come with me to my home and my friends. I am sure they would be delighted to see you and to have your company. We will make you happy and comfortable. The young men and maidens of my race will entertain you with songs and dances. Will you come? "

" Where, and how far away, are thy friends and home? "

The Keen Keeng replied, " One moon, as you walk toward the setting sun. The sun is now half-way down the western sky. Should you care to travel along with me, we shall arrive long before the sun sets."

The Winjarnings thought it would be a new experience for them, so they accepted the invitation, and replied, " We will come with you."

They were not aware of the Keen Keeng's method of travelling. The Keen Keeng knelt down and invited Winjarning and his brother to sit one on each of his shoulders. When they were seated he rose and stretched his arms above his head. To the amazement of the Winjarnings they travelled five miles in a moment. When they had recovered from the shock they thought that it would be good to view the country below as they travelled over it. Never before had they experienced such a sight as that which greeted them—mountains, hills, valleys, sea, lakes, rivers, shrubs, trees, birds, and animals all jumbled together.

After they had travelled thus for some time, suddenly there came out of space youths and maidens to escort the scout of the Keen Keeng and his guests to his home. When they were about fifty miles from home the Keen Keeng scout shot upward into the blue sky like a rocket. This was to give the youths and maidens time to reach the cave,[1] and to act as a bodyguard on his arrival. As the Keen Keeng scout circled slowly and gradually earthward the Winjarnings once again saw below them beautiful mountains, hills, valleys, and trees in the centre of the circle which they formed as they descended. They also saw youths, maidens, and children with wings outstretched, floating suspended in mid-air. Through these they passed onward to the cave and the home of the Keen Keeng. Then they walked into the midst of the Keen Keeng who were in the cave. The scout of the Keen Keeng put Winjarning and his brother under the care of an elder and his wife, who were the priest and priestess of these strange beings. The visitors were cordially invited to partake of their hospitality. The Winjarnings replied that they were very pleased indeed to have met their scout, and through his acquaintance to be privileged to be the guests of such wonderful beings. They said that when they returned to their country and people they would tell of the wonderful experience of travelling with such a remarkable being. The scout of the Keen Keeng went to the end of the cave to paint himself with pipeclay and red ochre in order to disguise himself, so that the Winjarnings would not recognize him.

After staying among the strange beings for three days, and witnessing their sacred ceremonial rites of dancing, singing the song of initiation, and offering sacrifice to the God of Fire and Flame, Winjarning and his brother expressed a desire that the Keen Keeng would be pleased to permit them to return to their own homes and people.

---

[1] It is said that the ceremonial rites of initiation of the young men, so dear to the aboriginals, originated in the cavern of the Keen Keeng, and that it was there that the Winjarnings came to know them.

THE KEEN KEENG CARRIES THE WINJARNING BROTHERS

MOUNT GAMBIER, WITH THE TEAR COURSES

By permission

When the scout of the Keen Keeng heard this he told the priest and priestess secretly to invite them to stay for one day more so that they might have an opportunity of witnessing the ceremony of offering a special sacrifice to the God of Fire and Flame. The Winjarnings expressed their pleasure, and accepted the invitation.

On this day the scout of the Keen Keeng arranged with the priest and priestess that on the evening of this fourth day their maidens should exercise their subtle cunning to attract the attention of the Winjarnings, which would give them an opportunity to overpower them and hand over their live bodies to the God of Fire and Flame.

Winjarning and his brother knew all about their plans, but acted as if they were in entire ignorance. When the fateful evening arrived the elder Winjarning told his brother to sit or stand at the side nearest to the opening of the cave, and to run when he, the elder, shouted out, " Run ! Flee as fast as your legs can carry you. Stop not nor look to see where I am, but flee for your life." This appeared to be a strange order, because the younger brother had always stood in the front in every battle and in every danger. The elder brother knew what was passing in the other's mind, so he said, " This is a most critical moment in our lives. It is not the strength of manhood, but the experience of age that must cope with it. Hesitate not, my young brother, but put your trust in the wisdom of your elder brother and do as I bid you." So the younger brother consented to obey.

The maidens were now ranged in order to perform the emu dance. Winjarning and his brother were not permitted to look upon the performers, but they were allowed to turn their backs upon them and to look upon the wall of the cave and see the shadows like emus walking about and picking berries. The images were cast upon the wall by means of the light of the Fire and Flame God who came out of the pit. To produce the effect the maidens raised the right arm in a straight line to the shoulder. Then they raised the forearm at right angles to the elbow, and bent the body at the hips. This cast a shadow like the picture of an emu upon the wall. The scene was greatly interesting to Winjarning and his brother.

As the performance was being repeated the men were forming a circle round Winjarning and his brother. Now although the older Winjarning was very much taken up with the acting, he was also observing what was taking place elsewhere. He whispered to his brother, " Run for your life ! " and in obedience to the command the younger man ran out of the cave. Then Winjarning the elder suddenly leaped into the midst of the maidens, and ran round the fire and flame pit, followed by the angry crowd. Round and round they went, until the whole tribe of the Keen Keeng, male and female, became so giddy that they were unable to balance themselves, and fell into the pit, and were consumed by the God of Fire and Flame. Winjarning the elder came out of the cave and joined his brother. They hurried away to a distance of five miles, and when they looked back they saw a wonderful sight. The God of Fire and Flame leaped out of the cave and sent sparks upward into the dark sky. These sparks dwell there as the spirits of the Keen Keeng.

On the following morning Winjarning and his brother returned to the place where the cave had been on the previous evening. They saw only a flat plain ; and the place where the God of Fire and Flame reigned was now a huge ant-bed, with many, many ants.

Thus were destroyed the most cunning enemies of mankind.

Winjarning said to his brother, " In evil there is some good, and the good separates itself from the evil as a spark mounts upward into the sky."

Mr and Mrs Newal and their Dog

The men and women of the Bajeeja tribe speak of Mr and Mrs Newal and their dog as the most cruel beings that ever existed. The dog possessed as much intelligence as did Newal and his wife, and he was able to express his thought by a bark or a yelp that was plainly understood by them both. The dog was their companion and friend, taking part in every murder, and sharing in the feastings equally with Newal and his wife. Unlike all other strange beings, who made their homes in caves, Newal and his wife and the dog lived within the hollow of a huge tree, which was large enough to accommodate them all. The only entrance to the cavity was an opening as large as the door of an ordinary house. This opening was about ten feet from the ground, and the only access to it was by means of a log leaning against the tree and serving as a ladder. Newal and his wife and the dog lived on the flesh of living creatures, such as reptiles and human beings, but they would not eat the flesh of birds. Of all kinds of food the dog preferred human flesh.

One day Newal and the dog went out hunting, and left Mrs Newal to go and gather grubs. As they were standing upon a hill the dog saw two objects passing across a plain. He recognized that they were men, and at once called with a yelp to his master, who looked in the direction in which the dog was pointing with his fore-paw. They watched the figures as they drew nearer. Presently the two men saw a kangaroo, and they began to stalk it from bush to bush, crouching and crawling with eyes fixed upon their prey. They were so intent on this that they were quite oblivious to danger. Newal and the dog hid in a bush near by which the men must pass in order to come within striking distance of the kangaroo. After some time the men came close up. Newal and the dog pounced upon them. But both the men were born hunters, and knew how to act in so sudden an attack. Each dropped his spears and *wommera* and quickly took a *nulla-nulla* from his waist-belt. They beat Newal and the dog so mercilessly that they had to run for safety, with the blood flowing from their wounds. As Newal and his dog ran each of the men quickly placed his *nulla-nulla* into his waist-belt and drew forth his boomerang, and threw so accurately that one of them struck Newal a severe blow upon the arm, causing a very bad wound.

However, Newal and his dog managed to return home. They presented a pitiful sight, both being sore and bleeding, and the dog having lost his tail. After attending to their wounds, Mrs Newal placed before them a wooden bowl full of grubs. During the period of their convalescence Mrs Newal went in search of food every day, but she could procure nothing but herbs and grubs. So there were grubs for breakfast, grubs for dinner, and grubs for supper during a whole month.

Now when Newal and his dog were able to go a-hunting again they came across a company of young men chasing an emu. When they saw Newal and his dog they suddenly stopped running, and approached in a fighting attitude, with spears poised. Newal and the dog did not wait to receive the spears, but ran as quickly as their legs could carry them. Never before had they run so fast, for the result meant life or death to them. Life was the dearer and sweeter—so said the dog as they related the incident to Mrs Newal.

Newal said that from the experiences of that day human beings would be on the warpath against them, which was a serious matter. They must, therefore, retaliate by waging war against the human beings who meant Newal's, Mrs Newal's, and the dog's destruction; or else they must become friendly with their enemies, which would, of course, be for the benefit of all concerned. Newal, favouring the first alternative, suggested that the dog should wait at some convenient water-hole for man; while man stooped to drink he would be in an unguarded position, and the dog would pounce upon him and bite, bite, bite, until the victim became exhausted through loss of blood. Then the dog would return to them, and they would go back with him to assist to carry the victim to their home. This suggestion was approved by Mrs Newal. The dog consented to give it a trial. After two whole days he returned disappointed, weary, and hungry, and said that men were too clever. Their sense of hearing was so keen that they could hear him breathing when in ambush about twenty paces away, and they would stand looking in his direction with spear in *wommera* ready to be thrown should they see him; and he would have to run away swiftly, stooping from bush to bush as he ran, until he was far from danger.

As the dog ate his meal a thought came to him, and he said, " I would suggest to you, Newal, that you go about the plain country inviting people to come to your water-hole to drink of the cool, refreshing liquid that is bubbling within the tree." Mrs Newal supported the dog's suggestion. So, with a very heavy heart, and fearing death, Newal went forth on a very hot day. Presently he saw a dust-covered man struggling under a great burden of four kangaroos. Newal went up to him, and said, " O brother, you must surely be tired and thirsty. Come, let me take your burden, and do you follow me. I will give you food and water to strengthen you, so that you may continue your journey in better condition." The man was completely thrown off his guard, and had no suspicion of danger. Accepting Newal's suggestion, he followed him to the hollow tree which was Newal's home, and sat down beneath its shade to rest. The dog, full of excitement, peeped out to have a look at the victim. By a sign Newal told the dog that he must be ready for action. Newal turned to the man and said, " Would you like now to quench your thirst, or would you prefer to have something to eat? " The man replied, " I would like a drink." " Come this way, then," said Newal, " and climb up upon this log. Put your head into the hollow you see there, and drink until you are satisfied." The man did as he was bidden. He placed his head inside the hollow. Then the dog, with his sharp teeth, gripped the hapless man by the throat, and Mrs Newal struck blow after blow on the victim's head, so that he fell to the ground, dead. Mrs Newal and the dog hurriedly descended from the tree to help carry the body some distance away. Then they made a fire and threw the body upon the live coals to roast; and after a while they sat down to enjoy their meal.

They continued decoying and murdering in this manner

for a long time, until the Bajeeja tribe became seriously lessened in numbers. The elders wondered why the people were disappearing, and they became alarmed. One day there came into Wonboona, the country of the Bajeeja tribe, two strangers. The few remaining families of the Bajeeja looked upon the visitors with a great deal of suspicion, thinking that probably they were responsible for the mystery. The next morning the elder smoke-signalled far and wide to the few that were scattered throughout the country of Wonboona to come and try to solve the problem of the mysterious disappearance of the members of their race. They came from the north, south, east, and west, and discussed the matter, but without coming to any decision. The elder of the two strangers rose and told the people not to be afraid of their presence, as they were come to protect them and to destroy their enemies. The strange men then walked away from them. After a while an elder, who was thinking seriously, spoke and said to the people, " The strangers are no other than Buda Gooda and his brother, the saviours and friends of mankind, appointed by the Father of All Spirits. Have not our fathers told us of the many wonderful deeds wrought by them? " Then the people went their way, satisfied, feeling assured that no danger would befall them, and spreading the tidings that they had seen Buda Gooda and his brother. This message was sent far and wide, and peace once more reigned in their homes.

But Buda Gooda and his brother went straight away to discover the cause of the disappearance of the people. They walked across the plain, and by and by they were met by Newal, who addressed them thus : " Well, strangers, how far have you travelled in the heat of the blazing sun? You must surely feel very thirsty."

Buda Gooda, not yet knowing that this was Newal, the destroyer of mankind, replied, " We do feel faint with thirst. Will you be friendly and give us water to drink? "

" Come, follow me," said Newal, " and I will grant you your request."

MR AND MRS NEWAL AND THEIR DOG

Buda Gooda agreed to leave his brother and go alone and return with water. He went with Newal, walking and talking, until they arrived at the hollow tree. There Newal told him to wait, but Buda Gooda, instead of stopping where he was told, followed, and watched every movement of his guide.

After a short time Newal returned and said to Buda Gooda, " You may now climb upon the leaning log and drink until you have quenched your thirst, and you may fill your water-bag to take to your brother, so that he also may drink." Buda Gooda thought a moment, and then said, " Will you bring a longer log to lean against the tree? " Newal went about a hundred yards away, and brought a log reaching about a foot higher than the first. Buda Gooda looked at it and said, " Bring another log a little longer than that one." Newal began to be impatient, and said, " You will have to climb or go without water." However, he went about a mile away to procure a log of the length required. Meanwhile Buda Gooda walked round and round, wondering why he saw so many skulls and bones. He was now convinced that he had solved the problem of the disappearance of the tribe.

Buda Gooda returned to the hollow tree and took a shield from his waist-belt. He mounted the leaning log, and, placing the shield in front of his neck, looked inside the hollow. Just at that moment the dog sprang at the throat of Buda Gooda, but instead of grasping it with his teeth he bit the shield, and his teeth became firmly fixed in the hard wood. Buda Gooda looked and saw the helpless state of the dog. He seized his opportunity, took a *nulla-nulla* from his waist-belt, and struck the dog a severe blow upon the head, killing him instantly. When Mrs Newal saw what had happened to the dog she, intending to kill Buda Gooda, struck a blow at him with her yam-stick. Buda Gooda caught the yam-stick in his left hand, and with his right struck her a blow upon the neck with his *nulla-nulla*, and severed her head from her body. At this moment Newal arrived. He raised his *nulla-nulla* to kill Buda

Gooda, but the brother, who, from a short distance off, had witnessed all that had taken place, came creeping up till within fifty paces, with his hand upon *wommera* and spear. He had divined the wicked intention of Newal, so he threw his spear with lightning speed into Newal's heart. Thus ended the cruel careers of Newal and his wife and the dog. Once more the Bajeeja tribe was able to retain and to populate the coveted country of Wonboona.

Woo

Woo was the strangest and most peculiar being that ever existed. He was the beloved and only son of a great giantess, who lived and wandered about in the country of the ancient Pumbala tribe that inhabited the south and south-eastern parts of what is now the state of South Australia. The mother of Woo, although she must be hundreds of years old, is still with us to-day. A great number of people in Australia are every day making her acquaintance.

Woo was not a very big being. He was only four feet high, and he had but one leg and one arm. His arm was formed of the two arms joined together, and grew from the front of his chest. His leg was similarly formed, and it pointed downward. Otherwise he presented the appearance of an ordinary man.

Woo found that walking was very difficult. Nature, however, made up for defect in one faculty by something special in another. In Woo the balancing power became very strongly developed. Even upon his one leg he could stand longer and more steadily than an ordinary human being could do upon two. He was able to turn and to stoop with a most graceful movement. He could jump over a creek or a log, and on landing he would remain upright on the spot without moving. In walking he progressed sideward after this fashion: Keeping the leg straight, he raised the front part of the foot and turned it outward, the heel acting as a pivot. Then, putting the weight on the fore-part of the foot, he raised the heel and turned it outward beyond the position of the fore-part.

WOO

These movements were repeated with great rapidity. In running he could with his one leg outpace anyone. He was able to travel over a hundred miles a day.

Woo's only method of capturing food was by chasing kangaroos, wallabies, and emus. Although his arms were joined together in a fashion similar to his legs, he was a good marksman at the exercise of spear-throwing. No wonder that men feared him.

Woo was very cruel to men, but was exceedingly kind to reptiles, lizards, and insects. If he found a dead snake or goanna he would track its murderer and slay him. The only way by which anyone could escape from Woo was to pretend to be dead by lying on an ant-bed and letting the ants crawl all over him. Woo would approach the ant-bed with his spear in his hand and gently probe the individual in the arm to test whether he were dead or not. If he remained quite still, although the ants might be crawling into his mouth, eyes, or nose, Woo would consider that he was quite dead. If he moved at the touch of the spear he would be certain to be killed. Some people carried maggots about with them in little bags, and when they heard Woo coming they would lie down and take a handful of the maggots from the bag and place them in their hair, and round their mouth and nose. Woo, seeing the maggots, would pass on quite convinced that the maggots were attacking a dead man.

Now the years as they went by brought changes. As Woo grew older some of the changes had a great influence on his life. He began to realize more and more that he was now entirely alone. He had neither friend nor relative. This loneliness began to prey upon his mind. It made him think of the days of his childhood. He went to visit his birthplace and wander about the country there. At Narracoorte he would go underground into the caves. Then he would come out of the caves and the subterranean passages and visit Lucindale, Salt Creek, and even Warracknabeal. Then he would come back to the sea coast near Kingston.

After this he would go on to Mount Benson, where he would sit and grieve and pour out all his troubles, because his feeling of loneliness increased whenever he came to this place. Everything here was so beautiful. Mountains, valleys, hills, shrubs, trees, and flowers all seemed so glorious. He was conscious that every morning and every evening the birds sang a song of thanksgiving and praise. He felt that nature all round him was expressing itself, and that he alone was unable to show that he had any glad feeling. The only sound he was able to make was '*Woo*,' and where was there any note of thanksgiving in that monotonous sound? Even in his dreams he could hear only that one sound, '*Woo*.' As he sat upon Mount Benson he began to think of his mother—and a desire came to him to go to her. She had gone into her mountain home, and was sitting in state. When he looked at her she sat quite still, appearing to take no notice, and did not utter a word. Her silence and indifference so saddened him that he pined away and died.

People from all parts of Australia go to visit Mount Gambier, the mother of Woo. They clothe and decorate her with beautiful lawns and flowers. Some offer their gold and silver as a token of their admiration for her. But she bears the marks on her aged body of the struggle she underwent in the bringing up of her son, and of the many tears she shed in disappointment that her only child was born deformed in body and in mind. Her decrepit body bears evidence of the soreness of her trials. The crater and the rifts in the mountain-side are the visible effects of her grievings over the deformity of her son. The lakes on the top and sides of the mountain are the tears she has shed. It is universally allowed that there is no spot so beautiful as Mount Gambier, the resting-place of the mother of Woo.

Thardid Jimbo

In the long, long ago, in a cave in the land of Ge Rill Ghillie, there lived Thardid Jimbo, a great giant who stood seven feet high and had powerful legs and arms. Every morning at sunrise he would come forth and go a-hunting for food, his chief prey consisting of goannas, blue-tongued and frilled lizards, and all kinds of snakes. Not many miles from the home of Thardid Jimbo there lived a very good man, Mummulbery, and his two girl-wives. These were sisters, daughters of a respected medicine-man. Now Mummulbery would not live with his people or tribe, but preferred to live apart from them, in company with his girl-wives, who loved him very much.

One morning Mummulbery rose very early, and, wrapping the opossum rug round about his wives to make them snug and comfortable, he whispered to them not to leave their bed, but to lie there until his return. He bade them a fond farewell, stepped out of his camp into the freshening air of the morning, and took spears and a *waddy* and a very long rod, much longer than a spear. He strode off rapidly toward the rising sun.

Thardid Jimbo too awoke that morning, stepped out of the cave, stretched himself, and gave a yawn showing his big mouth and sharp teeth. Then he began to walk rapidly westward. Now Mummulbery and Thardid Jimbo were walking straight toward each other. After proceeding some distance Mummulbery saw the footprints of animals that had recently passed, travelling southward. He decided that these were the footprints of kangaroos, and, as is the custom with expert hunters, he tracked one particular footprint until he came within view of the animal he was following. Then he crawled on the ground and sneaked from shrub to shrub, stalking it.

Mummulbery was carrying what would seem to an ordinary person to be two spears; but he had only one. The other weapon that he carried looked like a spear, but it was ever so much longer, and at one end the wings of an eagle-hawk were fixed to it. It was used after this fashion: The sharpened end was thrust into the ground so quickly that the kangaroos were attracted by what appeared to be an eagle-hawk, and their attention became fixed upon it.

273

Mummulbery, availing himself of this fact, came unperceived almost alongside of the kangaroo he was tracking, speared it in a vital spot, killed it instantly, and dragged it away. When he had gone quite a distance from the other kangaroos he found a convenient spot and made a fire and cooked his prey.

In the meantime Thardid Jimbo, with rapid strides, covered a good distance, snatching up goannas and lizards that came in his way. Gazing intently upon the ground, he noticed the footprints of Mummulbery and the kangaroo. He followed the tracks, and saw the pole with the eagle-hawk's wings tied to it. A little farther on he came to the place where the kangaroo had been killed. Still going onward, he no longer looked on the ground for footprints, because he could now smell burning wood and roasting kangaroo.

He continued on his way guided by the smell. Suddenly he came upon Mummulbery feeding on the liver and heart of the kangaroo. He stepped back a few paces and stood watching him with big, wicked, and cruel eyes. Presently Mummulbery looked up and saw before him a great big being. He immediately recognized the being as Thardid Jimbo, the enemy of man, of whom he had heard so much. Mummulbery quickly took up his spear and placed it on the *wommera* ready to do battle. Thardid Jimbo saw this action. He knew too well that even his brute force was no match for the skill and intelligence of man. Remembering that there were scores of spear-marks and many wounds upon his body caused by boomerangs during a pitched battle between himself and man, he sat down about ten yards away from Mummulbery. He made a fire, and enjoyed a meal of half-cooked goannas and lizards. Mummulbery placed his spear on the ground and sat upon a log, watching Thardid Jimbo, who was eating his food in a disgusting manner. Mummulbery, filled with pity, cut a leg from the cooked kangaroo and offered it to Thardid Jimbo, who quickly accepted it. He ate greedily, and crunched the bones between his powerful jaws, and swallowed both flesh and bone. Now at this time Thardid Jimbo was about three feet away from Mummulbery. He looked at Mummulbery's neck as if something had attracted his attention. He said, " I see a louse." Mummulbery, taken off his guard, leaned toward Thardid Jimbo and asked him to remove it. Thardid Jimbo, seizing the opportunity, opened his mouth wide and bit Mummulbery in the neck, severing the head from the body.

Thardid Jimbo now threw the body of Mummulbery into the fire. After roasting it a while he took it from the fire and hung it on a tree. Then he thought he would follow Mummulbery's footprints to his home. The sister wives, hearing footsteps approaching, thought that their husband had returned. With faces smiling to greet him, they looked up and saw a sight that almost froze the blood in their veins. For there, standing before them, was Thardid Jimbo, the enemy of mankind.

Thardid Jimbo said to the frightened girls, " I have killed a man yonder, and have roasted his body and hung it up on a tree." They realized that the victim was their husband, and tears began to roll down their cheeks. He said, " Why do you look so sad? Why do you weep? I see tears in your eyes." " They are caused," said the wives, " by the smarting of the smoke." Thardid Jimbo said to them, " I have come to take you to my home and make you my wives." The elder sister said, " We have not tasted food, and we are faint with hunger. Grant us one favour, and then we will follow you. In yonder cave there lives a dog with his wife and family. We shall take it as a great favour to eat the flesh of puppies caught by your hands, O brave."

Thardid Jimbo turned and beckoned that they would follow him and see him bring the prize. When they arrived at the cave Thardid Jimbo entered it, and presently came out carrying the dead body of the bitch, with the warm blood trickling from a wound inflicted by a blow of his mighty arm. He threw the corpse down at their feet, entered the cave a second time, and returned with nine puppies, a month old. He said, " Thy request is granted, Fair One of the Dawn." Then the younger sister said pleadingly, " Will you be my brave and bring me the dog? " This so flattered Thardid Jimbo that he entered the cave a third time. The sister knew that the dog would not be easily captured, and that the pursuit would lead Thardid Jimbo to the far end of the cave, which was a very long one. This would give them an opportunity for action. After waiting a few moments the younger sister called from the entrance of the cave, " O my brave, I am faint with hunger. Bring me the dog. I am craving for the flesh of the dog." She kept shouting and calling to him to bring the dog to her, while the elder sister was busily engaged in closing up the entrance to the cave with boughs, sticks, and logs. The younger sister then crawled through these and helped the elder one to carry more sticks and logs. Then they both sat down to make a fire after the usual fashion, by rubbing two sticks together. When the fire was alight they placed it among the wood and branches, which caught fire and burned quickly. The smoke and heat entered the cave, and when Thardid Jimbo felt the smoke smarting his eyes he ran to the entrance. There he found a blazing fire in front of him. He made one desperate leap to get over it, but he fell short, and dropped into the fire and was quickly consumed.

The sisters sat down, and, filled with sorrow and exhausted, wept bitterly for their husband and friend, Mummulbery. They then went back to their home, and followed the footprints of their husband and saw his roasted body hanging from the tree. They cried, " O husband, if you could come to us for a moment, just for one look of your kind and loving eyes ! " Thus did they weep for one whole week, forgetting even to take food or shelter.

When they came to themselves they remembered that they were the daughters of a good man and a medicine-man, and they immediately sent up smoke-signals, bidding their father come, as they were in sore trouble. Away in the distance another smoke-signal replied that their father would be with them at sunset. They laid the charred body

276

of their husband upon green leaves of the mallee-tree.   As
the sun sank in the western sky the father sat between his
weeping daughters, and tears rolled down his aged cheeks.
He said, " My children, your husband has already gone
to be with the spirits in the Spirit World.   Are you willing
to go and join him in that world, or would you like that
he should return and live with you here?   Now, daughters
of my heart, choose."   The girls said that should their
husband come in the flesh and take them they would be
willing to go into the Spirit World.   The father looked up
into the sacred group, the Milky Way, and prayed the Father
of Spirits to manifest his power and send their husband to
take his wives to shine for ever in the Spirit World.   The
husband's spirit entered his body, which suddenly became
alive and perfect.   Staying only to bid good-bye to his
father-in-law, and until the girls had clasped their father in
a final embrace, he ascended with his wives into heaven.

Palpinkalare

There is a story of a very remarkable event that happened
in the far-off days.   It is so old that it came to be regarded
as a traditional legend ; and, being so often repeated from
generation to generation, it became linked up with mythology. It is the story of a young man, a maiden, two brothers,
and the Evil One.

The young man, when a youth, willingly conformed to
the laws and customs of his tribe and his race.   He readily
consented to be made a young man.   After passing through
the ceremonies of initiation he did not, as was customary,
return quietly to the camp, to await instructions regarding
his most important tribal duties, but he stole away from
mother, father, sister, brother, and other relatives and members of his tribe.   No one saw him go, nor was anyone
aware of his absence until three days had passed.   He acted
in this way because some one had told him that the girl who
had been promised as his future wife wished to marry
another, and, as he loved her, he wished to leave her free
to choose her husband.

The young man wandered into a dense forest in a valley between two high mountains. Through this valley there flowed a stream of clear, pure, and refreshing water, in which there were shoals of fish swimming about. It was an ideal spot, and in it there abounded many wild-fowl and many different kinds of ducks. There was a cave, and on the walls of it there were drawings of strange creatures. There were also rocks shaped like human beings and animals. This spot was regarded with much superstition and a great deal of fear. The elders of the tribes around had given strict instructions that no one was to be allowed to camp there, or even to visit the place. Those who had been better acquainted with the locality had been dead for many years, and strange tales were told of it.

This young man, strange to say, had not received any instructions about the valley, nor did he know anything of its history. Had he done so he would, no doubt, have avoided it and gone to some other place. Being ignorant, he made his abode in the place, and built a wurley, a strong, substantial home, made of solid posts, lined with fine grass and gum-tree bark, and plastered over with clay. There was a small opening to answer the purposes of a doorway, and in the roof he made another opening about eighteen inches square to be of use as a chimney. In this forest there were many wallabies, so that all he required for food and shelter was quite close at hand. On account of his character and habits he came to be known as " the Hermit." He lived here until he was well advanced in years.

In another country there lived a medicine-man and his wife, who was the daughter of a noted doctor. The woman was versed in the knowledge of mind-healing, so they were well mated. They had an only daughter, whom they loved dearly. Her name was Palpinkalare. Now according to the law of the Wonboona and Kukata tribes these young people, the man and the girl of the story, were betrothed. When a message came that the young man was missing, and that no one knew whether he was dead or alive, the parents decided that the girl, their daughter, should conform with the initiation rites, and that these rites should be carried out according to directions and conditions laid down by them. The girl willingly consented to undergo the ordeal.

It was contrary to all custom that suggestions or conditions should be made by the parents of the candidates, but, on account of the position of both the mother and the father, the elders of the tribes assented, and the following provisions were agreed to. Firstly, that the daughter of the medicine-man should pass through the various grades of initiation alone, without any companion; secondly, that she should go on a long journey, and wander through the hunting-ground of the tribe to which the young man belonged; and, thirdly, that the young girl's tribe and the young man's tribe should provide four of the best and bravest of warriors, and four elders from among the men and women, to accompany her on her travels and minister to her wants. These companions were intended to protect her against danger and to hunt and provide food. The mother and father were allowed to accompany the party, but they were not permitted to speak to their daughter, or even to see her.

After this strange party had been travelling for about a fortnight the Evil One came across their tracks. He was struck with the fact that among these there was the footprint of only one girl. He walked round in a circle of about a hundred yards in diameter, and then went crosswise over it. He spent two whole days in constant thought. He concluded that the evidence pointed to the training of an individual, and particularly of a girl. When the Evil One first saw the footprints the party had passed by only one day before, so that they were now three days' journey ahead of him. He stood contemplating. " Surely," said he, " this must be an important matter. I wonder whether the girl is the daughter of some great personage, or whether she is being trained to become the wife of a young chief? I am satisfied that she is no ordinary girl. I must prevent her from completing her training, and I must hurry. From the appearance of the footprints she cannot be far ahead." The Evil One followed the tracks, step by step, all that day, until sunset. He slept that night upon the spot exactly in the same position as Palpinkalare had done. As he lay upon his back all his thoughts were fixed on her. He sang the magic song to her, pleading that every step she took after midday should become slower than the one before.

In the morning he rose early and began his journey, tracking her step by step until midday. He hastened along at a great pace that day, and at night he slept in the same place as the girl had slept. Palpinkalare was now two days ahead. Next day he resumed his journey, walking even faster, and noting everything she had done. He saw where she had plucked berries, and had gathered *nardoo*-seeds, and had dug for *kuntyari*-roots. He arrived at their camping-ground while the sun was only half-way across the western sky. He congratulated himself, for now the party was only one day's journey ahead of him. He sat down on the spot where the young girl had slept the night before. He noticed all along the journey that the girl was particularly fond of a grub that lived in the root of a gum-tree. He said to himself, " I must hurry and overtake the party before midday, and watch their movements closely, as well as those of the girl, so that I may have an opportunity of making use of the magic *waddy*."

On the afternoon of the third day he came upon their camping-ground, and again he slept upon the spot where the girl had slept. At three o'clock in the morning he rose from his sleep and swung a bull-roarer,[1] and at the same time chanted this song, composed specially for the occasion : " My eyes shall be as bright as the rising sun. Whatsoever my wishes are I shall obtain them. My thoughts shall be of grubs. The taste of them is in my mouth. My stomach craves for a big fat grub. I shall see a grub to-morrow."

---

[1] The woman-drawer is a very small bull-roarer. It is used to attract women. When they hear the sound caused by swinging it they are fascinated and go toward it.

PALPINKALARE

When Palpinkalare rose she began to sing, as if by inspiration, the song that the Evil One had sung. When she ceased singing she came to herself, and said, " Oh, I do wish I had a grub. I know and feel within myself that I shall discover a great big grub on my journey to-day."

The older women and men were startled to hear her song. It was not customary for a girl or boy to sing or to express a wish while undergoing training; so they held a short consultation as to what they should do. Several of the elders maintained that it was a breach of the law of initiation for any boy or girl to do any such thing. One of the elder women suggested that they should call the mother and father, who had been accompanying them at a distance. " No," said the eldest of the men. " Let her alone, and probably some great good may come out of all this. I know that she is breaking our law, and I begin to think that the Evil One is very near us. If this should be so we are helpless to protect her. We must be prepared for the worst. I am convinced that she does not do this of her own accord, but is influenced by some great power that is at work in her, and that is thinking for her. Come, let us be on our way." The warriors kept a very close guard on the girl, but, despite their precautions, the Evil One, with the experience of generations upon generations since the beginning of mankind, outwitted the cleverness of the elders in their knowledge of bushcraft.

On the fourth morning he came upon the party. He walked between the elders and Palpinkalare. The distance between was about one hundred yards. This had been thought to be sufficiently near for her protection, but the Evil One considered that it was quite far enough to give him an opportunity to do his evil work. When the girl came to a gum-tree she noticed signs of a grub upon it, about three feet from the ground. Here was what she had been looking for. She ran to the tree, and examined the bark carefully. She struck it several hard blows with her yam-stick, and broke the bark. She peeled it off and found a hole about two and a half inches in diameter. She called out, "What a large grub! Since I woke all my thoughts have been fixed upon such a grub." The elders heard the sound of the blows of her yam-stick on the tree, and knew that she had found a grub. Thinking that she would not be delayed long, they continued walking on until they were about four hundred yards ahead. Then they sat down and waited for her. She broke off a twig with a hook-shaped point, and thrust it into the hole where the grub was lodged, and tried to extract it. The twig broke. Then she procured another. With this she hooked the grub out of the hole, and stood admiring it. When she looked up she saw in front of her, and about four paces away, the Evil One, standing in all his ugliness, ferocity, and vileness.

The sight gave her such a shock, on account of its suddenness, that when she opened her mouth to call for help she was unable to cry out, and she fainted and fell to the ground. The Evil One took her up in his powerful arms, threw her across his shoulder, and ran toward a cave that he remembered was in the valley. He was not aware that the young man had built his wurley there. Now the Evil One was a great ventriloquist. As he was running away he sang the song, "My eyes shall be bright as the rising sun."

The elders, thinking that it was time that the girl should come, sent one of the warriors back to see if she was safe. He found that she was not at the place where they had left her. He became suspicious, and, on looking round, he saw where she had extracted the grub from the tree, and he noticed it lying on the ground. He then made the startling discovery that there was another track—a stranger's. He saw where the girl had fallen, and he noted signs that showed that the stranger had picked her up, and had first walked, and then run, toward the valley.

The warrior gave the signal of distress, and his companions, men and women, came hurrying back. They saw enough to convince them that the girl had been kidnapped; and they observed the footprints leading toward the Valley of Superstition. One of the elders said that he

282

thought the parents should be told of what had happened to their daughter, and a young warrior was instructed to go at once and tell them the sad news, and bid them stay where they were until they were called. Another young warrior was sent with all speed to tell the Winjarning brothers what had happened, and to secure their assistance. Then they decided to rest, as the sun had set; and they agreed that they would rise three hours after midnight.

When the Winjarning brothers were told by the young warrior what had taken place they said to him, " Go to your party and say that neither they nor anyone else shall go in search of Palpinkalare. We are going to undertake that task. We can take only one, as this is a work that does not require many. They may choose who shall accompany us. Throughout this night our minds will help you to find your way safely to your destination." Then the young warrior turned and faced toward the place where his party was awaiting his return. " Now go," said the Winjarning brothers. " We will protect you. No obstacle shall hinder you."

When the Evil One ran off with his victim he went straight into the Valley of Superstition. While the girl was still in an unconscious state he laid her down on the soft green grass, and he sat upon a ledge of rock about fifty paces away, and looked down upon her. For an hour he sat thus, waiting for her to recover. Presently she began to move, and to struggle, as if suffering from an awful nightmare. Then she awoke with a start, and gave a cry so shrill that it echoed and re-echoed up and round the valley like the sound of many souls in sore distress and despair.

The Hermit heard the cry. There was a note in that voice that he remembered from his boyhood days, when the surrounding tribes used to hold their grand corrobbery.[1] He

[1] At these corrobberies it is the custom for an uncle to point out to the boy his future wife. The Hermit remembered how he had looked across to the camp for that female form that had made an impression upon his mental vision and had stamped its image upon his heart. Her voice had caused him to gaze admiringly, and it had roused such tenderness within him that language was unable to describe the music in her laughter. It was like water rippling over pebbles in a stream and tumbling down from ledge to ledge.

immediately sprang to his feet, and, grasping his trusty spear and *wommera* and *kanake*, he ran with the speed of a kangaroo toward the valley, shouting, "I come to your rescue. Take courage! Take courage!" As the Hermit came running the Evil One heard the shout and the rustling and breaking of twigs, and he hid behind a bush, with spear and *wommera* fixed ready for immediate action. He saw the Hermit standing and looking about him in search of the distressed one. Palpinkalare rose from the ground, and stood in a dazed condition. The Hermit ran forward to embrace her. Suddenly, like a bolt from the sky, the Evil One sent his spear on its errand of death. It struck the girl in the chest, and pierced her heart. She fell dead into the arms of the Hermit, who quickly laid her on the ground, and withdrew the spear from her body. Then he lay down flat beside her to try to catch a glimpse of her assailant. But there was no one in sight.

The Evil One had stolen away under cover of bushes and shrubs to the upper part of the valley. The Hermit could stand the strain of sorrow no longer, and, regardless of the danger to his life, he stooped down and raised the girl's head. He looked on the face and recognized it. This was the girl who was to have been his wife. He remembered he had sought to avoid marriage by living the life of a hermit. He was overwhelmed with torturing grief, and would have liked to have again the opportunity of marrying Palpinkalare and defending her and making her happy. He stood up and struck the point of his spear into the ground on his left side, and he threw the *wommera* and the *kanake* about five paces away. Stooping gently, he lovingly placed the maiden with her head toward the east and her feet to the west.

He raised her head, and turned her face toward the sun. As the sun gradually sank in the western sky he sang the song of lament: "O spirit of this woman's form, thou hast taken flight, and art now winging thy way to the Spirit Land. I implore thee not to leave me in distress and despair. For I loved thee when thou didst dwell in this body.

284

THE EVIL ONE WATCHING THE FAINTING PALPINKALARE

PERFORMING A BOOMERANG DANCE

From "The Arunta," by Sir Baldwin Spencer and F. J. Gillen, by permission of Messrs Macmillan & Co., Ltd.

I loved thee dearly in childhood days. During the many years that have gone behind the veil of time that young love has grown big and strong, like some huge tree. I am far away from father, mother, and relatives, but farthest from thee, my love, because I wandered after fulfilling the ceremonial rites. I went away not because my love for thee waned with the changing seasons, but because I thought that thy love for another warrior increased, and that, by observing a custom of the tribe that has joined many youthful hearts in marriage, thou wouldst have consented to be my wife against thy will. I thought that perhaps when thou wouldst be brought to my fireside thou wouldst come unresistingly, like every obedient girl, through love to thy father and mother. And yet, all the time, in thy breast there burned the warmth of love for a soul-mate. Had I known that thy heart, in all its virgin purity, throbbed lovingly in unison with mine I would have stayed and taken thee unto myself. Good-bye, my love, sweet inspiration of my soul. Good-bye, sweet spirit of a pure virgin body. I shall join thee in that great mysterious Spirit Land far beyond the western skies."

The Hermit stood silent in contemplation until the sun sank over the hill bounding the western limit of the valley. He then stooped down and lifted the body of Palpinkalare, and carried it to the bank of a running stream, and washed the blood from it. Then he hurried away among the trees, and stripped the bark from a mallee-trunk. He removed the fibre from the bark and wrapped it round the body. Then he took the bark of the tea-tree, and wrapped this round on top of the fine fibre of the mallee-tree. He plucked some rushes and twisted them so as to make a string to tie round the bark, in order to keep the body secure. Then he raised the body, and carried it to his camp and placed it gently upon his bed. He returned for his spear, *wommera*, and *kanake*, and walked about to see whether he could discover any sign of the murderer. He saw where the Evil One had sat upon the ledge of the rock, and the spot from which he had thrown the spear, and the way he had taken to escape. With a sad heart, and a mind determined to be avenged, he returned to his camp. When darkness came he covered the coals of fire with ashes. He lay down beside the body of the girl, with his head to the east and his feet to the west. While lying upon his back he tried to bring himself into a visionary state, so that he might discover the whereabouts of the murderer.

He rose early in the morning, and broke his fast with no more food than was sufficient to strengthen him for his task of meeting the murderer. He was preparing to raise the body and convey it into a cave a little farther up the valley when the Winjarning brothers came into his camp. The young man at once recognized his visitors. He politely asked them to be seated, and said that all he had in his home belonged to them. He invited them to make use of everything. All was theirs, he said, as long as they cared to stay. He said, " I am now leaving you in order to fulfil the last sad duty to one whom I have fondly loved." He raised the body of the girl on his shoulder, and carried it to the cave. He laid it down and built a platform of flat, slab-like stones. He placed the body upon this, and sat down at its feet. Then he became lost in silent contemplation. He remained so for three hours.

By this time the Winjarning brothers had broken their fast. They walked round and saw by signs that they had arrived too late to save the girl's life. They noticed, too, the scene of the death-tragedy. They saw the footprints of the Evil One. They were indignant that one so young and beautiful as Palpinkalare had been sent to the Spirit Land without giving a son or a daughter to her husband's tribe. They decided that every effort should be made to bring the murderer, the Evil One, to his death, so that in future he should not exist in human guise and destroy others of the human race. They followed the footprints of the Hermit into the cave, and sat one on each side of him, and spoke words of comfort and encouragement, then they bade him rise and accompany them in their search of the Evil One.

286

PALPINKALARE

Together they hurried out of the cave. They traced the footprints of the Evil One, and were soon hot on his track. At midday they came to the spot where the Evil One had slept the night before. Looking about for a camping-ground, they continued running like bloodhounds thirsting for the life of the victim. At evening twilight of the first day's search they saw distinctly the light of a fire upon the hillside about a mile away. They stopped running in order to hold a consultation as to the method of attack. Then suddenly a light appeared along the whole horizon from east to west. They were puzzled as to what to do. They began to realize that they were dealing with a very cunning enemy, and that if they were not very cautious they also might fall victims to him. Instead of attempting to attack, Winjarning the elder said to the Hermit, "Come, let us go yonder to the highest hill, and when the sun rises on the morrow we may see the enemy, and find what form he has assumed, and in what direction he is travelling." So they wound their way through the dark valley to a point a mile beyond the northern firelight. There they decided to rest.

Winjarning the elder said that the Hermit must sleep all through the night, and that he himself and his brother would take turns in watching, in case the Evil One should pounce upon them unawares. The Hermit wrapped himself in a kangaroo-skin, and fell soundly asleep. The Winjarning brothers kept watch all through the night. In the morning they rose very early, before the sun was up. They listened carefully for any sound that might denote the presence of the Evil One. They heard the warning notes of birds as they stirred in the bushes and trees, and they knew that this was a sign of danger. The Winjarning brothers and the Hermit strained their eyes in searching the gully below. They caught sight of something. It might have been an old man kangaroo, or an emu plucking the tender leaf-tops of bushes and shrubs, that caused the birds to twitter, but they did not see an emu pass. Their curiosity was aroused. They looked again and again. They could not make out plainly any details of feet or body, but there

287

in the gully was what would appear to an ordinary observer to be an emu, walking and plucking his food as he went along. They watched the emu pass on through the gully and disappear.

They hurried to the hillside where they had seen the firelight the evening before. They walked round and round, but saw no sign of a fire or a camp, so they retraced their steps to the place where they had observed the magic light on the previous night. From this point they followed the footprints of the Evil One as far as to another rocky rise to the west of the firelight that they had seen on the previous evening, about a quarter of a mile from the other fire. Here they were filled with wonder and amazement, for right before their eyes the work of the Evil One was apparent. A burning bush was glowing before them. The leaves appeared to be not consumed, but to be continually burning.

They could not doubt but that the Evil One was acting in this way in order to show his power, and to frighten any who might try to follow him. They looked about and saw the spot where he had slept, about fifty paces distant from the burning bush. From this point the footsteps were tracked to where they had seen the emu in the morning. Just before the entrance to the valley the footprints led them on to a ledge of rock, and from this point no tracks could be found. They searched very carefully in every clear space, and also examined bushes, shrubs, and sticks for the slightest signs of tracks, but they were unable to find any. They were almost giving up the search in despair when Winjarning the elder sat down upon the flat rock in an attitude of contemplation. He thought of the emu, and he saw upon the ledge of rock a tiny tuft of emu-feather.

The problem was solved. He called to his younger brother and the Hermit, and they came to him eagerly and full of excitement. They sat down, and Winjarning the elder remained silent, with his eyes fixed upon the tiny bit of feather. They sat patiently waiting for him to speak, but still he remained silent, looking intently at the rock.

They followed his gaze, and saw the object upon which his eyes were fixed. Then what Winjarning was thinking about suddenly dawned upon them; and when Winjarning the elder divined their thoughts he said, " Come, let us find the tracks of the emu." So they walked into the gully again where they had seen the emu feeding as it passed in a northerly direction. They fixed their eyes upon the ground. Winjarning the elder said, " Come and see where the grass was pressed by a footstep. Do you not notice a bit of an emu-feather left in the impression made by the *kurdaitcha* [1] of the Evil One?" They hurried along the valley, and in a bush they saw the body of an emu with its entrails removed. It had been cut from breast to tail, so that it could be fixed upon the back of a person in such a fashion as to conceal his head inside, leaving a small opening through which he could look out. When the wearer of it stooped he would look just like an emu.

They saw plainly the cunning device of the Evil One, and recognized the difficulties they had to contend with. One with long ages of experience such as he possessed would not be easily captured and killed. They would require to bring all their knowledge of the past to bear upon the problem of capturing him. Winjarning the elder suggested that they should all walk apart at a distance of about a mile or two as circumstances might favour, and when they should come within reach of the fugitive the Hermit should run as fast as he could toward him, and approach him from the north side. Winjarning the younger would approach him from the north-east, and he himself would come up on the south side. Winjarning the elder sat down beside a bush, while Winjarning the younger walked due east and the Hermit walked due west.

When they reached their respective distances the Hermit sent up a small smoke-signal. Then they all walked in the

[1] A shoe made of emu-feathers and human hair, both ends being similar, so that a pursuer cannot say in what direction the wearer was travelling. It is often worn by a fugitive, or by one who seeks to be avenged for the death of a member of his family or tribe. Tradition says the *kurdaitcha* was introduced by the Evil One, or that the adoption of the *kurdaitcha* originated from this story.

manner previously agreed upon, so as to arrive at their destination at the time that they had fixed. About midday they saw the Evil One upon a rocky hill-top, viewing the country around him, and looking back upon the way he had come, to see whether anyone was on his track. He saw no sign of danger, so he took shelter under the shadow of a ledge of rock, because the day was now extremely hot. As soon as the Evil One lay down in the cool shade the Hermit ran with the speed of a kangaroo to take up a position on the north side of where the Evil One rested, in order to prevent him from escaping in that direction, and also to be ready to attack him. Winjarning the younger ran to take up his position for a similar purpose on the north-east side of the Evil One. The north and north-eastern sides of the hill were heavily timbered with tall trees, bushes, and shrubs. On the western side, however, for about two miles, there was a plain country, dotted here and there with clumps of stunted mallee-bush, about four or five feet high, which would offer but a very insecure hiding-place for a fugitive.

Now Winjarning the elder walked straight up the hill-side until he was about a hundred paces from the Evil One. Winjarning the younger crept up toward the Evil One until he was about a similar distance from him. The Hermit took up a position in hiding behind the great boulders of rock that formed part of the ledge under which the Evil One was lying, only about fifty paces away. The sun was shining with intense heat as the Winjarnings and the Hermit took up their posts under shelter. They sat thus from midday until the sun was half-way down the western sky. They began to think that the Evil One was aware of their presence, and was scheming how he might entrap them. They tried to think out a way of attacking him, or some means of drawing him from his place of concealment. Winjarning the elder saw that a rock boulder on the west side of the Evil One cast a shadow within fifty paces of the ledge where he rested, and it struck him that he could make use of this. He communicated his thought by a sign to his younger brother, who passed on the message to the Hermit.

By and by Winjarning the elder crept round the rock and sat behind it in the sunshine. He tied a bundle of grass round a long stick, and gradually raised it over the top of the boulder till it cast a shadow upon the ground about twenty paces away from the Evil One. The Evil One saw it, and to him it had the appearance of some one peeping over the boulder. When he saw the shadow he crept out from under the ledge in a stooping position. He fixed his eyes steadily upon the boulder to see whether the person who was peeping would repeat his act. The position that he was then in left him exposed to Winjarning the younger and the Hermit. Winjarning the elder was watching the actions of the Evil One through a thick shrub at the base of the boulder. He also saw that his brother and the Hermit had fixed their spears into their *wommeras* and had them poised, waiting for the critical moment. So he gave them an opportunity to aim. He gently raised the stick, showing the grass. When the Evil One saw the grass he quietly placed his spear on his *wommera*, straight in line for the object upon the boulder. At that instant and with the speed of lightning Winjarning the younger and the Hermit simultaneously delivered their spears. The spear of Winjarning the younger struck the Evil One between the shoulders, and passed right through his chest, while the spear of the Hermit hit him under the arm, passed through his ribs, and entered his heart. The Evil One fell dead without uttering a sound.

The three companions now came up to the body, and each dealt it a severe blow upon the head with his *kanake*, breaking the skull in pieces. They quickly bound the body with fibre collected from the inner surface of mallee-bark, and they tied it to a heavy log, so that if the Evil One should come to life he would be unable to run away with such a heavy weight. The three took turns in watching over the body during the night. When the sun rose they broke their fast, and then they bound the body to a pole about fifteen feet long. The younger Winjarning and the Hermit each took an end of the pole upon his shoulder, and carried the body into the plain country. They cleared the ground in a circle of fifty paces in diameter, and to the centre of the circle the young men carried boughs and twigs of mallee, and laid on the ground three logs, each about nine or ten feet long, and pointing east and west. Between these logs they packed smaller wood closely, and upon the logs they placed others cross-wise, closely together. Another layer of logs was placed upon the top in an east and west direction. Finally, yet another layer was placed on the top, which now formed a platform eight feet wide.

Upon this pile the body of the Evil One was placed, feet to the south and head to the north. This was contrary to their customary method of disposing of the dead. It was adopted because the Evil One was considered to be the greatest enemy of mankind. Winjarning the elder then began to sing the war-song of revenge, thanking the Father of All Spirits that he had used them as the means of bringing about the death of so cruel and wicked a foe. Winjarning the younger and the Hermit danced the war-dance. Then Winjarning the elder set fire to the pile. A dark cloud rolled up and hung about the Winjarnings and the Hermit like a huge canopy. It appeared to be in sympathy with their work, for it obscured the hot rays of the sun, which, combining with the burning of the body of the Evil One, would have intensified the heat and made it almost impossible for them to carry out their task.

Then Winjarning the elder said to his brother and to the Hermit, "We must walk round about the blazing fire to prevent the Evil One from escaping. Any animal, reptile, lizard, or insect that tries to escape must be instantly speared and thrown back into the fire." They walked round about the fire in a circle fifty paces apart. First came Winjarning the elder, then his brother, and then the Hermit. Each had his spear poised on his *wommera* so as to be ready for any emergency. Suddenly out of the flames there leaped a kangaroo. It landed just between the younger Winjarning and the Hermit. The Hermit threw his spear with such force that it passed through the body of the kangaroo and pinned it to the ground. He ran forward and dealt the kangaroo a severe blow upon the head with his *kanake*; then he withdrew his spear and threw the body back into the fire. Then out of the flames there arose an eagle-hawk, crying, "*Pichthor! Pichthor!*" A spear thrown by Winjarning the elder pierced its body, and it fell dying. Winjarning the elder then took his *kanake* from his waist-belt and struck the bird a blow upon the head. He withdrew his spear and threw the eagle-hawk back into the flames. Next a dingo rushed out from the burning wood. The younger Winjarning speared it before it had gone twenty paces from the fire, and then he threw it back into the flames. Then a goanna came out of the flames, followed in turn by a snake, a frilled lizard, a crow, a magpie, and a wombat. Each in turn was captured, and thrown into the burning mass.

When the wood had burned to bright coals a caterpillar crept out, and had almost got beyond the clearing when the Hermit saw it crawling. He took it up and threw it back on the red-hot coals. Next a centipede wriggled out of the fire. Winjarning the elder threw it back into the flames. Then there flew out a moth, which Winjarning the younger struck with his *wommera* and threw back into the fire. Lastly the Evil One attempted to escape in the form of a bull-ant. But it fared after the same fashion as the other animals, birds, reptiles, and insects had done.

If the Evil One, while his spirit was still in his dead body, had managed to escape in any shape he would have been able to change himself into human form again. But he was prevented by the watchfulness of the Winjarning brothers and the Hermit.

The Evil One now has no power such as he formerly had to do the human race bodily injury. But he is still alive in spirit. And it is said that he is to be seen at times in the form of wicked men, who are the medium through which he works. Further, men believe that the Evil One cannot work mischief through any of the animals, birds, reptiles, or insects, because when he made the attempt to escape from the fire in any of these forms he was baulked and thrown back to be burned. It is therefore said among the people that all nature is pure and true, and man alone is of evil disposition.

Perindi and Harrimiah[1]

This is a story of two brothers who were very fond of each other. It seemed to the whole of their tribe that it would be impossible to interfere with their friendship or to make them differ in opinion on any subject. If anyone tried to play a trick upon them by asking a question, say, whether emu food was good for young children or not, they would both agree in their answer. No matter how many miles their bodies might be apart, their minds seemed to act in unison.

Perindi and Harrimiah were twins, but they did not show such an amount of bodily resemblance as is sometimes seen in such cases. Perindi was taller and bigger, and he was the more active of the two. They always went hunting together, and in battle they stood side by side. If anyone quarrelled with Harrimiah Perindi would be offended ; and if some one annoyed Perindi Harrimiah's anger would be aroused. They were both great fighters, and they were experts in the use of the spear and the boomerang, and they would kill a person without hesitation. All the members of the lizard and reptile families were greatly afraid of them. On all important occasions they were treated with much ceremony. They were given the seat of honour, and at great gatherings or feasts they would always be served first and with the choicest morsels.

Their fame travelled far and wide. Many and many a

---

[1] The story of Perindi and Harrimiah teaches aboriginal girls and boys two lessons. The first is that they should not become victims to flattery. Flattery is, to the aboriginal, the seed of pride, malice, and hatred. Flattery, as this story shows, makes a gulf between loving brothers. The second lesson is meekness and humility as expressed in the character of Harrimiah. Unlike Perindi, Harrimiah did not allow pride to dominate him. He mastered it and put it in subjection. He would rather have died than have cultivated a revengeful spirit. For these qualities he was respected and honoured by all.

beautiful maiden was offered to them in marriage, but they did not succumb to these tempting offers. They said they would not marry because they loved each other so much that it would be impossible for either of them to love any other person.

The father, mother, and uncle of these boys were much troubled about their future. The uncle said that it was time that they should marry and have children, marrying and having children being considered one of the most important of their duties to the tribe. The animal, the bird, and the reptile tribes met in conference to find out what action should be taken, but they could not come to a decision without fighting and bloodshed, and perhaps a great loss of life. While the elders of the tribes were in conference the maidens sent a message to them that they would undertake to solve the problem if they were allowed to give effect to their proposals without anyone being involved but themselves and Perindi and Harrimiah. They also guaranteed that nothing wrong should be done. The elders said they would give their consent to the maidens endeavouring to separate Perindi and Harrimiah, provided that they did not violate their moral law or any of their tribal customs.

Then the maidens came in a body to the elders, and requested them to invite all the young men of all the tribes to come and take part in a competition as to who was the best painted and decorated. Many young men came in response to the invitation. Among the competitors were the bandicoot, the lyre-bird, the frilled lizard, and other members of the bird and lizard tribes. These were greatly admired, and it was allowed that they were skilful dancers and mimics. The only expert dancer and mimic who did not come was the green frog, and the reason he gave for his absence was that he had been asked by the maidens not to appear. The tribes made a great pilgrimage to Cooper's Creek, and the animals, the birds, and the lizards camped on either side of the creek. Perindi and Harrimiah pitched their camp about half a mile higher up the creek, so that

295

they would not come into touch with the other competitors until the day when they should be called upon to perform. Just at the beginning of the new moon all the performers began to paint themselves, and to rehearse. This they continued to do until the full moon.

On the day after the night of the full moon Perindi and Harrimiah went into the dense scrub to paint themselves, and the maidens followed them and hid among the bushes. " Now," said Harrimiah to his brother, " let me paint you first, and then you shall paint me afterwards." Harrimiah took a great deal of time, and used his best endeavours to make his brother look well. So with the skill of an artist and the genius of a great master he transformed Perindi into a wonderful picture of beautiful dots and stripes. Harrimiah could not help admiring his brother. He walked round and round him a score of times. He could not believe that this person was his brother. Then he said to Perindi, " Will you paint me, and try to outdo the design that I have depicted on you?" " Yes," said Perindi, and he began to rub powdered charcoal upon the body of Harrimiah. When the colouring was put on Harrimiah it did not show very well on account of this charcoal, but Perindi convinced his brother that he looked splendid.

While these two were being painted and decorated the performance had been going on. The performers had been cheered and encouraged by a great audience, but the maidens had not witnessed any of the triumphs. All their interest was centred upon Perindi and Harrimiah. When these two were waiting their turn to perform the maidens came out of their hiding-place and walked toward them, and passed many flattering remarks on their good looks. Some of the maidens looked amusedly at Harrimiah, and began to giggle; but they gazed with absorbing interest at Perindi. At last Harrimiah began to get uneasy. He asked the maidens if anything was wrong. They made no reply to his question, but looked shy, and turned their heads and walked away. Poor Harrimiah did not know what to do. He turned to Perindi, and asked eagerly,

"Brother, why this strange conduct on the part of the maidens? Can you tell me?" Perindi answered, "O brother, you are all right. There is nothing the matter with you. Come, let us go to the corrobbery ground and take our part."

Now it was a very hot day. The sun shone with all its brightness. Harrimiah said to Perindi, "Will you wait a moment? I should like to take a drink of the cool, refreshing water at yonder pool." "Yes," said Perindi, "I will spare you for a few minutes."

As Harrimiah went toward the pool the maidens all crowded round Perindi, and danced about him, and repeated these words, "O Perindi, the handsome one, all that is noble and grand in manhood belongs to you. You are beautifully painted above all others. There is no one like you." Harrimiah turned about and saw all that was going on. A strange feeling that he had never before experienced came over him. He turned and continued on his way to the pool. He stooped down to take a drink from the limpid water, and he saw to his disgust what had made the maidens laugh. For there, in the clear water, he saw himself as the maidens had seen him, badly painted by the careless and indifferent hand of his brother. Without waiting to drink, he rose up, and with anger in his heart went to Perindi, and asked why he had not painted him as well as he, Perindi, had been painted. "Oh," said Perindi, "I did not think that you should be painted so well, and I did not see why you should want to be decorated better than I, who am the more active." Harrimiah was very disappointed at the reply of Perindi. He had believed that his brother would show more respect toward him.

Now this occurred just after the fashion that the maidens had expected. So they thought at this stage that they would show Harrimiah some attention. They gathered round him and sang and danced. "O beautiful Harrimiah!" they sang. "You do not require artificial beautifying in order to attract the daughters of the tribes. Your beautiful, sparkling eyes are far more lovely than the colours

297

upon the body of Perindi. Come, oh, come, wonderful Harrimiah, and dance with us. We are your slaves. We will dance to the sweet music of your voice." When Perindi heard this he became exceedingly angry, and so far forgot himself as to challenge Harrimiah to fight a duel. Harrimiah accepted the challenge, and started to run to the camp for his weapons, when the maidens said, " Do not fight now. Wait until after the corrobbery. We shall be delighted to watch our brave Harrimiah vanquish the haughty Perindi."

At this juncture the elders came and asked them to present themselves to the audience, who were anxiously looking forward to the appearance of the two brothers. When they were introduced there was loud cheering from many thousand throats, just like the noise of thunder. Then the two brothers started to perform. They imitated the dancing of the lyre-bird and the jumping kangaroo and the wallaby so realistically that the audience was deceived. They were both recalled again and again, some dozen times, before they were allowed to retire from the stage. Then every one went to their wurleys. At the rising of the sun a herald went forth, and called Perindi and Harrimiah to come forward and, by special request of the chiefs, give a last performance representing the animal, the bird, and the reptile tribes.

At midday Perindi and Harrimiah danced the frog dance in such a manner that the young maidens of the tribes ran forth and crowded round them, waiting for an opportunity to pay compliments to them.

On the following morning they all returned to their respective homes, with the exception of the families of the frilled lizard and the blue-tongued lizard. These stayed behind because Harrimiah asked for the hand of the daughter of the blue-tongued lizard and Perindi asked for the hand of the daughter of the frilled lizard. So a double marriage took place.

Now Perindi was better decorated and more beautifully painted than Harrimiah, yet Harrimiah had a great deal of influence over the audience, and all the fair young maidens of the tribes took a fancy to him, and were not backward in showing it. Perindi was greatly incensed in that, with all his beautiful colouring, he had failed to gain the attention of every one, and his jealousy of Harrimiah became uncontrollable. One day he leaped upon the back of his unguarded and unsuspecting brother, and held him by the skin of his neck, and pulled his head back and tore the skin from the flesh. Harrimiah struggled fiercely to free himself from the grip of Perindi, and the blue-tongued and the frilled lizards took hold of Perindi, and, with all their strength, endeavoured to pull him away from the poor, bleeding Harrimiah. This, after much trouble and struggling, they were able to do, and the brothers then went to their respective homes. Harrimiah was accompanied by his wife and all his friends and relatives, but Perindi went alone, because no one could sympathize with him, not even his wife. She went with the wife of Harrimiah to assist her to dress the wounds[1] on the neck of her unfortunate husband.

On the following morning Harrimiah rose with the sun, and went to the pool to bathe the wounds so cruelly inflicted by Perindi. As he looked into the clear water he saw that his neck was badly disfigured, but instead of becoming angry he would not allow the spirit of hatred to control his better nature. He wept bitterly for the wrong he had received from his proud and unrepentant brother.

He did not return to his wife, who was anxiously awaiting his return, but went into the bush. As he passed along the birds ceased their songs of delight, and the trees, the bushes, and the plants whispered to one another as they saw the wounded and broken-hearted Harrimiah dragging himself along, wondering where to look for comfort, because he still loved Perindi. He was sorry he had lost his brother's

---

[1] After the wounds had been bathed with water, ashes of burnt mulga-wood were applied to them, and the wounds healed. This left a mark on each side of Harrimiah's neck, and these marks can be seen to this day if one looks at the animal called the lace lizard.

love; sorry that Perindi hated him; and he wondered if he could rekindle the love that burned for him long ago in Perindi's heart. He cried aloud, "O Perindi, will you not love me once more? I am sorry that I became offended for the way you painted me. O Perindi, my brother, I love you. Will you not come to me? Let us be reconciled. O Perindi, my brother, are we not sons of the same mother? Did she not love and care for us both? Did she not suckle us at the same breast?"

But alas! Perindi did not have an ear to catch the agonizing cry of a sorrowful and broken-hearted brother. His heart was too much occupied with pride, conceit, malice, and hatred.

Harrimiah wept as he passed through the bush. The crow saw him pass, and said to him, "O Harrimiah! Why not wait until your sore or wound heals, and then go back and give battle to this haughty being, your brother?" "No," said Harrimiah. "I cannot and will not return my brother evil for evil. I still love him, and will continue to love him." So Harrimiah walked on his way toward a sandhill not far away. As he passed by the trees and the shrubs they looked with tearful eyes at the broken-hearted Harrimiah. They could not conceal their sorrow, and they gave vent to their feelings. The trees moaned, and the bushes sobbed, and the grass whined in sympathy with Harrimiah. He reached the sandhill, and climbed up its side. Half-way from the top he lay down, exhausted. All the birds came round him and began to weep. Some of the more warlike birds said to Harrimiah, "Come, Harrimiah! Return with us, and we will go and punish this haughty Perindi. We will humble his proud spirit." "No, no, no!" said Harrimiah. "If you desire to make me happy, try to forgive my brother, and tell him that I still love him." Then he began digging, and he dug until half of his body was hidden from the gaze of the onlookers. He went on digging until he was about eight or twelve inches below the surface of the earth. After a time the birds returned to their homes and hunting-grounds.

BULPALLUNGGA

Harrimiah's wife began to feel uneasy at the long absence of her husband, and she called her mother, and said, "Harrimiah has not returned. Come, let us go in search of him." They followed his tracks to the pool of water, then on through the bushes until they came to the sandhill, and to the place where he had covered himself. Just as they were going to dig the crow came and said, "Do not disturb Harrimiah. He is broken-hearted about the treatment he has received at the hands of Perindi. He sleeps." So they decided that they would keep watch over Harrimiah as he slept beneath the cold sand. Then they asked the wattle and the wild apple tree[1] to accommodate them, as they would like to await the return of Harrimiah from beneath the sand. The trees were willing, so their spirits entered the wattle and the wild apple tree. When these trees blossom it is a sign that Harrimiah has come out once more from the sand to enjoy life.

Bulpallungga

This is a story that is often told by the elders of the different tribes in their various languages throughout Australia. It is told as an object lesson to their boys, with a view to educating them by instilling into their young minds a knowledge of the disastrous results of living a life that is contrary to the rules of their social order and out of harmony with the community. No boy is allowed to repeat this story to any of his playmates, not even to his bosom companion or to a brother, until the listener has fulfilled the ceremonial rites of his tribe and satisfied the elder; and then it must be told only in a whisper, and with the very greatest solemnity.

There was a Wonboona man who married a young woman. He enjoyed the companionship of his wife for only a short time, for he died three months after their marriage. As a sign of widowhood she had a mourning cap of white clay placed on her head. She was also required

---

[1] The wattle and the wild apple blossom are the symbols of sympathy, honour, and glory to those who are meek and humble in heart.

to have her face smeared with pipeclay. One evening, when she and her two married sisters were out gathering herbs for food, they sat down on the bank of a running stream that flowed through a valley. The widow looked into the clear water, and saw in it the image of her husband. The sisters also looked, and immediately recognized the likeness. But the husband appeared to be taller and bigger and more powerful than he used to be. He seemed to be about eight feet in height. The image in the water was so real that the widow rose to her feet and plunged into the stream, expecting to be embraced once more by kind and loving arms. But she was sadly disappointed, and when she had come up out of the water she again sat down with her sisters and began to weep. Then out of the stream there came the sounds of a musical voice. It was the Goddess of Childbirth who was speaking. She said, "Woman, you are with child, a male child. What you saw in the water was its image, the image of what you will bring forth. Upon your training of the child much will depend. If you lose control over him in infancy or in childhood you will be as deeply disappointed as you have been just now by the sight of the image. What you have seen in the water is a warning. Remember the child is coming."

The three sisters were glad, and rejoiced greatly. They went home and told their mother and their aged uncle, the brother of their mother.[1] They told no one else, and the secret was kept strictly among themselves. The three sisters visited the stream, the scene of their hopes, every day until within a few weeks of the time of the expected birth. Then their aged uncle, with the help of their relatives, began to make a wurley to receive and accommodate the visitor whom they were eagerly awaiting. At twilight of the first day of residence in their new home they sat

[1] The aged uncle, being the brother of the widow's mother, would regard the widow as his child. An uncle on the mother's side cultivates the feeling of love for children of his sister, and calls them his daughters or sons. The uncles on the father's side represent the law to the children, while the uncles on the mother's side are symbolical of love.

outside the wurley of the young widow. After having had their evening meal they were enjoying the cool, refreshing air, when the aged uncle spoke first, as is the custom. His speech was intended to encourage the young girl, who would have to endure severe pain within the next few days. This is what he said: " My daughter, the kangaroos, the wallabies, and the dingoes, with their mates, have sought shelter and peace among the bushes and shrubs at the farther end of the valley, near the rocky hill, in order to make all needful preparation for their progeny in the near future. For months the birds, both male and female, have been very busily engaged in building their nests, and now they have finished their labours. Some of them have been sitting on their eggs for some time, and are expecting the arrival of newcomers to swell the numbers in the bird families of the valley. Do you not hear the warblings of the magpies and the butcher-birds, the twitterings of the willy-wagtails, and the love-songs of the little blue wrens, each one desiring to delight his lady-love as she sits on the nest, with the eggs snugly and cosily tucked away among the soft down of her warm breast? The male bird sings, ' Rest, and sleep sweetly, my darling wife, companion of my life, and sharer of my fortunes and feelings.' When the mother bird hears the song her heart is thrilled with the beauty of the words and the melody of the music. The mother birds pass on the song to the unhatched baby birds in the egg. The voice of the father birds is not heard. Only the emotion of the mother is passed on, and this is how the young birds, both male and female, receive feelings and impulses that enable them to live in love and fidelity.

" The plants, too, are eagerly awaiting their time to burst forth in splendour, and to beautify this spot, and waft their fragrance on the morning and evening air. Every living thing fulfils its part in the great creation. There is one thing lacking, however, and this fills my soul with sorrow and distress. It is this, my daughter, that your young husband, master, lord, friend, and companion is not alive to be beside you, to comfort and support you in this emergency. But take courage, my daughter, you are most fortunate to be among the number of the creators, a contributor to the supreme glory of the one Great Father Spirit, to lay upon his altar your offering of an immortal soul, with power to think, and will to fulfil the eternal wisdom of that one Great Cause who is our life and through whom all things live and move." [1]

Then the elder and other members of the family retired to their own camps. The young widow and her sisters entered into the wurley.

At midnight the young widow gave birth to her first-born child, Bulpallungga. The aunts, her sisters, made a great show of the child. The aged uncle was called in first to see it, then the other members of the family. They all saw that this child was much bigger and stronger than other babies; in fact, that never had such a big baby been born. The aunts said to all round, " A vision appeared to our sister. We, too, saw it in the water when the Goddess of Birth came and told her all."

The young widow expressed a desire to her uncle and relatives to make the wurley her home until the baby boy was grown into a youth. Thus it was in this valley that Bulpallungga spent all his days of boyhood, hunting the young wallabies, opossums, and dingoes, and watching the birds building their nests, and noticing the flowers coming into bloom. Many and many a time he would go and swim in the pool where his mother had seen the vision.

One day the uncle of the young mother came and said to her, "My daughter, the time has come when we must submit Bulpallungga to the care of the elders of the tribe to which his father belonged." The mother pleaded and said, " O my uncle, brother of my mother, the woman that gave me birth, your sister whom you love, allow me to have him a little longer. Let me take him to his father's brother

---

[1] When a young woman is about to bear a child it is the custom that the uncle shall point out to her that she is passing through the same experience as other living creatures who produce their kind, and that this is only one of the many wonders of nature.

before he be taken and made a young man." " O my daughter," said the uncle, " I have cared for you and yours in your infancy. I have nursed you, and have sung many a ballad to send you to sweet and peaceful sleep, and it grieves me to have to refuse your request. Come now, my daughter, I will take him and present him to his tribe as a candidate for the ceremonial rites." " But, Uncle," she said, " allow me, your daughter, to spend one more night with him, and we will consider it a great honour to take him to his father's brothers and father's father. I will not ask of you another favour so long as my son lives." So the uncle gave her a little longer grace.

This gave the mother an opportunity to take the boy to another neighbourhood, and when she got there she pleaded with the elder of the tribe to have him excused from being made a young man. Now this was one of the greatest blunders that any parent could make, and especially so in the case of Bulpallungga. Although the mother had been warned at the beginning by the Goddess of Childbirth she now made this mistake, and she had to pay for it afterward with bitter tears.

Just after this the young mother, without saying anything to her sisters, told Bulpallungga that she did not approve of his being submitted to the tortures of ceremonial rites, and that she did not intend that he should undergo them. The lad was willing to do as his mother advised him. He was eager to avoid the initiation rites. So he ran away at midnight to another tribe. He was shown into the presence of the chief, who took a great fancy to this lad of such splendid physique, and adopted him as his son. This chief had not a son of his own, so Bulpallungga was very fortunate to have come to him. The chief presented Bulpallungga to the tribe as a son sent him as a present by the great Goddess of Childbirth. He was beautiful to look upon, and he stood head and shoulders above the tallest man of the tribe. But although Bulpallungga was a giant in stature he was still but a youth in mind and ways, and the old chief made a great blunder in allowing him to associate with the young married men of the tribe, and to sit and hear tales that were strictly forbidden for him to listen to. In ordinary circumstances such a proceeding would not have been allowed, as it was contrary to all social custom and to the moral law of the people of all the tribes.

Bulpallungga for the first two months led a life of idleness. Then he made the acquaintance of a newly married girl. Naturally her young husband protested against such behaviour. A petition was sent to the old chief, begging him to see that Bulpallungga should be made to control himself. When the old chief heard of the immoral behaviour of Bulpallungga he sent an urgent message to all the surrounding tribes to come and perform the initiation ceremonies upon him. In a short time all the tribes arrived at the appointed place and at the hour fixed. After serious consultation the elders decided to pass Bulpallungga through a course of the most severe training and discipline.

Meantime the mother of Bulpallungga became very much distressed about her son and his welfare. She wept every morning and evening as if her son were dead. She pleaded with her brothers that they would go and bring her tidings regarding his health and behaviour, as it was now six months since she had seen him. Then her brother said to her, " Sister, we have heard that an aged chief who has no children of his own has taken Bulpallungga into his home, and has instructed the elder of his tribe to send forth a proclamation to his people that the Goddess of Childbirth has sent him a son to comfort the lives of him and his wife. And, furthermore, we heard that, at the approach of the new moon, Bulpallungga's brothers[1] will chant the song of initiation."

The widowed mother was filled with sorrow for her only son, whose father, being dead, could not be present to witness the ordeal through which his son would pass. These thoughts troubled her mind, and she repented of her cowardice in sending her only son away into a strange tribe

[1] These would be the children of the brothers of the aged chief. A boy is taught to call these relatives brothers or sisters as the case may be.

in order to escape from those ceremonial rites. She now saw that wherever aboriginals existed as a tribe and a people the rites would be enforced. It would have been better for her to have submitted her son voluntarily to the elder of their own tribe, where she would have been near him, and where her pleading for gentle treatment would have had effect. She was grieved to think that it was on account of her action that he would now have to be disciplined by strangers.

She cried to the Goddess of Childbirth, " O my mother, Goddess of Childbirth, would that I could recall those happy privileges that you gave me, the duty of a mother's love to protect and train a child in the pathway that leads to honour, truth, purity, and duty. I now fully realize that through my indulgence and neglect my child has dishonoured me, and more especially my husband, his father. I have betrayed your trust. I have also dishonoured my husband. I do not ask for your forgiveness or pity, neither do I seek even the smallest favour, for your pity, favour, or forgiveness would intensify my sorrow and remind me of my indifference and my neglected duty. But let my cry be heard all through the coming ages as evidence of the wrong I have done, and let it be a warning for mothers in all time to come. Permit that my spirit, the spirit of a broken-hearted mother, be reincarnated in the body of the curlew. If my son and my husband's son should fail to fulfil his duty to his tribe in the ceremonial rites grant me one request. To-morrow, when the sun is far away on the western sky, let me come to that sacred pool where I beheld my husband in whose image my child was framed. Let me there see reflected in the clear water a vision of my son's future, whether it be a life of success or of failure."

The whispering voice of the Goddess of Childbirth replied, " My daughter, and the medium through which I multiply the people of the earth, you will not think it ill that I am not responsible for your son's actions, whether they be good or bad. It is not within my power to cause a child to walk in the paths of good men. That privilege belongs to the mother; she decides what a child shall be. But you may feel assured that you and your sisters will have my presence upon the morrow at the pool."

It was with a heavy heart that the young widow retired to rest. Her sisters chanted the spirit song of the departed. Then they sang the song of sleep. "Come, O sleep, on wings like the soft white down of the swan.[1] Settle upon us, especially on the eyelids of our younger darling sister. Come in abundance, and settle all about her body. Bury her deeply and snugly like the young wood duck in her down-lined nest."

After they had sung the song of sleep for an hour they slept soundly without being disturbed by a dream. They were awakened in the morning by the gentle touch and the whispering tones of their aged uncle. The uncle had not slept for a moment. He had been kept awake all through the night by the screeching of the owl and the mopoke, and the fluttering of the wings of the wild duck flying from one pool of water to another. He was troubled in mind. He had heard the sisters singing to their widowed sister the spirit song and the song of sleep. He now spoke to them, and said, "My daughters, will you all rise and break your fast? I have cooked a meal which you will find outside the wurley."

When the sun had reached half-way down the western sky the young widow went to the pool, accompanied by her sisters. It was a bright afternoon, and the air was fresh. There was hardly enough wind to ruffle the surface of the water. Everything looked bright and beautiful. The widow sat on the spot on which she had sat some eighteen years before, and her sisters sat one on each side of her. At the request of the Goddess of Childbirth the spirit that dwelt in the pool commanded the water to reflect the future life of Bulpallungga. There appeared within the pool a white cloud. In the cloud there came a dark spot, that gradually grew larger and larger, and shaped itself into human form, and in the view of the widow and the sisters

---

[1] The soft white down of the swan is a symbol of sleep.

there appeared the likeness of Bulpallungga. He looked very beautiful, and seemed to be full of youthful vigour, and so perfectly happy that the sight gladdened the heart of his mother.

Then there came a change. The watchers were unable to say where the happiness ended and the sorrow and despair began. They saw the changes plainly reflected upon Bulpallungga's face—happiness, sorrow, and then despair flitting across it in succession. The water began to ripple, as if a gust of wind had passed over it. The reflection was unrecognizable on the rippling surface. This was the work of the spirit of the water, who did this in order to obliterate the sad picture from the vision of the mother and the aunts. The watchers rose to their feet, and walked straight homeward. It was a most sorrowful procession. The women walked in single file, with their heads bowed with grief.

They walked in order of ages, the eldest sister first, and the young mother last. Soon they were joined by their brother and their uncle, the elder, who had come in order to show their sympathy for the young mother. The brother and the uncle saw by the looks and attitudes of the sisters that they were in trouble. When the sisters reached the wurley they fell upon the ground, facing the setting sun. They began to weep and to sprinkle handfuls of sand over themselves. This sign of deep mourning they repeated time after time. After a while the sisters sat down outside their wurley and turned their faces toward the west. They held up their hands in supplication to the Great Father Spirit. Addressing the departed spirit, the mother began to chant the song of sorrow. "O my son, why didst thou come to maturity in thy mother's womb? Had it not been better for thee that thy life had ceased before birth? My child, why should I talk thus to thee? Thou couldst not choose to live or die, or to be good or bad. Thy life was formed and fixed by thy father and thy mother. We were not bad in infancy, but were taught in early childhood not to follow the desires that are within, but to control the wayward impulses that all the human race is subject to. O my

309

son, I did thee a lasting wrong in allowing thee, when a child, to do whatsoever thou didst will to do. I checked thee not. O my son, would to the Goddess of Childbirth that thou hadst died within my womb! Then thy infant life of purity, nourished by a mother's love within thy innocent breast, would have expanded thy soul and mind and body in that mysterious land beyond the western sky. This is the grandest privilege to still-born infants untainted by worldly desire and sinful vice. My love for thee is great, and I have prayed that I may not pass from this life in peace, but that my spirit, instead of entering into that Land of Perfect Bliss, shall wander upon the earth, and continue to drink the cup of sorrow and despair, all to show the love I have for thee, my son. She has granted unto me this request, that from now until time shall be no more my spirit shall find a place of rest within the breast of the curlew."

That evening when the widow went to sleep her spirit straightway entered into the curlew. Her relatives heard a voice calling away in a glade in the valley. They strained their ears to listen. Yes, it was her voice, and they wondered what she was doing away in the valley at that time of the night. Then the uncle looked into the wurley, and found the sisters all sleeping soundly. He went to the young mother, and put his hand upon her breast. It was cold. He quietly awakened the elder sister, and told her that her young sister was dying of a broken heart, and that already her spirit had entered into something that was now calling in the valley. Then the other sister was wakened, and she also was told the sad news. They were all prepared for what might happen, for they had known that their sister would be dead by morning. She had told them earlier in the evening that her spirit would leave her body because she was overwhelmed with sorrow and disappointment at the behaviour of her only son. And thus it is that from that evening to the present day, at twilight and midnight and even until the dawn, we hear the mother still weeping for her wayward boy, Bulpallungga. In this manner the early life of young motherhood ended. And thus will the aboriginals be reminded of a mother's love in submitting herself to a year of weeping and refusing to be comforted. The mother died before her son came to a shameful end.

No one told Bulpallungga of his mother's death. He could not understand the wailing that he heard every evening regularly at twilight. He sneaked out of his camp, and saw that it was a bird that was calling, but the voice had the sound of a human being's. It haunted him because he recognized a tone in it that seemed so familiar.

During the twelve months of Bulpallungga's sojourn away from his mother and relatives, and the unpleasant experiences that they were passing through, he was enjoying himself and leading a life of dissipation.[1] He was spending his youth in riotous living, breaking all the social and moral laws of the tribe. His conduct before long became a source of danger to the girls and youths of the tribe in which he lived, and to the neighbouring tribes. His behaviour became so notorious that he was summoned before the elders of the tribes. They demanded that he should appear before them to suffer the penalty of death.

Now the morality of the tribes was so lax that when the maidens heard of the decision of the elders they came to Bulpallungga at night, and said, " O Bulpallungga, never, among the many warriors of the tribes, has a man been seen like you, so perfect in form and stature and possessed of such strength. We have come to you to beg that you will not submit yourself to be slain. Take these three spears.[2] We have stolen them from the camp of the medicine-man

---

[1] The aboriginal narrator said here : " Bulpallungga led a life similar to that of Samson, David, and Solomon, or, still more, a faster life, like the Prodigal of Holy Writ."

[2] The medicine-man's spear is the *thingairipari*; it is used in battle to slay the chief warrior of the opposing side. It is also used by an expert spear-thrower against a person who is to be slain for a violation of tribal law or custom. It is recognized by all tribes as a magic spear, and it is supposed to contain the spirit of the person into whose decomposing dead body it had been thrust, to remain there until the flesh had all decayed. The medicine-man speaks to this spear and tells it the wishes of the tribes or people regarding the destruction of their enemies.

during his absence. We secured the services of an admirer of yours to volunteer to thrust a kangaroo-bone into her thigh. She consented to do this willingly for your sake. When the girl had done this we sent for the services of the medicine-man, and while he was busy extracting the bone we entered his camp and stole the three spears. We have heard our brothers say that the medicine-man has already spoken to these spears, and so now you have only to use them."

"But," said Bulpallungga, "what if the medicine-man should return and discover that I have these spears?"

The young maidens replied, "We have other girls and your admirers in other parts of the country who have inflicted bodily injury on themselves, so that the medicine-man will be kept busy for a week. They have already sent messages begging him to go to their assistance. Some of the injured are three days' journey away. Be not afraid, you are well armed. Take courage. All your admirers are wishful that you should overcome and slay those who would take your life. You shall reign supreme, and have for yourself those things that are dearest to your heart."

When the sun rose upon the following morning Bulpallungga came before the tribe, bearing in his hand the three spears. There was a great gathering in the open country of young men, maidens, children, warriors, and the elders of the tribe. Bulpallungga stood up as straight as one of his spears. Then a warrior stepped forth from the crowd, with a spear fixed upon his *wommera*, and walked toward Bulpallungga. When Bulpallungga saw the warrior approaching he stuck two of his spears into the ground, and placed the third in his *wommera*. He remained in a half-crouching position, with a shield in his left hand, and awaited the advancing warrior, who had now come within striking distance of fifty paces. The warrior stopped suddenly, and, with the skill of a well-trained fighter, threw his spear with great speed straight at the breast of Bulpallungga. Bulpallungga quickly raised his shield, and the warrior's spear struck it and stuck fast in it. Bulpallungga

312

THE COMBAT WITH SPEARS

SHE-OAK TREES AT PEEL'S INLET, WESTERN AUSTRALIA
Photo B. H. Woodward, sometime Curator of Perth Museum   318

quickly dropped the shield with the spear, and threw his own spear. All that the onlookers heard was a *swish* as the spear travelled like lightning. It hit the warrior, threw him to the ground, and pinned him there, dead. This act struck terror into the hearts of the elders and the warriors and the young people of the tribe. Bulpallungga ever after this became known as " Bulpallungga the wicked, the great spearman."

Then the elders of the tribe sent messages to all parts, beseeching the tribes to procure the aid of an expert boomerang-thrower to do battle with Bulpallungga, and to slay him, and to rid them and other tribes of the violator of their

HOW THE SPEAR IS THROWN BY THE AID OF THE WOMMERA

Redrawn from *The Prehistoric Arts, Weapons, etc., of the Aborigines of Australia,*
by Thomas Worsnop.

morals and the breaker of their customs and laws. One man volunteered to match his skill against Bulpallungga's. This man was known far and wide as an expert boomerang-thrower. When the young women admirers of Bulpallungga heard of what the elders intended doing they again sneaked into the camp of the medicine-man, and stole a boomerang that had been treated in the same manner as the spears. This they gave to Bulpallungga. Once again he stood upon the same spot, prepared to do battle, but on this occasion he clasped the boomerang firmly in his hand. Then the boomerang expert approached him. Bulpallungga, without waiting for him to deliver the first blow, threw his boomerang at him. It went through the air at a great pace, struck the expert with mighty force, and cut his body in halves. The boomerang continued to travel onward, and killed six men. This act struck even greater terror into the hearts of the people and the surrounding

313

tribes, and it made the maidens more bold. They came forward and threw their arms about Bulpallungga. Even the young married women preferred him.

The elders did not know what to do. Here was a new peril threatening their homes, and they were helpless to deal with it. They came upon Bulpallungga in a mob, but he was so powerful that he took hold of a man by the leg and swung him about, using him like a *nulla-nulla* to kill those who were attacking him. The people became panic-stricken, and began to take flight to another country. The medicine-man called them together and inquired why they were so afraid and anxious to leave their own country. Then they said to him, " Have you dwelt among us and not heard of the wrongdoing committed by one named Bulpallungga, a youth who came into our midst some eighteen moons ago? No one knows where he came from or where he goes. On the first day of his arrival he was sent to the aged chief, who, when he saw the gigantic youth, called to his wife and his relatives and the elders of the tribe, ' Behold my son sent by the Goddess of Birth to be a comfort to my wife and me.' In body he stands eight feet high, and he is proportionately perfect in every way. His strength is equal to a dozen warriors of any tribe, although in age he is only a boy of eighteen. The chief and his wife allowed the boy too much freedom. They gave instructions that he was to be allowed to do as he liked, and that he was not to be considered as one to be subjected to the initiation rites, since he had been sent to them by the Goddess of Childbirth. So the youth was given full liberty, and was allowed to have all that he desired. After he had lived among us for some time he became wayward, and whatever he wished he would take from anyone, irrespective of age or sex. The elders protested against his unruly conduct to the chief, who said, ' Leave him alone until the next gathering of the tribes, and then we will endeavour to make him conform to our rules. He is only a boy, and does not know what he is doing.' Now he has grown up to be a wicked youth, and defies men, women, and the

314

Great Father Spirit. He has violated our moral law and the social customs of our tribe and country. He is a danger to our tribe, and to all tribes. When the death-sentence was passed upon him, and he had appeared before the tribe to undergo it, he speared the warrior who was appointed to execute him. In fact, he slew all who were selected to punish him for breaking the laws. And now we have left our homes and our country to seek for a safe place for our wives and children."

Then the medicine-man said to them, " Children, tell me what was his chief offence and crime." An elder replied that Bulpallungga was a slave to his evil passions ; he had broken up the homes of young married couples, and had violated the virginity of the maidens. The medicine-man listened attentively while the elder was speaking. He spoke no word until the elder had ceased. Then he arose and walked over to the shade of a tree near by. He sat down on the ground in order that he might think. It was midday when the medicine-man met the people who were fleeing from their homes and country. They were taking shelter under rocks and trees. After the medicine-man had rested for about two hours he rose, and came to the elders of the tribe, and said, " Send two of your finest young men to the people of the north to say to the elder of the tribe that the medicine-man of the Wonboona tribe would like to see the prettiest girls of his tribe before the new moon. Send two other young men to the east to say that the medicine-man of the Wonboona tribe would like to see two of the prettiest girls. Send a similar message to the west."

On the morning of the next day, before the sun rose, the six young men had broken their fast and were well on their respective ways, north, east, and west. It took them three days to deliver their message. On the sixth day they returned, and told the medicine-man that the tribes had granted the request, and that in two days or more they would arrive, bringing the maidens with them. Then the medicine-man called the elders and the warriors to him, and told them what he intended to do. The young girls who were coming were to be instructed in the part they were to play in bringing about the downfall of Bulpallungga. They were to entice him so that he would endeavour to gain them, but they were not to allow him to put hands on them. The important part of the plan was that the girls should ask Bulpallungga to go and help them to collect pheasants' eggs, and place the eggs in a glade in the valley. Each girl was to volunteer to feed Bulpallungga with an egg, but before they started feeding him he should dig a slanting hole, eight feet long, into the earth. He was to stand in this hole.

A messenger was sent to tell Bulpallungga that there was a great gathering of the tribes from the north, east, and west, and that among the peoples of the tribes there were most beautiful maidens. When Bulpallungga heard this he came to the great gathering, and beheld the girls, who had already been told what they were to do. The girls had their own camping-ground. Next day Bulpallungga went boldly into their camp, but no girl would allow him to touch her. They all said to him, " Come, let us gather some pheasants' eggs." They went with Bulpallungga into the valley to gather eggs. When they had collected a sufficient number of eggs they took Bulpallungga to a spot in the valley surrounded by dense forest growth. They told him to dig a hole, and he did as he was ordered. He stood in the hole, and the girls said, " Lie on your back, and we will put the eggs in your mouth." Bulpallungga enjoyed this. Then some of the girls began to tickle him, and this made him laugh most heartily. When he opened his mouth again they gave him some more eggs. He began to get weary of this, but the girls said, " Just one more, and then we will be your slaves." They continued to tickle him, and then they rubbed their cheeks against his. He began to think that they were in earnest, so he opened his mouth once more. As he did this half a dozen spear-points were thrust down his throat and into his chest by warriors who had lain in hiding. The girls rose quickly, and ran to join their tribes.

Thus was Bulpallungga's life brought to an end, not by the strength of men, but by the cunning of maidens.

Nurunderi's Wives

Nurunderi is the name given by the Narrinyeri tribe to the good man who was sent by the Father of All Spirits to be his messenger and teacher. After coming from the northern part of Australia, and passing through various parts of New South Wales and Victoria, he found his way into South Australia. He dwelt mostly on and round the shores of Lakes Alexandrina and Albert, and there he would visit various camping-grounds where the people lived permanently. Some of the people would run into the water when they saw him, and hide among the reeds and other water-plants. When he saw that the people fled from him he would call, " Where art thou? " But they would remain silent. He became annoyed with the attitude of the people, and he would say to them, " Well, children, if you will not answer me I shall curse you. You shall all become birds, and shall remain so for ever." And at the command of Nurunderi they suddenly became birds. But some who summoned sufficient courage and came at his call are the tribes that remain at this day round Lake Alexandrina.

When Nurunderi had completed his mission he chose as his last home on earth two bald-looking hills, which were free from trees and had only low shrubs and grass-trees growing on them, while the surrounding country was covered with a dense growth of mallee, honeysuckle, and she-oak, and some species of gum-tree and other plants. He made the choice of these two hills because from them he was able to view both of the lakes, and because he intended to rest there until the Great Spirit should call him to take his place in heaven among the great company that had gone before him.

Once on a fishing expedition he was passing on his way to Lake Albert when he saw in his path two grass-trees swaying gracefully in the south wind. His attention was

317

so arrested that he stood for a time gazing upon them. Then it appeared that there came from the bough of a she-oak the weird notes of a song, not of pleasure or joy or happiness, but of sadness. The song was sung by two maidens who were imprisoned in the stem of the grass-tree. The selfish spirit of the grass kept these two young maidens fast because they were so sweet, and he delighted to invite the native bees and ants and honey-birds to come and dine with him there. Nurunderi's heart was moved by the pitiful cry.

Now these two maidens, by their wonderful charms, had captivated many and many a good man on his way to the Spirit Land. On account of their behaviour these two maidens had been imprisoned under many different forms, sometimes as beautifully coloured butterflies, sometimes as flower-tops of reeds. Various trees, shrubs, and plants had endeavoured to keep them prisoners because they captivated so many good and great men. So at this time the grass-tree made an effort to keep them shut up. It was the last plant to attempt to make them prisoners, and all the plants were wondering whether it would succeed in its efforts. This was why, when the great man Nurunderi stood looking at the grass-tree's stem, the boughs of the she-oak began to wail as if the wind was passing through their wiry leaves.

Now the sounds seemed to come from the she-oak, but they were really coming from the grass-tree. These cunning maidens knew that if they were to try to use their charms to win this sacred man they would fail; but if they could touch the chords of pity then surely this good man would have compassion on them and release them. On this possibility they were depending for their freedom. They were conscious that the grass-tree was not a good medium through which they could send their message to Nurunderi, so when the south wind was blowing they made a sorrowful cry, as if they were mourning for some loved one who had died. Then Nurunderi stood, and being a great man he listened to the cry of the two maidens, and said, " Oh, I pity! Oh, I pity you both! Why do you both weep so?" They replied, " We have been placed in this grass-tree, and our bodies with their senses of taste, smell, hearing, and touch are dead. It is only this half-conscious state which is still alive that makes us accept this prison home. Our bodily form and human flesh have become vegetable. O great one, take pity upon us and release us, and we will be your servants."

Nurunderi thought and thought. And meantime these two maidens began to use the cunning of many years' experience upon this sacred man. He listened, and then he began to think within himself that it would be good to see the forms of these two spirits enclosed in this grass-tree. He said, " It will be no great harm for me to look upon them, although I am forbidden to associate with women. I will assist them and cause them to come forth, and then I will look after them for a while." So he told the grass-tree to give the fair maidens their liberty. In the twinkling of an eye they stepped from out the tree, a picture of beauty. Their perfect forms and their wonderful eyes so captivated the great man that he fell a victim to their charms. He decided that he would make both of them his wives. So he told the maidens that, since he had given them their freedom, he would ask them to be his wives. Instead of going fishing as he intended, he returned to his home, and asked them to be seated, and then he gave them something to eat.[1]

As time went on the women passed through new experiences, and the woman nature began to show itself in them. In the mind of Nurunderi there began to be suspicions of some coming trouble. He would not allow his

---

[1] After the wives had enjoyed their meal Nurunderi began to tell them of the various laws and customs that had been given to the people, and to explain that some of the laws were very drastic—that is to say, the breaking of them would result in the death of the offender. For instance, in the ' making of the young men ' no woman is allowed to look upon the candidates or to give or offer them food. Further, no woman is allowed to eat the *tukkeri,* a fish silvery-scaled and extremely bony. This fish is much sought after by aboriginals, and if a woman eats of it she is punished by being killed.

wives to remain at home by themselves, but would ask them to accompany him on his fishing expeditions. One day they were out fishing on Lake Albert. Nurunderi was in his canoe, while his wives were wading in the shallow water along the shore, with a cone-shaped net [1] made from the rushes that grow on the banks of the lakes. In the net they caught three beautiful, silvery-white *tukkeri*. The women looked round, trembling with excitement. This was a species of fish that women were forbidden to eat. They covered the fishes with weeds and rushes, and went on their way with the net, pretending to be fishing, but they were so overjoyed with their catch that they paid no attention to what they were doing. After a time they felt they could not stand the strain much longer, so they decided to go home. On looking out over the lake their attention was attracted by a column of smoke that rose against the clear sky to the north-west. So they called their chief and husband, Nurunderi, and he came to them. The elder of the wives pointed toward the smoke, and said, " Look ! A message ! " So he sat down, waiting for the message. Suddenly he rose up and told them that Nepelle had said that he would like him to come to his home. He said he would leave at once, and advised them that they should make themselves comfortable at home. The young wives said, " We will stay here and watch you cross over to the other side of the lake, and then we will go to our home." So Nurunderi got into the canoe and paddled across the lake.

When the wives saw that he had landed safely and was on his way to the home of Nepelle they turned round and went toward the heap of weeds and rushes, and took the forbidden fish from beneath it. They sat looking and looking, and turned the fishes over and over, and after they had finished admiring them they rose and set off homeward. They ran all the way until they reached the camp, and then they began hurriedly to make a fire of she-oak tree-bark.

[1] This net is made in the shape of a cone, constructed after the fashion of the old style candle-extinguishers.

Then they commenced to cook the fish. Nurunderi heard
the fat of the *tukkeri* frizzling, and he said to Nepelle, " Do
you hear a sound as of some one cooking forbidden fish ?
I shall not sleep here to-night. I shall leave you just before
sunset."

After the fish were cooked the wives sat down on top of
the hill so that they would have a view of the surrounding
country, and in order that if anyone should be passing or
should come to their camp they might have plenty of time
to hide the remaining portions of the fish, so that they
would not be accused of having eaten forbidden food.
They sat in the sunshine, chatting and eating and expressing
the delight they felt in enjoying such sweet food. They
remarked, " Ah, the men are clever ! They know what
foods are nicest, and so they make laws to deprive us of our
rightful share. But we also have been clever." So they
ate and laughed and made merry. When they had finished
their meal they reclined on the grass and enjoyed their rest,
and listened to the song of the birds in a valley not very
far distant. But just as the sun was half-way down the
western sky they began to think about what they had done.
They sat up and looked into each other's eyes inquiringly.
One sister said to the other, " Oh, what have we done?
We must not stay here any longer. It is a very strange
thing, but can you not smell the oil of the *tukkeri*? The
grass, the shrubs, and the trees all seem to smell of it.
Come ! We cannot stay here and be asked questions when
our master returns."

By this time they were fully aware of the seriousness of
their offence. The elder said, " Come, let us flee." " But,"
said the younger, " where shall we go? Let us stay and
face the wrath of Nurunderi. It is better that we should
stay and be returned to our place in the grass-tree than that
we should be caught fleeing away and suffer something far
more dreadful." " Come ! " said the elder. " There is
no time to discuss the matter. We may go into some
strange land and win the affection of a wise man and be
married to him, and then no one will dare to interfere with

our liberty." So without another word each of them gathered a great bundle of grass-tree sticks and carried them to the waterside and bound them together, forming a raft. They pushed the raft off into deep water, and sat upon it, and paddled across to the western side of Lake Albert, and slept there for the rest of the night.

Nurunderi arrived at his home late in the evening. When he came within about a hundred yards or thereabouts of his wurley he noticed the smell of *tukkeri*-fat. "Ah!" said he, "those silly and frivolous maidens have eaten the forbidden fish, and now they must be punished." When he entered the wurley there was no one about, so he called out, "Where are you two?" There was no answer. There was no sound but the screeching of the night-owl, which was a sign that something was wrong. The culprits had fled. So he lit a fire and sat down for a while, pondering over the misdeeds of his two young wives. He was thinking deeply what excuse he could make to the Great Spirit for releasing those maidens from their prison in the grass-tree in which they had been placed by the last victim, the spirit of the native companion. He meditated as to what form of punishment he should make them undergo, or what prison he should shut them up in. Then he thought he had better capture them first. So he lay down to sleep.

Next morning before the sun rose he took his *plongge* [1] and a boomerang and prepared to set out. Binding his opossum-skin about his shoulders he set off, walking slowly down to the shore of the lake. As the sun rose he began to walk faster, and as he walked he kept a sharp look-out for signs of footprints. When he reached the side of the lake he made for the place where his wives had left their net. He examined the net carefully, and discovered some scales of *tukkeri* upon it. Now he felt satisfied regarding the reason of the absence of his wives. After he had looked

[1] A weapon with a knob at one end, about eighteen inches long; it is used for bruising the body of anyone who transgresses a law, and its use causes a slow and painful death, which gives the offender time to think over the misdeeds that he has done and to repent of them.

about very carefully he got into his canoe and paddled across the lake, and came to the place where his wives had landed. He saw their raft, and among the bushes that grew on the bank of the river he saw a fire and the place where they had slept. Then he began to follow their tracks toward the Coorong. He saw that they had constructed another raft. By certain signs he judged that they had gone across the Coorong a few hours before his arrival. He thought that he could afford to rest that evening, and make an attempt to ford the Coorong in the morning.

Early next morning, therefore, when the sun rose, he crossed the water, and began his search on the other side for further tracks of his wives. But in this he failed, and stood wondering in what direction he should go. Never before had he been so greatly at fault. As he could not find any tracks he had to decide which way he should take, and he chose to go toward the south-east, following the line of the Coorong. He walked with great speed, and covered about seventy miles. Then he rested a while, thinking he must be ahead of his wives if they had come in that direction, for he knew that no one had passed that way. So he built a small camp of tree-branches and shrubs and grass, and at midnight he went to sleep. He was so tired with his day's journey that he slept soundly long after the sun rose; and he would have slept on had he not felt a touch and heard a voice, saying, "Awake, sleeper! Beware! Thine enemy is near." So he rose and looked round, but saw no one. The visitor was Puckowe, the Grandmother Spirit, the guardian angel of good people, who is ever beside them to warn them of danger. So he broke his fast, and made preparations to meet the unseen enemy. Then he resumed the search for his two wives.

Now away among the Pumbala tribe there lived a very cruel man who had become a disciple of the crow, and who, like his chief, had caused a great deal of mischief. He had been transformed from a human being into a wombat, and in this form he wandered alone among the sand-hummocks. As Nurunderi walked along he saw the wombat and threw his spear, striking him in a vital spot, right through the heart. He withdrew the weapon, and the blood flowed from the wound into the white sand. Then he picked up the wombat and carried it to his wurley, and tied it upon a pole. As he was about to sit down he missed his spear, and, remembering that he had left it at the spot where he had speared the wombat, he returned, and behold! he saw that the blood of the wombat was developing into a man. So he sat and watched it. Presently there was a man lying upon the ground, breathing as if in a deep sleep; and Nurunderi, instead of taking his spear, left it, thinking perhaps it might be of use to this man. He went away among the tea-trees and made several spears, and returned again to his wurley. This time he thought a great deal about the man that had developed from the blood of the wombat. As a servant of the Great Spirit he was aware that there were spirits of good and bad men embodied in trees, shrubs, and plants, but this was a new discovery. A spirit to be within the life-blood of an animal! He began to experience an uneasy feeling, as if something unpleasant was about to take place, so he returned to see what the person was like, and whether he was a friend who would assist him in the search for his two wives. He began cautiously to wend his way until he came to the spot, but the person had disappeared. He looked round, hoping to see footprints that would lead to him, but there were no footprints, and now he was convinced that this strange person was an enemy.[1] So he thought to himself, as all wise men do, that he would always have to be on the alert.

During that day he saw nothing of the enemy. On the second day Nurunderi sat upon the peak of a high sand-hummock, looking first north, then west, then south, and finally east. There was no one to be seen. Then he sat down and debated with himself as to which direction he should take. Presently he heard the sound of some one laughing. It was not a laugh of joy or amusement. It was the laugh of scorn. So he leapt to his feet, and

[1] A friend will always leave a footprint. This is the teaching of the aboriginals.

324

immediately his eyes caught a vision that made a cold chill run down his back and that almost froze the blood in his body. For there before him stood the Evil One, the arch-enemy of the good. So Nurunderi grasped his *waddy* and stood erect, holding the weapon firmly in his hand, and ready to hurl it at the approaching figure. The Evil One stood about two hundred yards away from the foot of the hill on which Nurunderi was, and called to him, " O brother-in-law of mine, do you not recognize me? " When Nurunderi heard this friendly salutation he came down to within about twenty paces of where the Deceiver sat. He said, " O brother-in-law, was it you that I released from the body of the wombat? " " Yes," said the Deceiver. " Now, brother-in-law of mine," said Nurunderi, " do you really claim to be my brother-in-law? " " Yes," replied the Deceiver. Nurunderi said, " Then perhaps you may be able to tell me the whereabouts of your two sisters, my wives. I am in search of them." " No," said the Evil One, " I shall not tell you, O mine enemy. I have waited long and patiently in order to kill you, but during your sojourn among the people in various parts of the country I was prevented by your followers, the emu, the eagle-hawk, and the native companion. They placed me in the body of the wombat, but you released me. Now you shall not reach heaven without submitting to death." Nurunderi reminded the Evil One that all good men had the privilege of going to heaven without having first to die.[1] He said, " Are you not pleased that I have been the means of your release? Were you not at my mercy? Do you not realize that I could have slain you? I was the means of your taking your present form. Come, let us not quarrel. I leave you now." And Nurunderi turned and set off in the direction from whence he had come, the north-west. Then the Deceiver began to laugh and to sing a song. Nurunderi kept on walking, and he thought that when he had put a certain distance between them he would turn and look back. He still heard his enemy singing, and

[1] This is a belief of the aboriginals.

he thought that he was following. But when Nurunderi turned and looked back he saw that the Evil One had not moved a step, but was dancing and brandishing his spear in a threatening attitude, ready to send it on its mission of death. Nurunderi stood awaiting results. Suddenly the spear was hurled with lightning speed, and would have struck a vital spot had not Nurunderi seen it in time. With a downstroke of his *waddy* he struck the spear, but its point tore a flesh wound in his thigh. Then the Evil One began dancing and singing because he had drawn the first blood. But Nurunderi took his spear and placed it on the throwing-stick, and poised it well above his shoulder. Like all warriors, he uttered a prayer, and speaking to the spear he said, " O my trusted spear, art thou not my handi-work? Have I not made thee for a purpose? Come, now, serve thy master faithfully, and do his bidding." So with muscle and mind he hurled the spear at lightning speed, and it entered the body of the Evil One, and pierced his heart. He fell lifeless, and his blood trickled into the ground. Then Nurunderi thought he would continue his journey.

He walked on and on, taking no notice of things around him, until his attention was attracted to a willy-wagtail that seemed to be repeatedly getting in his path. He looked about, and saw that he was still in the same place ; and he said to himself, " I have met a great and powerful enemy who, although his life has left the body, is influencing the conditions around me, so that I am prevented from escaping." He sat down to rest himself for a little before making another attempt to depart. As he sat he noticed that birds and animals that came near the dead body became unable to go away from it. So he decided that the only way out of his difficulty was to burn the body. He rose and gathered a great heap of grass and twigs, and piled log upon log until he had a heap twice his own height, and then he took the body of the Evil One and placed it upon the wood heap. He then took sticks of two grass-trees. In one of them he made a small hole. Then he inserted the end of the other into this hole. He then held the other stick between the palms of both hands and began rubbing his hands alternately backward and forward until the friction between the two pieces produced sparks, which set fire to the wood and burned the body of the Evil One.

Once again he began his journey. He walked and walked, and then looked to see how far he had come, but he was still in the same place. He said to himself, " I must see whether I have burned everything that belongs to him," and looking round he found the congealed blood of the Evil One upon the ground. So he made another fire upon the spot, and stirred the hot ashes until there was no sign of the blood.

Then he again resumed his journey, and this time he was able to pass on without hindrance. He walked so fast that he covered about seventy or eighty miles within an hour. Then he found that he was confronted by the Murray River, flowing toward the Southern Ocean. So he spoke to the· Great Spirit, and prayed him to make it possible for him to walk across. His prayer was answered, and the ground came up and formed a bridge across the river. When he had crossed to the other side he saw the footprints of his two wives that had been made three days before. He followed the footprints, and came to where his wives had camped for the night. He noticed that the cold ashes had the appearance of having been stained with the fat of a butter-fish. Now a woman is strictly forbidden to eat this fat, and when Nurunderi saw this evidence of the transgression of this command he was so greatly grieved and sorrowful of heart that he sat down beside the camp and wept bitterly for the sins of his two young wives. He spent the night in weeping, because he loved his wives greatly. He was grieved to think that it was he who had delivered unto the people the words of the Great Spirit, and that those who broke these laws must receive the full penalty of death ; that he, who had brought his wives out of bondage and given them the freedom to live a human life, must now be the means of bringing about their destruction.

It weighed heavily upon his mind that he must punish them, and that the coming generation would know that the transgressors were the beloved wives of the greatest of the prophets among the aboriginals. He prayed for forgiveness for them; the answer came, " As one lives, so must he die."

So he set out to overtake his wives, and to mete out to them their punishment. He followed their tracks, which led him to the south coast, and he came to the spot where they had camped two days before. He saw ashes and examined them, and noticed that the women had cooked cockles and periwinkles and mullet. Again he wept, this time beside a huge rock; and his tears trickled into the sea. He wept so much that to-day some of the old people will point out the place and say, " This is the spot where Nurunderi wept bitterly for his two wayward wives." It resembles a soakage of fresh water by the side of the sea; the water that was salt with the bitter tears of a sorrowing heart now comes as a sweet, cool, and refreshing liquid to souls journeying to the Land of the Spirit. And when the aboriginals visit this spot one may see tears trickling down their cheeks as they think of their great leader, the messenger and teacher of the will of the Great Father of All.

Now Nurunderi, after spending a restless night, rose early and walked rapidly until he arrived at the bluff. He sat there, with his face turned toward the west, and in spirit he saw his wives. Again he wept, because he saw in a vision what was about to happen, and that it would be he who should bring them to their untimely end before they reached the Spirit Land in the island toward the west. So he hurried on once more, and a great conflict went on within him. His loving and forgiving nature was willing that his wives should reach that island and be free for ever from punishment for their wrongdoing.

Now the wives arrived in the afternoon at a place opposite the island. At the time of this story this island was connected with the mainland, but during a severe southerly storm the sea would cover the connecting strip of land. On this occasion the wives, instead of going across immediately, stayed to collect honey, with the intention of crossing on the morrow. There was also another reason for their delaying. At the mainland end of this strip of land there was a keeper who was in charge. He was known as the blue crane, and no one would attempt to cross without his permission. He was an austere person, and one with whom it was decidedly dangerous to dispute, because he always had beside him a very sharp-bladed spear, that would cause an exceedingly severe wound.

Nurunderi was only four or five miles away from his wives, and he could see them standing on the cliff, looking across to the Spirit Land. So he made a little wurley, and went into the bush and procured an opossum and roasted it, and allowed it to cool before beginning to eat it. His wives had acted in a similar fashion. They had made a comfortable little wurley and a large fire, which Nurunderi could see. He had not yet received a message from the Great All Father as to how he should punish his wives, so he went to sleep. At midnight in a vision he was told that these maidens should be allowed to walk along the strip of land that served as a bridge to all pilgrims to the Spirit Land, and that when they had arrived half-way across he should chant the wind song. First he must chant to the west wind, and sing its song of fury in order to bring up the waters of the Mystery Land and let them roll with vengeful strength. Then he must sing the song of the south wind to make it blow and bring the water that comes from the Unknown Land, so that they who wish may return to that land. Then he must sing the song of the north wind, to bring the waters together, and let the maidens toss and toss until they became exhausted. Then he must command them to become rocks.

So Nurunderi rose early in the morning and came near to his wives, and sat upon the cliff to see them begin their journey of death. They came to the blue crane, and asked his permission to cross the strip of land. This he gave willingly; and the maidens began laughing and chatting in expectation of the joy and pleasure and happiness that awaited them when they should arrive at the Spirit Land, and most of all because they would be free from the punishment which they were trying to escape. Little did they realize that within a few minutes they would be called upon to pay the full penalty of their disobedience.

Now Nurunderi came a little nearer to the strip of land that led to the island, and he sat upon a vantage spot watching and waiting until his wives were half-way to the island. When they reached that point Nurunderi began to sing the wind song. "Fall down from above, O thou mighty wind! Run swiftly and display thy fleetness! Come thou down from the western sky, O water of the deep! Come up in a mighty swell!" And the west wind burst forth in all its fury, and came screeching overhead, while the maidens pressed forward and struggled against the storm. Then presently the waters were churned up, and they welled and rose over the way. Then Nurunderi sang a song of the south wind, and the south wind blew, and the waters from an Unknown Land came on, raising themselves like mountain peaks; and they dashed upon the maidens and lashed them and tossed them about like corks. They struggled first toward their goal, the island; then it seemed as if the Spirit were against them, and they turned and began swimming back toward the mainland. But the north wind, answering the call of Nurunderi, performed its office in making these two maidens pay the penalty of their sin. They sank exhausted, and were drowned. Then the winds ceased suddenly, and there was a calm.

Nurunderi wept bitterly, and although he hated everything that was displeasing to the Great Spirit he felt within his inmost consciousness that he loved those youthful maidens with all their faults and their wrongdoings. Again a voice whispered to him, "Command that the bodies of the maidens be turned into stone as a warning to all women not to eat of the forbidden food." He spoke, and it happened

THE TWO SISTERS
By permission

THE YARA-MA-YHA-WHO

as he commanded. The two rocks can be seen from the mainland, as well as from vessels passing. They are known to-day, as they were known before the coming of the white man, by the name of the " Two Sisters." Many pilgrimages were made by the aboriginals in days gone by to see these stones, and to contemplate the doings of the great teacher Nurunderi.

After these things had happened Nurunderi, heart-broken, and with tears still welling in his eyes, commanded that the waters should go back, in order that he might walk upon dry land to the island.

On the eastern side of the island was a huge gum-tree, and under its shade he rested until the sun sank into the western sky, the Land of the Spirits. He then walked to the western side of the island and plunged into the sea, and sank into the deep. There he remained for a long while, seeking the spirits of his two wives. When he found them he rose from the depths, with them clinging to him. Then he flew upward and upward until he came to the Land of Heaven, to join that bright and happy group Nepelle, Wyungare, and the Seven Sisters, and to look down on the earth in order to comfort and cheer the people, and encourage them to obey the will of the Great Spirit and to resist the evil desires from within.

Chirr-bookie, the Blue Crane [1]

Chirr-bookie was a Wimmera man. His sister, the only woman in his family, married into the Raminyeri tribe. This is how he became associated with the Raminyeri. He would often visit his sister, and he at last decided to live

[1] The story of Chirr-bookie is intended to educate the Raminyeri or other tribes in a belief in the reincarnation. Chirr-bookie was the name of a person belonging to the Raminyeri tribe who was greatly respected by his own and other tribes. He was a good-living man, and he taught the people that if they fulfilled the laws and customs they should, if they so desired, still continue to live on the earth. If death came to them by accident, or in warfare, or by a pointing-bone, or by any other such means, they would only have to wish and that wish would be granted. If, however, a person was a law-breaker, and a good man killed him, the good man could express a wish that the bad man should become a stone. And the bad man would become a stone.

with his brother-in-law. Chirr-bookie's sister had three sons, and, like all uncles on the mother's side, Chirr-bookie delighted to take part in their education. They had to be instructed in hunting, fishing, bushcraft, and all the customs, traditions, and legends of the tribe. When the three boys grew up they received their names. The eldest one was called Eurowie because he was a great jumper, and was able to leap over obstacles like a kangaroo. The second was called Pithowie.[1] He was not gifted as Eurowie was. He could not run or jump, but he was persevering, and was a good hunter in following game such as emus and wallabies. If a subject were in dispute Pithowie would always hold by his opinion. The youngest brother was called Koolatowie. This name means 'easy to bend,' yet he was strong if there arose a dispute among the brothers. Koolatowie would always willingly yield in order to avoid angry words that might lead to a quarrel. This won him the respect and love of his mother and father and his uncle Chirr-bookie and the tribe of the Raminyeri, but it made his two brothers hate him. They were always seeking a cause of quarrel with him, and this grieved their good old uncle Chirr-bookie, who at last summoned the chief and the elders in order to suggest that Eurowie and Pithowie should be sent to another tribe. This was agreed to, and it was decided to send both to make their homes with the Adelaide tribe. So a messenger was commanded to approach the chief of the Adelaide tribe to ask if he was willing to receive the two young men and their wives. When the brothers were told of the intention of their tribe to transfer them they vowed secretly to take the life of Koolatowie, and it was with the spirit of revenge in their hearts that they bade farewell to their mother, father, uncle, and brother, and set out on their journey to their new home, to begin life in a new country with new people who spoke a strange language.[2]

[1] This word comes from *pitchingga*, the gum of the pine or gum-tree. Pithowie was a 'sticker,' or one that clings.

[2] Although tribes might be separated only by a rock or by trees, yet they might be unable to hold converse except through an interpreter.

CHIRR-BOOKIE, THE BLUE CRANE

After Eurowie and Pithowie had become conversant with the language of the Adelaide tribe, and could speak it fluently, they began to plan ways and means of being revenged. They tried to prejudice the other tribes against their father's tribe, but no one would think of going to battle against the Raminyeri, because they were a peaceful tribe, and were respected by all. Then the brothers thought of another plan; they suggested that as certain animals and birds were becoming scarce it would be well to station men at the boundary of their country, in order to prevent these creatures from departing and wandering away into the land of another tribe. This plan appealed to the Adelaide tribe, and all the hunters—men, women, and children—were told to help to carry it into effect.

Now Eurowie and Pithowie knew that emu food was much sought after by their uncle Chirr-bookie. It was his favourite dish, and his nephew Koolatowie would travel long distances and endure great hardship and face great danger to procure it. They therefore made a plan to prevent the emus from passing, and drove them down toward a peninsula formed by a river bending in its course to enter the sea.

Every day Koolatowie would rise early in the morning and set out in search of an emu, but he would return to his mother and uncle with the same story that there were no emu tracks. He could not understand this. After some time Eurowie and Pithowie sent a messenger to their aged uncle to inform him that emus were plentiful in their hunting-ground, and that at the next full moon they would send a nice fat one. When Chirr-bookie received this message he sat down and took from his *punauwe* [1] a stone pencil, and made some marks upon a smooth stick [2] about four inches long and half an inch wide. The message was that, although he loved the fat and flesh of the emu so much, he had vowed that he could not eat of it unless the bird had been caught, killed, and cooked in the earth oven by Koolatowie.

[1] A kangaroo-skin bag.   [2] This was a message-stick. See pp. 101, 144.

When the messenger returned to the brothers they were greatly annoyed with the message, because it upset their plans. That afternoon they took up their spears, left their homes, and went to the peninsula and caught an emu, and bound its legs and carried it back with them. Late in the evening they took it beyond the boundary to Horseshoe Bend, just across the river, and let it loose. They waited till they saw it recover itself and set off toward Aldinga. They followed it for a few miles, then turned back homeward, and reached their camp about midnight. Then they had a late meal. They rose next morning before the sun, and armed themselves each with a *wunde*, three *waddies*, and a *kanake*. When the sun rose they were at the Onkaparinga river. At Horseshoe Bend they speared a couple of fishes and lit a fire and cooked their breakfast. Now they felt refreshed, and ready to do battle should they be challenged for trespassing. They followed the track of the emu, knowing well that if it wandered toward Cape Jervis and Koolatowie saw it he would be sure to hunt it, and kill and cook it before taking it home to his mother and uncle.

During that same morning Koolatowie set out hunting. He scoured the hills and valleys in search of an emu. Suddenly he stopped with his eyes fixed upon the ground. A few paces away he saw the footprints of an emu, the object of his hunt. This sight caused his blood to course rapidly through his body, filling him with great excitement. He noticed the direction of the emu's tracks, so he ran on a course in the form of a crescent, knowing that this would bring him ahead of his prey, since the emu would continue in the direction in which it was going. Being a great hunter and well

versed in the knowledge of how to hunt the emu, he waited
at the head of the valley. He hastily plucked branches of
shrubs and made them into a shield about three feet long
and eighteen inches wide. He waited patiently.

It was some time before the emu came in sight. When
Koolatowie saw it he took hold of his shield with his left
hand and his spear with his right. The emu came on
toward him, picking berries and young leaves from bushes
and plants. As it approached Koolatowie would move in
the line of its travel. When the emu moved to the left
the hunter moved to the left, and when the emu moved to
the right the hunter moved to the right. Nearer and
nearer the hunter approached the prey, until he was within
striking distance. He allowed the emu to pass about three
yards away from him to the left, then he threw his spear
and struck the bird in a vital spot. It dropped instantly.
With a bound Koolatowie reached the side of the emu and
removed the spear from the body, and allowed the blood to
flow. He tied the two legs of the bird to its head and neck
and then took the emu and lifted it up, and placed his head
between the legs and neck, which formed a loop, and soon
it was swinging over his shoulder with its legs and head to
the side of his head. In this manner he carried the emu
to the place where he meant to cook it,[1] about a mile from
where he had killed it.

When Koolatowie arrived at the spot he dug a hole and
gathered grass and a few twigs and some strips of the bark
of a dry she-oak log lying on the ground. Then he made
a fire, and burned the bark till it made excellent coals. He
placed some more bark in the hole, and he also threw a lot
of small stones among the blazing wood. After the wood
burned there was a layer of red coals and hot stones. Then
he took small boughs of shrubs and placed them upon the
hot stones and coals. Upon this he placed a layer of soft
grass. After this he took up the emu with all its feathers
on, and placed it on top of the grass. Then he put more

---

[1] An expert hunter will always kill his prey, such as kangaroo, emu, and wombat,
about a mile from the cooking-ground.

boughs upon the emu, and covered the whole with earth, leaving only the head of the emu uncovered. On top of this earth he made a fire, and thus the emu was lying below the level of the surface of the ground, with only its head protruding. After this Koolatowie felt satisfied, and sat down and chanted songs of the hunter.

Now Eurowie and Pithowie, who had so often hunted with their uncle, Chirr-bookie, knew that emus in this part of the country always travelled in a certain direction—viz., southward—as if prompted by instinct, and that on their way they passed through a certain valley. The brothers made for the valley, and began looking about for the tracks of the emu. Pithowie found the tracks first, and called to his brother to come and look at them. They both followed the tracks until they reached the place where the emu was slain. Here they saw the blood upon the ground and grass, and they also saw the footprints of Koolatowie. They followed these tracks until they could smell the fire and the cooking. They walked boldly forward toward Koola-towie. Koolatowie rose to his feet with his spear in his hand fixed upon the throwing-stick, and stood on guard, ready to meet anyone who should come with unfriendly intentions. The brothers threw their spears upon the ground, and called, " Younger brother of ours, how do we see thee? There have been great changes, and many moons have passed. Do not hold back that brotherly feeling which belongs to us both. Give place to tears of joy and delight because we have come together after being long separated. Come, let us weep with one another ! " So Koolatowie placed his spear upon the ground and beckoned that they should come forward and be seated beside him.

Eurowie and Pithowie came forward, and sat one on on each side of Koolatowie. They began to inquire about their mother and father and their uncle Chirr-bookie. Then they asked about other members of the tribe. After some talk they told him how scarce emus were. They said they had seen the tracks of the one that Koolatowie had killed, and they had followed it, hoping to capture it, as they were anxious to taste the food. It was many moons since they had eaten emu-flesh. Koolatowie said, " O my two brothers, did you not send a messenger to Uncle some two moons back saying that if he would like an emu you would send him one? Is that so, or am I mistaken?" Then Pithowie answered, "Perhaps the messenger made a mistake. If emus were plentiful do you think we should dare to come over the boundary-line hunting one? But, brother, you have been lucky to capture this one. It has travelled through all the hunting-grounds of the tribes, where there are many expert hunters. You have therefore distinguished yourself as a great hunter."

Although Koolatowie had received a thorough training in hunting and bushcraft he was not acquainted with the subtle cunning of his brothers in using this weapon of flattery. It put him completely off his guard. Eurowie and Pithowie saw how their younger brother had fallen a victim to flattery, and without warning, and with the swiftness of well-trained and expert hunters, they seized their weapons. Eurowie struck Koolatowie across the forehead with a *kanake*, and Pithowie dealt him a blow on the same part, which rendered him completely unconscious. Then Eurowie took up his spear and pierced Koolatowie's heart, thus killing him. Eurowie and Pithowie took up the body and carried it down the valley to the place where the emu was killed. They dug a hole about three feet deep, and placed the body in it, and covered it with grass and boughs. Then they put earth over the top of all this. After they had done this they took up the emu and stole hastily away. They returned home to their families, and sat round the camp-fire and enjoyed a meal of the cooked emu.

At the moment that Koolatowie was killed Chirr-bookie felt that something dreadful had happened, and he was greatly distressed and began to weep. "Where, oh, where art thou, O nephew of mine?" he cried. "Something within me says that thou art no more." Chirr-bookie continued to weep and to repeat these words all the afternoon, until the setting of the sun. The mother and father of Koolatowie came round, and, feeling uneasy, they asked Chirr-bookie why he was weeping. He told them, and they said they thought the boy would be all right. However, they waited up all night, thinking that Koolatowie would return; but when the sun rose they were still waiting. Then Chirr-bookie went to the beach, and plunged into the sea, and stayed under water for a minute. He then rose to the surface and swam ashore. When he came out of the water he shook himself and ran round several times. Then he leaped into the air with one arm stretched upward, and shouted out this challenge, " O nephew of mine, whoever has slain you will have to kill me, because I go forth to take revenge—an eye for an eye and a life for a life."

Chirr-bookie hastened to his camp, and made his preparations for a journey. He knew not what was before him. He sat down and broke his fast, eating fish and herbs. Then he rose to his feet and shouted out, with a loud voice, " I rise to go forth to avenge ! I shall not return until I have killed those who have slain my nephew ! "

He left his camp, well armed with two spears, six *waddies*, two *panketyes*, and a *kanake*. There was murder in the heart of Chirr-bookie. As he walked away it was noticed that he stepped out with the elasticity of youth. As is the custom when a person goes out to kill some one, Chirr-bookie left his camp without bidding anyone goodbye.

As Chirr-bookie went along toward Mount Barker he communed with the spirits, of whom there are many, and begged of them not to intervene in any way, but rather to withdraw their influence, as he wished to be avenged for the death of his nephew. So the spirit of the north wind stepped forth and blew with much force round the base of Mount Barker, then leaped to the top, where Chirr-bookie sat with his head bowed, and said, " O Chirr-bookie, I shall not intervene. My presence shall be withdrawn.

Go and slay your enemies." The west wind, the east wind, and the south wind all spoke to him in like manner.

Once more Chirr-bookie offered a prayer to the spirit of life. And the Father of All came out of the Milky Way with such tremendous force that he rent the air like lightning, causing a noise greater than many thunderbolts. He stood beside Chirr-bookie and asked him to rise. Chirr-bookie rose, and covered his face with his hands. He said, "O Father of All Spirits, grant me my requests. I ask that thou wilt withdraw thy presence and thy influence from Eurowie and Pithowie because they have slain one of thy beloved sons, Koolatowie, a young man who feared thee. I wish to take their lives and the lives of their wives and families. Then after I have slain them I do not wish that they should live an active life, but that they should become earth. Even then my spirit of revenge will not be satisfied; but I shall continue to kill every being that I meet on my way home who refuses to help me. O Father, let the spirits of those that I kill live in the form of birds, and when I die permit me to be changed after the same fashion." The Father of All Spirits answered, "O my son, thou child of my desire, go and do as thy conscience bids thee, and it shall be as you wish." So Chirr-bookie hastened on to fulfil his desire, and he came to Mount Torrens. Once more he prayed, asking the spirits of weapons to guide and give accurate flight to the boomerang, the spear, and the *waddy*. From out of the trees from which weapons were made came the answer, "We come to do thy bidding, O Chirr-bookie."

Chirr-bookie went straight from Mount Torrens to the home of Eurowie and Pithowie. He arrived just as the sun sank in the western sky. Upon his face and body there were signs painted showing that he had been on a very long journey and was just returning home. This gave the impression that he was not aware of the death of Koolatowie. When he met Eurowie and Pithowie they began asking him questions regarding the health and well-being of their mother and father. They asked how

Koolatowie was when Chirr-bookie left home. The old man said that every one was well and happy at the time of his setting out on his journey.

Now Eurowie and Pithowie held secret converse, planning to take the life of Chirr-bookie. They invited Chirr-bookie to stay in their big camp; but he refused, choosing rather to sleep behind some bushes about a quarter of a mile away. Then they all retired in order to rest their weary bodies. At midnight Chirr-bookie rose and set fire to the camp of Eurowie and Pithowie; and the spirit of fire consumed Eurowie, Pithowie, and their families.

The old man wept bitterly for his two nephews, because he still loved them after a fashion, and he cried, " O my children, sons of my only sister, it is because of what you have done that the anger of all the spirits and gods has punished you."

Chirr-bookie then set out on his journey homeward, and at Aldinga he met a man of the Hawk totem tribe, who was fishing. The Hawk man sat with his eyes gazing seaward. Chirr-bookie called to him, and said, " O cousin, have you any fish to offer me? " The Hawk man would not answer, so Chirr-bookie threw his *waddy* at him with such force that it killed him instantly. Then he called out, " O cousin, thy body shall become a stone, and thy spirit shall take unto itself the body of a bird."

Chirr-bookie continued on his journey till he came to Yankalilla. Here he saw a man of the Shag totem, sitting up and sunning himself upon a rock. " O cousin of mine," said Chirr-bookie, " give me fish to eat." But the Shag man took no notice. So Chirr-bookie threw his *waddy* at him and killed him. Like the man of the Hawk totem tribe, his body became a stone, and his spirit took the form of the body of a bird.

When Chirr-bookie reached his home he took the remains of Koolatowie into a cave and placed them upon a ledge, and stretched himself out beside them. He prayed to the Father of All Spirits to come and transform him into a blue crane, and to call back the wandering spirit of

Koolatowie and command it also to become a crane. The spirit came and sang a song that belonged to the Spirit World, and the body of Chirr-bookie became a stone man, which is still to be seen, and his spirit entered into the body of the blue crane.

Buthera and the Bat

In the southern part of Yorke's Peninsula there lived a great chief called Buthera. He was a very proud man, and ruled haughtily over his tribe. One day his mother asked him to go on a journey to the farther end of the peninsula, toward what is now called Marion Bay. She told him to be very careful on his way, and to be prepared to do battle at any time, for she felt that she was sending him on a very dangerous journey. Buthera set out, and travelled on and on, and by and by he came to Corny Point. Here he thought he would take a rest, so he made himself a fire and cooked some food.

While he was resting another man came along. Buthera was surprised to see him, and asked him who he was. The stranger said, " I am Mudichera, the chief of the Bat tribe." Buthera was very angry that another chief should dare to come into his land, so he said to Mudichera, " I do not believe that you are a chief; you are something that has been blown down here by the west wind." These remarks made Mudichera very angry, and he rushed at Buthera. Then the two chiefs began to fight. They fought fiercely for some time, until Buthera, with a stroke of his flint knife, cut Mudichera in halves. And this is the reason why to this day Mudichera has his present form, and if any of the tribe, no matter where they be, see him flying about they say he is the bearer of evil tidings.

After the fight Buthera continued on his journey. He walked for about twenty miles, and then he began to feel sick from the effects of his fight with Mudichera. Presently he came to a deep valley where a tribe was camped round about the water-holes. The aboriginals called this valley Curre Mulka. Now this tribe had heard all about the fight from the willy-wagtail, who, as soon as he heard of it, had hastened about spreading the news. The willy-wagtail at this time was a man. He was a very clever doctor and message-carrier, and was greatly feared and greatly respected. When Buthera found out that the tribe knew all about the fight and what had happened he became very angry and decided to punish them. He took up his magic wand and waved it about. Instantly a great fire sprang up, and soon the whole of the countryside was in flames. The members of the tribe became alarmed, and rushed hither and thither, seeking a means to escape from the fire. They rushed into the water-holes, but the anger of Buthera pursued them even there. He waved his magic wand toward the water-holes, and lo! all the tribes were turned into shags. They have remained so ever since.

Then Buthera continued his journey toward Marion Bay, but his troubles were not yet over. He travelled all that day, and at nightfall he built himself a shelter with bushes and shrubs. Next morning he set out again on his journey, but he had not gone far when he met another chief, named Larna. It was not long before the two chiefs began to quarrel and then to fight. Now Larna, being younger than Buthera, had more strength, and by and by he overcame Buthera and killed him. Just as he was going to throw Buthera's body into a lake Mudichera, the chief of the bats, appeared. Although he had been badly treated by being cut into halves by Buthera he decided to help him and to punish the chief Larna. He punished him by turning him into a rock; and to-day one can see this rock. It looks like the figure of a man, and is named Rhino Head.

Yara-ma-yha-who [1]

There were many strange beings who lived a long while ago, many, many years before the white man came to

[1] This is one of the stories told to naughty children to teach them that if they do not behave the Yara-ma-yha-who will come and take them and make them become one of themselves.

Australia. Among these was a queer little red man. Now this little man was an exceptionally funny fellow. He stood about four feet high, and he had a very big head for such a small body; in fact, the biggest parts of him were his mouth, his throat, and his stomach. But he had no teeth in his jaws, and he would simply swallow his food. And the strangest part of all was that this little fellow would swallow an ordinary man such as you see at the present day on the street, or in any of our towns or cities. His head was something like a snake's, and he would open his mouth just as a snake does.

These little people did not hunt their food or make spears, *nulla-nullas*, or boomerangs like their bigger brother, man, but they were in possession of a queer hand. The points of their fingers were cup-shaped, like the suckers of the octopus, and so also were the tips of their toes. They lived mostly in thick, leafy trees. They preferred the wild fig-tree. The reason for this was that during the summer months men, women, and children would often come and seek shelter under the trees from the burning rays of the sun, and in winter they would be protected by the thick boughs from rain and hail. That was why these little men, the Yara-ma-yha-who, chose to live after this fashion, because it saved them the trouble of going about hunting for food.

Now if a little boy happened to be alone he fell an easy prey to a Yara-ma-yha-who; therefore everybody dreaded the queer little fellows, and would often go out of their way to seek shelter and safety in caves, or under ledges of rock on the mountain-side. The Yara-ma-yha-who pounces upon a person as a cat does upon a mouse, only in this case the hunter is smaller than his prey. When he springs upon his victim and captures him he places his hands and feet upon the body. The suckers on these drain the blood from the victim, and he is left helpless upon the ground. The Yara-ma-yha-who does not try to suck all the blood from the body, but leaves sufficient to keep the victim alive while he walks round and gets an appetite. Then he returns and lies down on the ground facing his victim, and crawls like a goanna, and opens his mouth wide, and sucks his prey into his mouth head first. He then rises and stands on his little legs, and dances and dances round until the prey is well inside his stomach. Then he goes away to a river or pool of water, and drinks copiously, and afterward goes to some valley near by and lies down and goes to sleep. When he wakes he vomits the remains of his recent meal.

In all probability the victim is still alive, but he lies upon the ground, feigning death. The Yara-ma-yha-who stands beside him, and then walks away for a short distance, say, about five paces, and suddenly turns round, walks back, and pokes the victim in the side with a stick, to see whether he is alive. If the person shows no sign of life the Yara-ma-yha-who again walks away about ten paces, turns again suddenly, goes back to the side of the victim, and this time tickles him under the neck or arm. If the person still shows no signs of life the Yara-ma-yha-who repeats this. Getting no response, he goes still farther away, say, about fifty yards, and comes back a third time and tickles his victim; and then he goes away and sits behind a bush, watching.

Now all children are taught that if they should happen to be captured they should offer no resistance, because they have a better chance of escape if they allow the Yara-ma-yha-who to swallow and vomit them, as has been its custom from time immemorial. Should the Yara-ma-yha-who fail to do this, then the spirit of the wild fig-tree would kill him by entering into his head through his ear, and causing a mumbling noise, ending with intense silence, so that the spirit would leave the rude body and become a cold fungus that grows upon the trees, and sheds a dull glow at night.

The Yara-ma-yha-who, after vomiting, seeks a bush and lies down to rest, and sleeps soundly. The victim takes this opportunity to run away. Should the Yara-ma-yha-who hear the running feet he would rise very suddenly and give chase, shouting all the while, " Which way hast thou gone, my victim, my victim? " One advantage that the victim has is that the Yara-ma-yha-who is not able to run very fast; he has a wobbling style of walking, like the cockatoo.

If the Yara-ma-yha-who should fail to recapture his prey he would go away where there were rock holes or water-holes and drink up all the water in them. This he would do to deprive the people of their water-supply. The people would then go in search of the wild apple tree, and strip the bark, and sometimes the water would come forth from a cavity between the bark and trunk of the tree. Now this would give the Yara-ma-yha-who another opportunity to capture a person, because he was more able to seize his prey by attacking it in a tree, thick with boughs, than by attempting to do so on the ground.

If a person were caught and swallowed again he would become shorter in stature. If swallowed a third time he would become still shorter, until at last he would resemble the Yara-ma-yha-who; only in the first stage of trans-formation the victim's skin would become very smooth, with a visible sign of hair on body or head. It would remain thus for a short time, and then long hair would begin to cover the body very thickly indeed, and in this way the victims were gradually changed from ordinary human beings into the little mythical beings that roam about in the dense forests along the coast of the Pacific Ocean.

The Origin of the Pleiades

In various parts of the world and among different races there are traditions that the lustre of the Pleiades is asso-ciated with acts in which women were concerned. There is an Australian legend on the subject. According to this story, it was the girls who had reached the age of adolescence who perceived the necessity for bringing the body under subjection to the mind in order to restrain physical appetite and control the effects of pain and fear. They saw that without such control there could be no real racial advance-ment. Accordingly, they presented themselves to the elders of the tribe in order to undergo the trial by ordeal.

The elders explained to the girls that the test that they would have to submit to was a severe one. The girls, however, were firm in their resolve to undergo it. So every morning for three years, in a place apart from their brothers and sisters, the elders, to teach them moderation, gave them a small portion of the usual food, consisting perhaps of a piece of fish or flesh of the emu, kangaroo, or wombat. This they received twice a day, at the hour of sunrise and at the hour of sunset. At the end of the third year they were taken for a long journey through the dense bush, where the thorns scratched their flesh, and across the plains and rivers, travelling during the heat of the day, often almost fainting from fatigue, but ever pressing on-ward. After a week of such journeying had passed the elders called the girls before them and inquired whether they thought they were better able to control the appetite. To this the girls replied, " Our minds are made up. We will control the appetite." The elders then said, " You are asked to fast for three days, and during this fasting time we will all travel."

So the girls set out with the elders on the journey. The way was long and difficult, and they were weak from lack of food. The blazing sun seemed to them more ruthless and the way more rough and thorny than usual, but they were determined to conquer, and so they kept on their way undaunted. On the evening of the third day they arrived at the appointed camping-ground. The elders prepared the food for them for the following day. On the fourth morning they were given a flint knife, and were instructed to cut from the kangaroo or emu the amount of food they required. How tempting was the smell of the roasted flesh to the girls, who had travelled unceasingly for three days without breaking their fast ! The tempta-tion to cut a generous portion and satisfy the craving for food was very great. But each cut for herself only an ordinary portion. The elders praised the girls for their restraint. They said, " You have acquitted yourselves well so far ; and now there are other appetites, and it is for you

BREAKING A TOOTH

*From "The Arunta," by Sir Baldwin Spencer and F. J. Gillen,
by permission of Messrs Macmillan & Co., Ltd.*

346

to control them as you have controlled your hunger."
They replied, "We are ready to undergo any tests you
please. Our minds are made up to subdue appetite and to
conquer inclination." They then submitted themselves
to various tests in order to learn to control other appetites,
each test being more difficult than the former. In every
case they were successful.

When the elders told them that it was necessary to
overcome pain they again submitted themselves to their
guidance, and the elders decided the particular form of
discipline that the girls should undergo. In the presence
of the other girls and boys they took the girls away to a
selected spot, where all sacred ceremonies were performed.
They ordered them to lie upon the ground. Then they
took a stone axe and a pointed stick about eight or nine
inches long. They told the girls one by one to open their
mouths. The elders placed the point of a stick against a
front tooth of each, then raised an axe and brought it down
upon the stick, breaking the tooth off, and leaving the
nerves exposed and quivering. The girls then rose from
the ground, and sat awaiting the further commands of the
elders. They were asked whether they felt the pain, to
which they replied, "Yes, we felt the pain." Then the
elders said, "Are you willing to have another tooth knocked
out?" And the girls replied, "Yes, our minds are made
up. We are going to control pain." And again the elders
asked at the conclusion of this test, "Are you willing to
undergo more severe testing?" The girls replied as
before, "Yes, our minds are made up. We will control
pain." They were then led to another camping-ground
and commanded to stand in a row. An elder of the tribe
approached with a flint knife. He stood before each of
the girls for a while, and then drew the knife silently
across her breast, and the blood flowed. This he did to
each girl in succession. Another elder took the ashes of a
particular kind of wood, and rubbed them into the wound.
The effect of this was twofold; it intensified the pain, and
helped to heal the wound.

347

A day or two was given to allow the wounds to heal, and then the elders called the girls before them and inquired if they were still willing to submit themselves to further testing. They replied, " Yes, we are willing to go through any tests. Our minds are made up." The elders then went alone through the bush and selected another camping-ground for the girls. At bed-time they were led to the spot, and told, " It is time to retire to rest. This is your camping-ground." The girls, weary and eager for rest, threw their opossum rugs on the ground. The night was dark and moonless and very warm. They lay there for a little while, and presently they felt things crawling over their bodies. They were afraid, but they refused to give way to fear. It may have been that each girl was afraid of what the others would think of her if she failed, and that thus each helped the others to be brave. By and by they discovered they were lying on a bed of ants. All through the night they lay there with the ants swarming over them. The time seemed very long. These girls had journeyed far, fasting, and their poor bodies were still tender with half-healed wounds. In the morning they presented themselves to the elders, smiling and showing no signs of the terrible night that they had passed.

Still their journey continued, and they underwent further tests, such as the piercing of the nose and the wearing of a stick through it to keep the wound open. Further, they were bidden to lie on a bed of hot cinders. Before each fresh trial they were asked if they were willing to undergo the tests. Their reply, which never varied, was, " Yes, we have made up our minds to conquer pain."

Now the elders were very pleased with the girls, and very proud of the powers of endurance that they showed, but they realized that it was necessary for them to overcome fear as well as the appetites and pain, so they called them together and said, " Girls! You have done very well, and have proved that you possess wonderful courage and endurance. The next stage is the control of fear. Do you wish to continue on the way?" The girls stood there in all their youth, and with glowing eyes; and they repeated the old phrase, " Yes, our minds are made up. We will conquer fear."

On a fresh camping-ground in the dark night, with the camp-fires gleaming on the trees, and casting dark, gloomy shadows, the elders told them tales about the *bunyip* and the *muldarpe*. This latter is a spirit which assumes many shapes. It may come as a kangaroo, or a wombat, or a lizard. The girls were told fearful stories of these dreadful beings, and of ghosts, to which they listened tremblingly. The more highly strung among them could scarcely refrain from crying out. They found themselves looking over their shoulders, and imagining that the dark shadows were the *bunyip* or the *muldarpe* or other spirits. For hours they listened, until it was time to go to bed. After the elders had made the sign of good-night they told them that the place where they were camping was the burial-place of their great-grandfathers. They lay down to sleep, resolved not to be afraid of any ghosts or spirits.

Then the elders crept round the camp, making weird noises, so that the hair of the girls rose and their blood ran cold. Besides these sounds there were the usual bush-noises, such as the howl of the dingo, the shriek of the owl, and the falling of decayed branches. But the girls were not to be turned from their purpose, and they lay there until the break of day. Then they rose and presented themselves to the elders, showing no signs of their disturbed night, their faces placid and their eyes clear and shining. The elders knew that the girls had conquered fear, and they rejoiced with pride. They sent out invitations to the adjoining tribes, and they made great rejoicing, and held many corrobberies in honour of the girls.

But the girls were not content with having conquered the appetites and pain and fear. They desired that their sisters should do the same. So the leader of the girls stepped out from the group, and said to the girls of the assembled tribes, " We have passed through the testing that our elders prescribed, and we have endured much pain.

349

Now it is the desire of the Great Spirit that you should go through the same course of testing. You must know that the selfish person is not happy. This is because he thinks only of himself. Happiness comes through thinking of others and forgetting self. Greed and pain and fear are caused by thinking too much of self, and so it is necessary to vanquish self. Will you not go and do as we have done?" The girls of the other tribes eagerly assented, so proud were they of the victory of their sisters.

Then the Great Spirit was so pleased with them that he sent a great star spirit to convey the girls to the heavens without death or further suffering, in order that they might shine there as a pattern and a symbol to their race. And on clear nights ever since that time the aboriginals look into the sky and revere this wonderful constellation, the Seven Sisters, and remember what the girls did, and always think of the story of how there came to be given to them a place in the heavens.

INDEX

ADDER, 138–139, 140, 141–142, 143, 144, 147
Adelaide tribe, 332, 333
Albert, Lake, 230, 249, 317, 320, 322
Aldinga, 334, 340
Alexandrina, Lake, 22, 181n., 229, 230, 231, 249, 317
Animal life, studied by aboriginals, 219 et seq.
Animal tribe, 19, 28, 29, 31, 32, 34, 40, 47, 59, 63, 67, 75, 76, 77, 78, 89, 91, 94, 95, 99, 105, 106, 116, 117, 118, 119, 120, 150, 151, 152, 153, 155, 157, 161, 162, 166, 182
Animals, structural changes in, 32–33
Ant, 17, 348
Appetite, overcoming of, as initiation rite, 20, 173, 346–347
Apple-tree, wild, 301, 345 ; blossom, 301 n.
Arna, 23, 30–31
Ashes, rubbed into wound, 347
Axe, 126, 130 ; stone, 150

BACK, turning, significance of, 48
Bajeeja tribe, 264–270
Bajjara, 23, 30–31
Bandicoot, 42, 144, 145, 166, 167, 168, 295
Barter, 203, 206, 208, 215
Baskets, fishing, 229
Bat, 29, 97, 99, 136, 341
Bat tribe, 94, 95, 341
Biggaroo, the wombat snake, 175, 176, 177, 178, 180, 182
Billabong, 67, 74, 155, 156, 157, 168, 229, 230
Bird Age, 181–182
Bird-song, origin of, 62
Birds, 28, 118, 119, 151, 152, 153, 155, 157, 160, 161, 162, 164, 170, 172, 174 ; land, 169 ; forest, 169
Birth, Goddess of—see Sun Goddess
Bliss, Land of, 175, 176, 182, 310
Blood of wombat, develops into a man, 324
Blue crane, 329, 340, 341. See also Chirr-bookie

Blue Mountain, 151, 156, 164
Blue wren, 130–131, 132–133, 146–147, 303
Blue-tongued lizard, 144, 146, 299
Body, subjection of, 345 et seq.
Body-burning, 104, 326–327
Body-marking, as initiation rite, 20, 347
Bone, 203 ; magic, 171–172
Bonfires built to light the world, 96
Boomerang, 88, 95, 98, 122, 123, 127, 222, 258, 265
Boomerang-throwing, 236, 240–241, 313
Boora-ground, 192, 199
Bream, Murray, 214, 228
Brigge, 209, 210, 211, 218
Brother-in-law (ronggi), 121 and n., 122, 134, 136
Bruising the body, as form of revenge, 200–201
Bubble-spirit, 112, 113
Buda Gooda, 268–269
Bulpallungga, 301–317
Bunyip—see Moolgewanke
Burial-grounds, 183, 349
Bush-fire, 251
Bushcraft, 19, 219, 337
Butcher-bird, 75, 303
Buthera, 341–342
Butter-fish, 229, 327
Butterflies, birth of the, 59–62

CAMPING-GROUND, 160–161, 235, 348, 349
Cap, pipeclay, 164, 165, 213, 301
Cape Jervis, 334
Cape Spencer, 171
Carpet-snake, 94, 102, 127, 128, 129, 133–135, 151, 158, 159, 162, 163–164
Carvings, aboriginal, 91, 161, 166
Cat, native, 105, 169. See also Kinie Ger
Cat-fish, 124, 214, 228
Caves, carvings, etc., in, 166, 278
Ceremonial rites, 18, 301, 305
Ceremonies of initiation, 32, 277 ; tribal, 216

Charm-sticks, 207

Charms, 23

Chase, aboriginal love of the, 214

Cheeroonear, 252–259, 260

Childbirth, Goddess of, 302, 314

Children, 106, 142

Chirr-bookie, 331–341

Cinders, bed of, in initiation rites, 20, 348

Civilization, aboriginals and, 23

Cockatoo, 74–75, 94, 98, 169, 170

Cockatoo feathers, 87

Cod, Murray, 78, 124, 125, 214, 228, 229

Companion, native, 98, 162

Compass, points of, 17

Constellations, aboriginal legends concerning the, 22

Coo-ee, 87 and n.

Cooked food, 73–75

Coolamon, 65, 119–120

Coorong, river, 323

Coorong tribe, 231–235

Cormorant, 156–157, 158

Corny Point, 341

Corrobbery, 22, 63 and n., 182, 231, 283 and n., 349

Creation, story of the, 23–31

Crow, 42, 45–55, 64, 65, 102, 104, 120–147, 151, 153–154, 160, 162, 166, 323 ; totem of, 52

Crystal, magic, 184, 190, 203

Curlew, 97, 310

Curre Mulka, 341

Customs, aboriginal, 17–23

Dance, tortoise, 64–65 ; emu, 263–264

Darling, river, 22, 120, 228

Death, mystery of, 60–62 ; song of, 192–193

Decoration, bodily, 295, 296, 297

Dingo, 30, 66, 97, 119, 120, 303

Dragonfly, 67

Duck families, 169–170

Duck, wild, 308

Duck-netting, 222, 223

Ducks, 161, 221, 222

Eagle-hawk, 33, 42, 45, 46, 48, 49, 50, 69, 72, 73–74, 75, 94, 117, 118–119,
120, 121, 140–141, 151, 152, 153, 160, 161

Earth's movements, aboriginal knowledge of, 93

Eastern Sea, 156

Education of aboriginals, 173

Elements, as totems, 154

Emu, 42, 66, 75, 95–96, 102, 123, 129, 139, 143, 156, 157, 158, 159–160, 161, 162, 166–167, 170, 171, 182, 227, 266, 271, 333, 334, 336

Emu, cooking an, 335–336

Emu feathers, 205, 239

Emu tribe, 122

Eurowie, 332–340

Evil, origin of, 120 n.

Evil One, 121, 135, 279–280, 281, 282, 283, 284, 285–288, 289, 290, 291, 292, 293–294, 325, 326

Evil Spirit, 20, 349

Falcon, 33, 115–117, 135, 136, 138, 139–140, 141

Fangs, how the snakes came to possess, 143

Fasting, as initiation rite, 346

Father Spirit—see Great Father Spirit

Fear, the overcoming of, as initiation rite, 20–21, 348–349

Festivals, aboriginal, 21

Fig-tree, the home of the Yara-ma-yha-who, 343 ; spirit of the, 344

Fire, discovery and loss of the secret of, 67–69, 71–78

Fire and Flame God, 259

Fire-stick, 71–72, 106, 126–127, 327

Fish, 29, 34, 149, 174, 182, 229, 230

Fish, restrictions on the eating of, 235, 320, 321

Fishing, 228–236 ; baskets for, 229

Flood, aboriginal legend of a, 151–168

Food, of the animals, 63, 67 ; exchange of, between aboriginals, 215

Foot-racing, 236

Footprints, aboriginal knowledge of, 22

Frilled lizard, 29, 146, 154, 155, 156, 162–163, 181, 295, 299

Frilled lizard tribe, 188

Frog, 29, 64, 65, 66, 99–101

Frog, green, 111–118

INDEX

GE RILL GHILLIE, 259, 272

Goannas, 66, 94, 102, 129–130, 131, 141, 144, 145, 146, 151, 152, 153, 162–163, 273 ; the lazy, 78–84 ; the selfish, 84–91

Goanna family, 42, 79

Goddess—*see* Sun Goddess

Golden hair, the man with, 242–249

Goonnear, the carpet-snake, 175, 176, 177

Grandmother Spirit—*see* Puckowe

Grass-tree stick, 77, 322

Great Father Spirit, 24, 26, 27, 31 *et seq.*, 174, 175, 177, 180, 182, 183, 248, 251, 268, 309, 317, 324, 331, 339, 340

Grubs, 168, 266, 280, 281, 282

Gum-tree, pelican babies in, 125–132

HAIR-ROPE, 124 *and n.*, 190–200

Harrimiah, 181, 294–301

Hawk, 33, 169

Hawk totem tribe, 340

Headdresses, bark, 20–21

Heaven, reached without dying, 325 ; land of, 331

Hermit, the, and Palpinkalare, 278, 294

Honey, porcupines' love for, 81

Horseshoe Bend, 334

Hospitality among the aboriginals, 215

Human Intelligence—*see* Intelligence of Mankind

Humpy, 48 *n.*

Hunting, 19, 219–228, 337

IN-NARD-DOOAH, 105–111

Initiation rites, 18–21, 32, 277, 279–281, 305, 319 *n.* ; song of, 306

Insects, 25, 26, 27, 28–29, 118, 161, 164, 174, 175, 182, 271

Intelligence of Mankind, 37, 44, 55–59

Intermarriage of eagle-hawk and crow, 45 ; proposed, 46 ; of animals with reptiles, 55

Kaike, 86, 122, 214, 232, 233

Kalduke—*see* Umbilical cord

Kanake, 205, 284, 285, 334, 337, 338

Kangaroo, 29, 65, 66, 94–96, 97, 98, 102, 106, 117, 120, 129, 130, 131, 132, 133, 134, 135, 139, 143, 144, 145, 152, 153, 154, 155, 156, 157, 158, 159, 160, 161, 163, 165, 167, 169, 170, 171, 172, 267, 271, 303, 346

Kangaroo, magic leg-bone of, 171–172

Kangaroo-hunting, 225–226

Kangaroo-rat, 136, 137, 169

Kardin-nilla, 23 *n.*

Kartinyeri, 192–200

Keen Keeng, 259–264 ; cavern of, 262

Kendi, 181

Killunkillie, 45 *and n.*

Kingston, 139, 271

Kinie Ger, 101–105

Kirkin, 242–249, 260

Kite-hawk, 119

Knives, flint, 129, 154, 341

Koala, 29 *and n.*, 30, 67, 152, 153, 154, 155, 163

Koolatowie, 332–341

Kurdaitcha, 289 *and n.*

LAND OF MYSTERY, 91 *n.* ; of Perfection, 174–176, 182 ; of Perfect Bliss, 175, 176, 310 ; of Bliss, 182 ; Sacred, 182 ; of Heaven, 331

Language, aboriginal, 22

Larna, 342

Lathinyeri tribe, 211

Laughing jack, 45, 66, 75, 114, 142, 146, 162, 169

Lawarrie tribe, 196, 197

Lightning, as totem, 52, 154, 155, 185

Lizard, 29, 76–78, 97, 98, 99, 141, 143–144, 146, 154, 165, 169, 271, 273, 299

Lobster, 124

Lucindale, 271

Lyre-bird, 67, 113–115, 116, 161, 219, 295

MAGGOTS, 271

Magic bone, 172 ; eye, 178 ; song, 280 ; wand, 342

Magpie, 33, 42, 45–46, 74, 75, 114, 119, 129, 130, 131, 137, 162, 166, 169, 170, 303

Maljarna, 246

Mallee-root, 243 *and n.*, 244, 260

Man, birth of, 38–40 ; made the protector and teacher of woman, 59

353

Mankind, coming of, 31–59

Mankind, Spirit of, 31. *See also* Great Father Spirit

Manly, 91

Mar-Rallang, 250

Marion Bay, 341, 342

Marriage customs and ceremonies, 21, 32, 56, 63, 78, 209–214, 295

Marriage of the porcupine and the mountain devil, 105–106

Medicine-man, 23, 144–145, 184–185, 188–189, 197–198, 201, 314–316; spear of, 311 *and n.*

Message-stick, 101 *and n.*, 122, 144, 145, 160, 333

Mia-mia, 48 *n.*, 85, 158, 160, 165

Migrations of the aboriginals, 17

Milky Way, 104, 182, 183, 277, 339

Moolgewanke, 181 *and n.*

Moon, 23 *n.*, 30, 69–71, 105; aboriginal knowledge of course of, 71

Mopoke, 308

Morality, aboriginal sense of, 182

Mount Barker, 338

Mount Benson, 139, 140, 272; lakes on, tears of mother of Woo, 272

Mount Gambier, 143, 146, 272

Mount Torrens, 339

Mountain devil, 105–111

Mourning, of widow, 212–213; cap of, 164, 165, 213, 301–302; signs of, 309

Mud-fish, 125, 228

Mudichera, 341, 342

Muldarpe—see Evil Spirit

Mummulbery, 273–276

Munkumbole, 185, 200, 201–202, 206, 207–208

Murray, river, 78, 89, 120, 121, 136, 228, 229

Murray bream, 214, 228

Murray cod, 78, 124, 125, 214, 228, 229

Murray perch, 228

Murrumbidgee, river, 78, 228

Mypolonga, 133

Mystery, Land of, 91 *n.*, 329

Nardoo seed, 168, 280

Narracoorte, 271

Narrangga tribe, 168

Narrinyeri tribe, 17 *n.*, 120, 121 *n.*, 317

Native cat, 101, 169

Native companion, 98, 162

Native sloth—*see* Koala

Neilyeri, 186–189

Nepelle, 22, 183, 229, 251, 320, 321, 331

Newal, Mr and Mrs, 264–270

Ngathungi, 184, 195, 199, 202–208

Ngia ngiampe, 215–218

Night, Lady of the, 30. *See also* Moon

Night-owl, 322

Nose-piercing, as initiation rite, 20, 348

Nulla-nulla, 79, 86, 92, 94, 150, 194, 195, 198, 201, 227, 265

Nullarbor, Plain of, 24, 25, 26, 30, 174, 252

Nurunderi and his wives, 17 *and n.*, 173, 183, 216, 250, 317–331

Observation, aboriginals' powers of, 22, 219

Ochre, red, 87, 154, 248, 262

Old, aboriginals' care of the, 215

Onkaparinga, river, 334

Oompi, 48 *n.*

Opossum, 129, 130, 131, 132, 155, 160, 163, 169

Opossum totem tribe, 188

Opossum-hunting, 226, 227

Owl, 29, 33, 97, 98, 99, 102, 104, 135–136, 164, 166; the selfish, 94–99

Pain, tests of endurance of, 20, 347

Palpinkalare, 277–294

Panketye, 86, 338

Parrot, 161

Peewee, 40 *and n.*; story told by the, 41–45

Pelican, 29, 65, 122, 123, 124–125, 126, 128, 129, 130, 133, 135, 146–147, 161

Pelican babies, the crow and the, 125–132

Pelican tribe, 131, 134

Pellati, 136 *and n.*

People changed into birds, 317

Perch, 74

Perch, Murray, 228

Perindi, 181, 294–301

Pheasants' eggs, Bulpallungga and, 316

Piltinyeri tribe, 231–235

INDEX

Pinyali—*see* Emu
Pipeclay, 87, 154, 302 ; cap, 164, 165, 213
Pit-traps, 226
Pithowie, 332–340
Platypus, 29, 153, 155, 156–157, 158, 159, 160, 161, 162, 163–168, 219
Pleiades, 70 ; origin of the, 345–350
Plongge, 322
Plover, 220
Pointing-bone, 184, 187
Pointing-stick, 184, 203
Pomeri, 233, 234
Ponde—*see* Murray cod
Porcupine, 81, 105–111, 137
Porcupine bush, 109
Porcupine tribe, 79
Port Augusta, 172
Port Lincoln, 171
Primitive race, traces of extinct, 91 *n.*
Puckowe, 184, 188, 189, 198, 199, 208, 323
Pulyugge, ball-game, 240
Pumbala tribe, 210, 270, 323
Punauwe, 333

RACES, running, 238
Rain-making, 154–155, 185–186
Raminyeri tribe, 231, 331, 332, 333
Rat, 137, 163
Reeds, 222
Reedy Creek, 142
Reincarnation, 307, 331 *n.*
Religion, aboriginal sense of, 182
Remarriage of widow, 212–213
Reptile Age, monsters of the, 181
Reptiles, 102, 103, 118, 134, 156, 157, 160, 161, 162, 163, 164, 165, 169, 271
Revenge, 103, 186, 200–201, 338
Rhino Head, 342
Riverina district, 148
Robin red-breast, 147
Ronggi—*see* Brother-in-law
Running stream, spirit of the, 118

SACRIFICE, human, to the Fire and Flame God, 259–264
Salt Creek, 139, 271
Sand-heaps, made by the whowie, 148
Seal, 29
Seasonal changes, origin of, 26

Self-control, aboriginal idea of, 173, 309. *See also* Initiation rites
Sex laws among the aboriginals, 21
Shag families, 169
Shag totem, 340
She-oak, 318
Sister-in-law, marriage with, 213
Sisters, the Seven, 331, 350 ; the Two, 331
Sleepy lizard, 144, 162
Smoke signals, 71–72, 102, 149, 200, 210, 276, 289 ; column, 320
Snakes, 24, 77–78, 141–143, 144–146, 147, 166, 273
Snipe family, 169
Song, the Tuckonie tree-, 127–129 ; of the storm, 154–155 ; of the Evil One, 280–281 ; of lament, 284–285 ; of the departed, 308 ; of sleep, 308 ; of the south wind, 329 ; the wind, 329, 330
Soul, 120 *n.*, 173, 175
Spear-head, flint, 50
Spear-throwing, 236, 238, 312
Spears, 94, 104, 123, 150, 214, 222, 225, 285, 311, 326, 337
Spencer's Gulf, the origin of, 168–172
Spirit, Great—*see* Great Spirit
Spirit Land, 27, 178, 285, 329
Spirit World, 341
Spirits, existing in the elements, 111 *n.* ; of weapons, 339
Spirits, Home of the, 174
Sport, 236–241
Star, morning, 23 *n.*
Stars, 22, 23 *n.*, 30 ; study of, 93
Stars, God of the, 251
Sting, given to the adders and snakes, 140, 141–143, 147, 153
Storm, song to raise, 154, 155
Suggestion, mental, 23, 189, 198, 207
Superstition, Valley of, 282
Sun, 23 *n.*, 96 *and n.*
Sun Goddess, or Goddess of Birth, 23 *n.*, 24 *et seq.*, 180
Sunshine, loss and recovery of, 97
Swamp-hawk, 126, 136, 137
Swan, 161, 219 ; down of, 308 *and n.*
Swan families, 169
Swan-hunting, 223–225
Swift, 116–117

355

Taralye, 232, 233
Target-throwing, 238
Tatiara, 141
Teal teal, 86, 87, 90, 221
Thardid Jimbo, 259, 260, 272–277
Theen-who-ween—*see* Emu
Thingairipari, 311 *n.*
Thousand Isles, Sea of a, 79, 154
Throwing-stick, 326
Thumie, 124 *n.*, 184, 190–201
Thunder, as totem, 154, 155, 185
Thunner-spale—*see* Bull-roarers
Tiger-snake, 146, 151, 152, 153, 163
Tilpulp, 196
Tintinara, 139, 141
Tinuwarre, 230, 232, 233, 234
Tooth-breaking, as initiation rite, 347
Tortoise, 64–65, 118, 119–120
Totemism, 55 *n.*, 91, 92, 136, 166
Tracking, aboriginal knowledge of, 22
Trespassing, 215
Tribal laws, 17, 23
Tuckonie, 87–89, 127–129 ; tree-song of the, 127
Tukkeri, 319 *n.*, 320, 321, 322
Turtles, 214

UMBILICAL CORD, 216–218
Uncle, power of, among aboriginals, 21, 209, 212, 302, 303
Uroo, 181

VEGETATION, the beginning of, 24, 181
Ventriloquism, 115, 282
Victoria, Lake, 17 *n.*, 121

Waddy, 86, 88, 91, 94, 122, 196, 201, 202, 205, 222, 225, 226, 280, 326, 334, 338, 340
Wagga Wagga, 228
Waiirri, 22
Wakkalde, 202
Wallaby, 160, 169, 271, 278, 303
Walliow, 246–247
Waratah, 58 *and n.*
Warracknabeal, 271
Water, animals' disagreement concerning, 170–172 ; kept by the selfish goannas, 84–91
Water-finding, 228

Water-rat, 68, 69, 148, 149, 150, 167–168
Water-snake, 181
Water-spirits, 28, 112
Wattle, 28, 301 *and n.*
Weapon, throwing, 239 ; spirits of, 339
Weather, the rain-maker and, 185
Whowie, 147–151
Widow, remarriage of, 212, 213 ; mourning of, 213
Willy-wagtail, 37 *and n.*, 38, 75, 106, 119, 120, 170, 171, 172, 303, 326, 342
Willy-willy, 100
Wind, 100 ; as totem, 154, 155 ; song, 329, 330
Winjarning brothers, 248, 255–259, 260–264, 283, 286–293
Wirrie, 138, 139, 140, 143, 184, 189–190
Wit-wit, 60 *and n.*
Witchcraft, 128, 146, 184–208
Woman, power of, 99 ; restrictions on, 235, 319 *n.*
Woman-drawer, 280 *n.* *See also* Bull-roarer
Wombat, 29, 33, 35, 66, 119, 139, 143, 155, 165, 219, 323–324
Wombat-hunting, 227
Wommera, 196, 265, 284, 285
Wonboona, country of, 268, 270
Wonboona tribe, 301, 315
Woo, 270–272
Woodpecker, 130, 131, 147
Wound, dressing of, 299 *n.*, 347
Wren, 75. *See also* Blue wren
Wrestling, 119, 236
Wunde, 214, 334
Wurley, 48 *and n.*, 124, 127, 133, 206, 302, 303, 329
Wyju, 242–249
Wyungare, 183, 250–251, 331

YABBY, 230 *and n.*
Yam-stick, 18, 129
Yams, 107
Yankalilla, 340
Yara-ma-yha-who, 342–345
Yee-Na-Pah, 105–111
Yong Keeng, 204–205, 206
Yorke's Peninsula, 168, 341